PAUL ENO

FOREWORD BY NICK REDFERN

DANCING PAST THE GRAVEYARD

POLTERGEISTS, PARASITES, PARALLEL WORLDS, AND GOD

Printed in China

Other Schiffer Books by the Author:

Behind the Paranormal: Everything You Know is Wrong
Paul and Ben Eno
ISBN: 978-0-7643-5222-5

Library of Congress Control Number: 2019935789

Cover design by Brenda McCallum

Cover Image courtesy of ShutterStock
Ouija is a registered trademark of Hasbro

Type set in Frutiger/ Desire/ Times New Roman

ISBN: 978-0-7643-5774-9
Printed in China

Published by Red Feather Mind, Body, Spirit
An imprint of Schiffer Publishing, Ltd.
4880 Lower Valley Road
Atglen, PA 19310
Phone: (610) 593-1777; Fax: (610) 593-2002
E-mail: Info@schifferbooks.com
Web: www.redfeathermbs.com

Visit supernatural adventurers Paul & Ben Eno at
www.BehindTheParanormal.com or www.NewEnglandGhosts.com

To Ben:
Much-loved son, colleague,
and friend!

TERMS USED IN THIS BOOK

Some or all of these terms are used throughout this book, and might be unfamiliar to most readers.

Multiverse: Short for multiple universes. The concept comes from theoretical physics and basically says that reality is made up not of one universe or world, but many. A corresponding term is "parallel worlds." The theory is based on the Multiple Worlds Interpretation (MWI) of quantum mechanics, first proposed in 1956 by Hugh Everett III. Today, the MWI is widely accepted by physicists, though there is disagreement about its form and interpretation.

A critical concept in many interpretations is that all possible worlds, creatures, objects, and outcomes exist in concrete reality somewhere or somewhen in the multiverse.

The Unity: As postulated in concepts and philosophies from the Holographic Theory in quantum physics and the Oscillating Universe Theory, to the theology of Teilhard de Chardin and the African idea of Ubuntu, the Unity is the tendency of all parallel worlds to eventually blend into one perfectly balance reality.

Somewhen, Elsewhen: In an alternate time. Corresponds to "somewhere" and "elsewhere," in an alternate place.

Superlife: The totality of a person's existence, embracing all facets of that person throughout the multiverse.

Facet: A parallel life being lived in a parallel world, but being an integral part of the subconscious of every other life being lived by that person in all parallel worlds in which that person exists.

Translate, Translation: An ancient term for bodily death as a passage to somewhere or somewhen else. The author uses "translation" instead of "death," since he believes the latter cannot exist in the multiverse.

Brane: Short for membrane, a term theoretical physicists use to describe the electromagnetic or plasma boundaries between parallel worlds.

Intersects: Points where one or more branes join and exchange energies between various worlds. The terms "cross-brane," "overlap," and "overwash" are also used to describe parallel-world interaction.

Neighbor: An inhabitant, human or otherwise, of a parallel world.

Parasites: Energy feeders attracted by negative human activity and emotion. Author believes that, in the human experience, parasites are responsible for our folklore about vampires and demons.

Peter Pan Theory: The author's jocular term for bringing in positive human activity and emotion to replace the negative, and thus cut off the parasite food supply, as in "think happy thoughts"!

Distressed humans: Generally believed to be classic ghosts, the spirits of, or psychic remnants of, dead people. The author believes instead that they are live people in distress in parallel worlds, even if a facet of them lived in this world and has translated.

Space-time: As defined in Albert Einstein's general theory of relativity (1952), space and time are essentially the same thing. The concept combines the three dimensions of space and one dimension of time. The effects, the author believes, can have profound implications for parallel-world interactions that we consider paranormal.

Leinster Effect: Named for Murray Leinster, pseudonym of American author William Fitzgerald Jenkins (1896–1975), who wrote masterful science fiction novels about parallel worlds with alternate historical timelines. The author describes the effect as "a nanosecond of blackness between perception of one world, then another. It's almost like the transition from one image to another in an old slide projector."

World Family: A group of concurrent parallel worlds with nearly identical contents, inhabitants, and laws of physics, through which we progress daily. The author believes that when we encounter an intersect point with a world in a different world family, what we consider paranormal experiences can result.

CONTENTS

SECTION ONE | **PARAMETERS AND POLTERGEISTS**

SECTION TWO | **THE NEIGHBORS**

SECTION THREE | **PARALLEL WORLDS AND THE PARANORMAL ON STEROIDS**

SECTION FOUR | **PARALLEL WORLDS AND GOD**

166 CHAPTER ONE
WHO OR WHAT IS GOD?

185 CHAPTER TWO
WHAT GHOSTS HAVE TO SAY ABOUT GOD

FOREWORD

BY NICK REDFERN

Paul Eno's new title, *Dancing Past the Graveyard: Poltergeists, Parasites, Parallel Worlds, and God,* is a detailed study of multiple supernatural and paranormal entities and their connections to us, the human race. The book is, however, more than that. In fact, it's way more. What Paul has done with his latest release is to carefully demonstrate the very real dangers that face us when we dare to cross paths with terrible creatures that will do all they can to torment us, to feed on us, and even to destroy our lives. As you will soon come to see, there are plenty of diabolical things in our midst that will be all too pleased to do that. And in rapid-fire speed, too.

The collective story that Paul tells is both fascinating and gripping. It's also deeply disturbing, and specifically in relation to the natures and agendas of the phenomena that Paul has encountered during his many and varied journeys into the unknown. What I particularly like about *Dancing* is that it's Paul's personal, first-hand quest for answers. By that, I mean what we have here is something akin to an extensive, packed journal or a diary that chronicles the day-by-day, month-by-month, and year-by-year experiences that Paul has endured while seeking the truth. It's his story, but one that we, the readers, are invited to indulge in.

Matters begin in the early 1970s, when Paul is studying for the priesthood. In no time at all, Paul finds himself plunged into the seriously dangerous realms of demonic possession and exorcism. No pun intended, but the story that Paul shares with us is as creepy as hell. If you thought William Peter Blatty's 1971 novel, *The Exorcist*—which was turned into a blockbuster movie two years later, starring Linda Blair, Max von Sydow, and Ellen Burstyn—was traumatic, imagine finding yourself in the heart of the real-world equivalent. That's precisely what happens to Paul. As time progresses, and as the case files pile up, dealing with cunning and hostile intelligences from other realities becomes practically second nature for him. It's also in this period—the 1970s—that Paul comes to realize just how manipulative these monsters really are.

The perils of recklessly dabbling in the world of the Ouija board are also spelled out—and in grim, stark fashion. People are placed in danger, as deceptive beings masquerade as the spirits of dead friends and relatives. Those same things will tell you exactly what they think you want to hear, as they seek to get their claws into you. Bizarre runs of bad luck, collapsing families, divorce, and lives wrecked are some of the typical issues that Paul has to deal with as he helps those who were unfortunate enough to encounter the others.

Violent poltergeist activity is something that Paul finds himself immersed in, too. It's yet another phenomenon that provokes calamitous activity in the home. Strange and sickening odors, and a deep sense of menace, overwhelm once-welcoming environments. Yet again, we see Paul using his by-now-honed skills to do battle with the world of evil.

One of the most significant and important aspects of Paul's book crops up time and time again. It's the matter of how just about all these creatures of the supernatural kind appear to have a symbiotic connection to us. But, it's by no means a positive connection. Rather, we are talking about things that latch onto us—in parasitic fashion, no less—and that have no intention of letting go. Ever. Paul makes it clear that this band of beasts is possibly, and quite literally, feeding on us. Farming us, maybe.

Dancing Past the Graveyard is an extremely important book, written by a man who lived through turbulent times and survived them; a man who shows us just how vulnerable we are to the predations of those non-human things that both haunt us and hunt us. For Paul, the decades-long journey has been both traumatic and eye-opening. It has, however, clearly been cathartic too. I think, by the time you have finished reading the book, you will feel exactly the same.

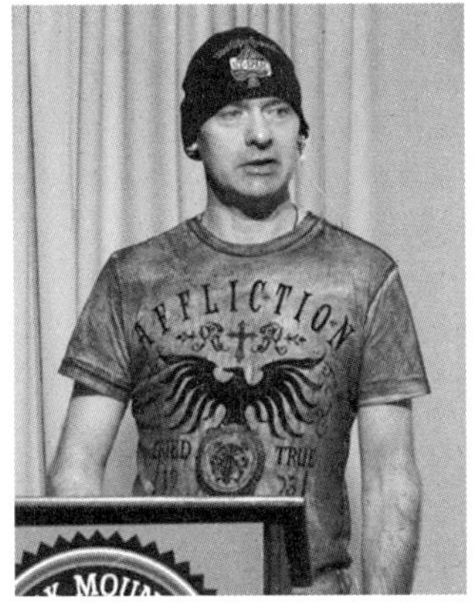

Nick Redfern is the author of fifty books on UFOs, lake-monsters, zombies, and Hollywood scandal, including *The Roswell UFO Conspiracy; Women in Black; Men in Black;* and *365 Days of UFOs*. He has appeared on many television shows, including the BBC's *Out of This World*; the SyFy Channel's *Proof Positive*; the History Channel's *Monster Quest, America's Book of Secrets*, and *UFO Hunters*; the *National Geographic Channel's Paranatural*; and MSNBC's *Countdown with Keith Olbermann*. Nick lives in Arlington, Texas. He can be contacted at his blog: http://nickredfernfortean.blogspot.com.

INTRODUCTION

On Sunday, November 24, 1974, I stood in the kitchen of a tiny bungalow on a side street in Bridgeport, Connecticut. I was flanked by three police officers and three firefighters. The seven of us stared in stunned silence as a 300-pound refrigerator lifted about a foot off the floor, turned one way, then another, then quietly set itself back down.

One police officer backed out of the house, backed down the sidewalk, got into his patrol car, and wouldn't come out.

That was only one mind-wrenching incident in what has been called "the world's most haunted house." I was a twenty-one-year-old student for the priesthood, working with Fr. William Charbonneau and none other than the controversial "grandparents of ghost hunting," Ed and Lorraine Warren, who were later immortalized in the 2013 and 2017 *The Conjuring* movies.

With the Warrens and "Fr. Bill," the unquestioned assumption was that we were dealing with demons. After all, what else could it be?

I wrote at length about the Bridgeport affair, probably the best-documented poltergeist (from the German for "a spirit that thrashes about") case in modern history, in *Behind the Paranormal: Everything You Know is Wrong* by Paul Eno and Ben Eno (Schiffer Books, 2016). But the questions raised by that subtitle have haunted me since my very first case in 1970.

Perhaps that's because I have always been a very annoying questioner. As a four-year-old in 1957: "Mom, where did the cat go when he died?"

Mom: "To the Happy Hunting Grounds."

Where?

In fourth grade, at St. Mary's Catholic School in East Hartford, Connecticut, during the Cuban Missile Crisis in October 1962: "Sister, what's the point in hiding under a desk when we're within five miles of three primary targets?"

Sister: "Get under the desk!"

As a teen student at St. Thomas Seminary in Bloomfield, Connecticut, in 1968: "Father, if Jesus Christ is 'truly man' as well as 'truly God,' as the doctrine says, wouldn't he have had a wife and reproduced?"

Father: "Of course not!"

As an older seminary student at St. Thomas in early 1973, when I'd already been working in the paranormal for over two years: "Father, why don't we study the Devil and exorcism?"

Father: "You're too young to worry about that. Keep your nose in your books."

This tendency to ask irritating questions only got worse as I aged, especially when I started tangling with the paranormal. After my first real case in the field, at the "The Village of Voices" in northeast Connecticut in 1971–1972 (also covered in detail in *Behind the Paranormal: Everything You Know is Wrong*) the questions were fast and furious.

These village ghosts just seemed to go about the normal daily routines of any rural people in the eighteenth or nineteenth centuries. We could hear metal farm implements, along with snatches of conversation and the sounds of cows, dogs, and horses. Do what we consider ghosts have more to do with time than with death? If ghosts are spirits, why are so many things they do so physical? Why are they often seen with bodily features, wearing clothes, and even driving wagons, buggies, or cars?

By the end of the 1980s: When I was dealing with a haunted house and studied the surrounding region instead of just the house, why did I find that other houses were affected as well? When I investigated ghost cases, why did I keep running into reports of UFOs and even crypto-creatures?

Then there were the dark and ominous implications of at least some of what I encountered, especially as I assisted at exorcisms in the 1970s. Were demons really servants of Satan, or was there a great deal more to it? There were serious physical and psychological consequences in some of these negative cases. What was that about?

Further: What role has the paranormal played in the human experience, in our beliefs, our religions, our societies and cultures, even our governments? And has our narrow, human-centered view of just about everything crippled our understanding of ourselves, our world, and the universe?

To those questions, no one offered answers that sounded anything but naïve and shallow. Most of the psychics and mediums I rubbed elbows with over the years were married to two-dimensional ideas based on the nineteenth-century séance room. Most of the priests I knew were, by the 1970s anyway, far more concerned with social justice than with the Devil. The parapsychologists of my acquaintance were straining and sweating to make the paranormal fit the accepted, comfortable, matter-based scientific paradigm, which was—and is—never going to happen.

There seemed to be no truly original ideas about the paranormal. The one major exception was the pioneering thought of Dr. Jacques Fabrice Vallée, a French computer scientist, astronomer, and UFO researcher who, in the 1950s, was already talking about paranormal phenomena of all types being connected because they involved multiple dimensions. Unfortunately, it would be another fifteen years before I even heard of Dr. Vallée, though I came to similar conclusions about the paranormal on my own.

By the end of the 1970s, I was not only in total confusion about the subject, but I had been kicked out of the seminary for researching it, with only a year or two to go before ordination to the priesthood. I had to start answering my own questions as best I could because none of the traditional answers were good enough.

My conclusion by 1980: We don't know a damn thing, and might never. Time to start over. So, start over with me. Stand by my side in those early years as I assist at mind-wrenching exorcisms, tangle with poltergeists, and meet some pretty astonishing "neighbors." When we're done, maybe you'll agree that everything we know is wrong.

Finally, we'll consider a question that's in the minds of surprising numbers of people when they come face to face with the paranormal: Where is God in all this? And even: Who or what *is* God?

"Whistling past the graveyard" is an old saying that can have two meanings. It can apply to someone who's trying to take a positive attitude toward a difficult situation. It also can apply to someone who's ignoring danger and foolishly plunging forward. Whichever meaning you prefer, it can be an apt saying for anyone who encounters, let alone works with, the paranormal. In fact, after reading about the encounters in this book, you might find that we are doing far more than whistling in the face of unutterable danger. We might be *dancing* past the graveyard, and oddly enough, we might be entirely justified in doing so.

Special Note: In some case files in this book, names have been changed to protect those involved, at their request or their families'.

SECTION ONE

PARASITES AND POLTERGEISTS

CHAPTER ONE

ADVENTURES IN EXORCISM

When objects began flying off shelves, or the patient started floating off the bed, that's when the doctors called Fr. Lawrence Wheeler.

It was 1973, and I had just graduated from St. Thomas Seminary in Bloomfield, Connecticut, the "minor seminary" where I attended high school and junior college. The faculty there was none too friendly toward my interest in the paranormal. Neither was my boss, Bishop John A. Marshall of Burlington, Vermont. He allowed me to move on to the "major seminary," the last two years of college and, presumably, four subsequent years of graduate theological studies leading to ordination to the priesthood. But he sent me to a school in the middle of nowhere: Wadhams Hall Seminary College in Ogdensburg, New York, right on the St. Lawrence River and the Canadian border.

This was to keep me out of mischief, but Bishop Marshall didn't figure on Fr. Lawrence and the nearby St. Lawrence State Hospital.

"Wait!" the reader might shout. Isn't the paranormal the business of priests? Not according to the bishops and seminary rectors responsible for "priestly formation," especially when it came to youngsters like me, who entered the seminary in 1967 at the age of fourteen, when you could still do that. My job was to study the usual high school and college subjects, along with Latin, philosophy, and basic theology. Each of us had a "spiritual father" among the faculty members, went on retreats, maintained a rule of prayer, and attended mass a lot.

The paranormal wasn't even in the picture, and nobody ever talked about "demonology." When I asked, priests told me that, in the graduate-level seminaries, in third- or fourth-year theology, the about-to-be-ordained had some minimal instruction in the church's narrow beliefs about demonic possession, and what to do if they suspected a case: Call the exorcist for that diocese (a diocese is a regional division of the church, headed by a bishop).

At St. Thomas, however, the faculty was alarmed every time they heard about one of my ghost expeditions. In fact, I was lucky to graduate. Much to my surprise, the priests at Wadhams Hall were different. I suspect that was because I was now being mentored by Fr. John J. Nicola of Washington, DC, a highly respected Jesuit priest who was the leading exorcism expert of his day. In fact, he was the technical advisor for the film *The Exorcist*, still in production at the time. Fr. John told me that stories of weird happenings on the film set were largely true, and that he regretted having anything to do with it.

The rector (the priest in charge of the seminary) at Wadhams Hall was open-minded about my paranormal studies. No doubt he wisely believed that I would be better off studying the subject with academic and spiritual guidance rather than on my own. The seminary's academic dean, who held a master's degree in counseling and taught psychology, set up private courses for me, notably in abnormal psychology. Basically, this was to help me tell the difference between people who were having paranormal issues and people who were just plain nuts.

As things turned out, it wasn't that simple.

Fr. Lawrence lived at the seminary but didn't teach. When I first saw him, I wasn't sure what he did, but he came across as a quiet, unassuming man of deep spirituality. One day early in my first semester, in September 1973, he called me to his rooms in the upper recesses of the building. Evidently, my reputation had preceded me.

"So, you've been studying ghosts and poltergeists," the priest declared in a soft, buzzy voice that many people found hard to understand. I, however, would get to know his voice well.

It was the first of several long conversations, during which he asked many questions about my knowledge and experience, such that it was. And he was interested in my involvement with Ed and Lorraine Warren, the controversial "grandparents of ghost hunting," whom I'd been working with for over a year.

Finally, two weeks later: "Have you ever assisted at an exorcism?" he asked.

The answer was "no," though Ed Warren had shared recordings and information with me on his exorcism cases. It turned out that Fr. Lawrence was an active exorcist. Every Roman Catholic diocese has, or is supposed to have, a priest who has done special studies of demonology *a la* Catholicism, and to whom possible possession cases are referred by other priests. In the Diocese of Ogdensburg, Fr. Lawrence was it.

The job of diocesan exorcist is, of course, very low-profile and the cases completely secret. When Fr. Lawrence took me under his wing, it was completely hush-hush. I'm not even sure how much of the seminary faculty knew about it. Fr. Lawrence carried on investigations, and, with the bishop's permission, the occasional exorcism, throughout the diocese, which included most of far northern New York State. For the next two years, however, I assisted him only a few miles from the seminary at St. Lawrence State Hospital (SLSH), otherwise known as the Ogdensburg State Asylum for the Insane.

Built in 1890 on a point of land along the St. Lawrence River, on the US/ Canada border, SLSH served the mostly rural expanse of New York's northernmost counties. While I found SLSH rather depressing, it was considered one of the more progressive psychiatric institutions in the country. Administrators and staff tried to maintain a positive, family-like atmosphere, and patients were kept active.

In the 1970s, however, this part of New York was economically depressed. Many farms had been foreclosed on and were up for sale, drug and alcohol addictions were on the rise, and so was overall negativity. By the time I surfaced, SLSH doctors and staff had their hands full with addicts, domestic-abuse victims, and others just overwhelmed by life. Most of these were outpatients, but some were serious enough to admit.

Officially, Fr. Lawrence was the Roman Catholic chaplain at SLSH. And, officially, I was one of the seminarians who visited inpatients as part of pastoral training. I did that, but I was really there to help Fr. Lawrence, observing and assisting if there was something strange in the neighborhood. And there usually was. In fact, I would learn more about the paranormal at SLSH than I ever would from the Warrens, my other mentors, or from chasing ghost reports back home in New England.

First, I began to see that what we call the paranormal or the supernatural doesn't just happen to people. We don't just sit there like lumps. We all bring something to the experience. We participate in it. And with the typical negative (i.e., demonic) experience, we invite it, then feed it.

Second, I began to take my apparent abilities to "sense" things seriously. That's because there were unseen presences at SLSH, and they weren't nice. They were hungry, they were hostile, and they were quick learners. This was where I began to learn about what I would come to call "multiversal parasites." I had always been able to feel the presence of entities, but I didn't want to, and I tried to bury these impressions because I felt they were dangerous to my Catholic spirituality, which I took very seriously.

I also knew things about people—what was really in their hearts, what they were feeling. Thinking that I was being unfair or judgmental, I rarely trusted these feelings when they were negative, usually to my cost. I didn't mention these insights either, not even to my spiritual fathers. Any hint of the psychic or mediumistic in my research, and I would have been out the seminary door for sure, even at open-minded Wadhams Hall.

Even though many rank-and-file Catholics use Ouija boards, read Tarot cards, or attend seances, contact with "the dead" or any other "spirits" was and is strictly forbidden in Catholic practice. Helping a priest while he did battle with demons during an exorcism was as close to the paranormal as I was allowed to get, and even that was unofficial.

Third, I had the nagging feeling that what was happening in these exorcisms wasn't what it appeared to be. Nothing in the paranormal was, I realized. It would be a while before I'd be able to put my finger on why I had that feeling.

As if that weren't enough, I began to realize that mental illness, addictions, and behavioral problems can be intertwined with paranormal "oppressions," "obsessions," and "possessions." That thought not only complicated many situations I would face, but it also terrified me because I felt so powerless in the face of it.

BARBARA

Barbara was one of many young patients at SLSH who was destitute, drug-addicted, and desperate. She was seventeen, a high school dropout, and she was the subject of the first and worst exorcism I actually witnessed.

In mid-October 1973, Fr. Lawrence told me that two doctors, three hospital staffers, and three other patients in Barbara's room had witnessed her drawers open by themselves, in broad daylight, and most of her clothes fly out and land on the other side of the room. At night, there were reports of growling under each bed in the room, and of heavy footsteps that seemed to come and go from the window. This was, essentially, classic poltergeist activity, a phenomenon often associated with possession, but not always.

By the time Fr. Lawrence and I arrived, Barbara had been moved to a single room. The first sight of her broke my heart. The girl looked emaciated, and her short brown hair hung from her head like seaweed. She was in a chair by the bed, and a nurse was trying to spoon-feed her some soup. Barbara looked up at us with distant eyes as we walked in. She knew Fr. Lawrence, but I was new to her.

"Who's that?" she asked nervously.

"This is Paul. He's one of the seminary students," Fr. Lawrence answered gently.

"He's good lookin'." At least she had a sense of humor.

Instantly, the plastic bowl, still half-full of soup, flew straight up out of the nurse's hand at amazing speed, hit the ceiling, then clattered to the floor. The nurse yelped, then jumped about ten feet toward the door. Fr. Lawrence and I were spattered with tepid chicken broth.

Phenomena like these, exterior to the patient, were the first signs doctors looked for when deciding whether to call Fr. Lawrence. In addition to the flying clothes and hurtling soup bowl, Barbara had been attacked by some invisible force the previous night, sheets and blankets were torn off the bed, and bruises were found on her legs and back, with no apparent cause.

Friday, Oct. 19

Barbara several times in 1971 and 1972 and again in June this year she saw little gray figures by her bed but does not remember anything more. She said these were bright lights in the sky over the river three nights before each of these events.

Fr. C said he sometimes hears this and sometime people report different kinds of animals or creatures. Buy especially with mental patients he does not put much stock in the stories. *

Demons?

Thursday, February 20

Richard has not been to Church in 10 years and he said his grandmother used to read tarot cards and do ouija boards. Here we go again. He also said his family has always talked to people from other worlds and seen flying saucers.

Fr. keeps tellinmg me to ignore this but I think it might be important. Five people I have talked to at the hospital said they had experiences like this and here they end up possessed. They not only see lights in the sky, in their houses and in the woods and field, they all claim to see strange figures in their houses, especially the bedromns. I do not know what this can mean. Fr. says keep our eye on the ball but maybe the ball is bigger than he thinks. I am just not comfortable with some of the expOlanations here and should I fel guilty about doubting my superiors?

Some of the author's original notes on exorcism cases at St. Lawrence State Hospital, including Barbara's, with the experiencers also reporting UFOs.

As if her drug addiction wasn't enough, Barbara, an otherwise very intelligent young woman, had been diagnosed with schizophrenia. Also, there were signs of dissociative identity disorder (multiple personalities). But none of these conditions could explain the poltergeist activity, also known as telekinesis, the movement of objects by invisible means.

We found out in conversations with her over the next week that there was far more to Barbara than met the eye. For Fr. Lawrence and me, red flags went up as soon as Barbara told us she and some friends had used a Ouija board for over a year. She told us that the board did as much as the drugs to take her mind off her problems, which included an alcoholic single mother, a violent older brother, and an abusive boyfriend.

If I knew then what I think I know now, I would have paid a great deal of attention to something else Barbara told us: She'd had a number of UFO sightings, going back to when she was four years old. Twice she remembered seeing "little men" in her bedroom. We chalked all this up to demons and paid no further attention. Today, I realize that was a great mistake. More on the possible alien-exorcism connection later.

Then there was "Chall."

"Chall came through the board. He said he was a prince from Asia a long time ago," Barbara told us. "He was killed by his own father. He said he would be my guide so bad things wouldn't happen to me."

Yeah, sure, I thought. One of my first realizations in paranormal research was that nothing can be taken at face value. Most "spirits" lie, and it's best not to communicate with them at all. I couldn't get over, and I still can't, how people who participate in séances or use Ouija boards tend to assume that what some entity is telling them is true.

"Did bad things continue to happen?" asked Fr. Lawrence. In his mind there was no question that Barbara was a victim of demonic oppression, which is just what it sounds like. Technically, it's not the same as possession, but it's a step or two away.

"Well, I'm in this place," Barbara quipped. "But Chall makes me feel special."

At that moment, there was a heavy thud right outside the window. I went to see what it was. We were on the second floor, and it was the middle of the afternoon. I could see no cause. Another thump—one that shook the room—seemed to thunder out from both walls. Fr. Lawrence and I jumped to our feet. I glanced at Barbara and was interested to see that there was a little smile on her face. I couldn't believe that no one else heard this, so I ran out into the hallway. Two nurses at the far end turned their heads toward me, questioningly. As it turned out, they hadn't heard a thing.

Fr. Lawrence called me back into the room. Barbara now looked very weird. She was staring off into space, but that wasn't the weird part. Her hair was standing on end, as though she had her hand on a Van de Graaf generator. The air was charged with electricity, and there was a smell of ozone.

"Get the doctor," the priest said calmly.

I ran into the hallway again and called the nurse. She ran to fetch the doctor. Back at Fr. Lawrence's side, I was shaking. The priest turned toward me to say something, when suddenly, a deep, gurgling voice I never want to hear again ululated from Barbara.

"Get out, you f—king priest!"

Barbara's hair then fell back to her shoulders and she slumped over the side of the chair, as if unconscious. I couldn't believe that Fr. Lawrence remained calm. I was sweating and wanted to bolt! But there's a strict rule: The priest is never to be left alone with the experiencer or, as the *Roman Ritual's* Rite of Exorcism calls him or her, the "sick person." There should have been a female nurse in the room with us as it was.

Just then, the doctor and a nurse rushed in, maneuvering Barbara into bed. All was quiet.

Roman Catholic priests don't just swoop in and perform exorcisms. The local bishop must review the case and grant permission for an exorcism to take place, and he must approve the priest who will perform it. Though I've heard of the rare exception, the experiencer has to be a Catholic. Doctors and attendants or nurses must be involved, but they are hand-picked by the exorcist for their devotion to the Catholic faith and their trustworthiness when it comes to complete secrecy.

As for the experiencer, there's a long and careful process to make sure that all non-paranormal possibilities for the "sick person's" condition and the accompanying phenomena are accounted for. There are thorough medical and psychological tests. If none of these can explain the condition, the exorcist will consider all the facts and observations and decide whether the person really is possessed.

Along with external phenomena, exorcists also look for one or more of these clues: strange voices from the subject; unnatural physical strength; violent hatred of religious objects; and knowledge of things, including languages, they have no way of knowing. In the case of a minor, like Barbara, parental permission must be obtained in writing. That wasn't easy in this case, since Barbara's alcoholic mother wasn't in much better shape than she was.

A DEFENSIVE RESPONSE

Exorcism in some form is practiced in every religious tradition. It's a defensive response to the primal human perception that some kind of non-human life form threatens our species. The Christian concepts of possession and exorcism have a fascinating history. In the New Testament, when the Gospels talk about the "public life of Jesus," the roughly three years he was out teaching and performing miracles, they make a clear distinction between possessed people and those with physical or mental illnesses. This belies the common modern belief that all ancient people were unintelligent clucks who thought every ailment was caused by demons.

As far as Fr. Lawrence was concerned, however, the hair thing, the evil-sounding voice, and the wall thumping crossed the line. His finding: Barbara was possessed.

The Rite of Exorcism is long, involved, and highly institutionalized. Once an exorcism is approved by the local bishop, the priest must go to confession (the "Sacrament of Penance and Reconciliation") and celebrate mass. Everyone else involved in Barbara's case, including the doctor, two nurses, a hospital attendant, and me, had to fast for three days, go to confession, attend mass, and go to communion.

Early in the exorcism ritual, the priest is supposed to demand that the demon reveal its true name. This is because Jesus did so in the fifth chapter of the Gospel of Mark and in the eighth chapter of the Gospel of Luke, as he was about to toss "Legion" out of the Gerasene demoniac and into an unfortunate herd of pigs.

I never saw much point to this demand for a name, especially because expecting these creatures to tell the truth is naïve. Fr. Lawrence saw my point but said that the demon is "bound" by the authority of Christ as exercised through the priest and can't lie. In addition, he subscribed to the very ancient belief that knowing someone's true name gives you power over them, and I think there's something to that, as far as it goes. Accordingly, Fr. Lawrence always asked for ID during each of the ten exorcisms at which I assisted him.

Exorcisms themselves might take place over several sessions. Barbara's would take three, spaced over three days, and I consider these to have been three different exorcisms. Before we began, however, I was assigned to hunt down the name "Chall," and I pretty much came up with zip. There was a perfectly human family of that name, one of whose members was a psychologist at Harvard University. There was nothing in the paranormal literature, such as it was, about any Chall, at least not that I could find. Interestingly, there is a twenty-first-century video game with a character named Chall Acustica, a "celestial being" but, in 1973, that was decades in the future. Who knows? Maybe Chall is still out there, up to his/her/its old tricks.

On the appointed first day, Thursday, October 25, Fr. Lawrence and the other five of us took Barbara, in a wheelchair, to an unused part of the hospital, at the end of a second-floor hallway. The girl looked as though she was drugged, but she wasn't. Her eyes were barely open, her head drooped, and saliva drooled from the left side of her mouth.

The room was well lit but bare. No beds. No chairs. Fr. Lawrence later told me that this was because of the danger of poltergeist activity. The fewer loose objects in the room, the less chance someone would get hurt if something started flying about. A year later, I was to learn the wisdom of this policy the hard way, in the Bridgeport, Connecticut, poltergeist house (see *Behind the Paranormal: Everything You Know is Wrong*, Schiffer Books, 2016).

I was the only one in the room, including the attendant, a thirtyish man named Leonard, who had never assisted at an exorcism before. Leonard and I took our places on either side of Barbara. Fr. Lawrence, in black cassock, white surplice, and purple stole, stood a few feet in front of the girl. The doctor and two nurses stood behind him.

Exorcisms are sometimes photographed, but Fr. Lawrence never permitted that to the best of my recollection. I certainly wasn't allowed to take any pictures, and I wasn't permitted to take notes, something I found a little odd. As soon as I returned to the seminary, however, I wrote down my whole experience. The doctor, on the other hand, had a small cassette tape recorder. Presumably, he captured audio of everything that happened. That was good, because it allowed him to track down the language the entity in question used when it addressed me personally during the second session.

The exorcism began with Fr. Lawrence blessing Barbara and the rest of us with the sign of the cross, then sprinkling us with holy water. Maybe I'd read too many horror novels, but I expected the girl to have some violent reaction to this. There was no response whatsoever from her. Then we all knelt, and the priest recited a lengthy Litany of the Saints, meant to call upon all the heroes of Christianity from all ages. Litanies like this are used in many church services, and new saints are added all the time. The litany in this exorcism ritual included all the archangels and angels, along with the intriguing line "all holy orders of blessed spirits," whatever they are.

Throughout the ritual, the rest of us responded to Fr. Lawrence and the various invocations with "Lord have mercy," "Christ have mercy," etc., as appropriate. Through it all, Barbara continued to appear half asleep in her wheelchair, making no movement and no sound.

Then came a long list of just about everything bad the church could think of, with all of us responding "Deliver us, O Lord." From sin; from God's anger; from lewdness; from storms, earthquakes, famines, plagues, and wars; and certainly "from the snares of the Devil"; it was all there. A long list of ways to dodge these dangers followed: By the coming, birth, baptism, fasting, death, and resurrection of Christ, especially.

"We beg you to hear us," we responded.

After some more invocations and a few psalms (Old Testament hymns), Fr. Lawrence's attention turned, at last, to Barbara, beginning a lengthy prayer for her salvation, with us pronouncing the responses.

Finally: "I command you, unclean spirit, whoever you are, along with all your minions now attacking this servant of God, by the mysteries of the incarnation, passion, resurrection, and ascension of our Lord Jesus Christ, by the descent of the Holy Spirit, by the coming of our Lord for judgment, that you tell me by some sign your name, and the day and hour of your departure. I command you, moreover, to obey me to the letter, I who am a minister of God despite my unworthiness; nor shall you be emboldened to harm in any way this creature of God, or the bystanders, or any of their possessions."

No response from Barbara or . . . whomever.

Fr. Lawrence then blessed the girl again. There was a reading from the first chapter of the Gospel of John, which I have always thought moving and profound. There were additional gospel readings about Jesus exorcizing demons, along with blessings and prayers for Barbara. There were more commands for the creature to detach and leave.

Then came the first of the actual exorcism prayers.

"I cast you out, unclean spirit, along with every Satanic power of the enemy, every specter from hell, and all your fell companions; in the name of our Lord Jesus [priest blesses] Christ. Begone and stay far from this creature of God [priest blesses]. For it is He who commands you, He who flung you headlong from the heights of heaven into the depths of hell. It is He who commands you, He who once stilled the sea and the wind and the storm. Hearken, therefore, and tremble in fear, Satan, you enemy of the faith, you foe of the human race, you begetter of death, you robber of life, you corrupter of justice, you root of all evil and vice; seducer of men, betrayer of the nations, instigator of envy, font of avarice, fomenter of discord, author of pain and sorrow. Why, then, do you stand and resist, knowing as you must that Christ the Lord brings your plans to nothing?"

And so on for a few more lines. There followed more prayers, blessings, and an anointing of Barbara with blessed oil. Then came the second, and longest, of the exorcism prayers, which I abridge here.

"I adjure you, ancient serpent, by the judge of the living and the dead, by your Creator, by the Creator of the whole universe, by Him who has the power to consign you to hell, to depart forthwith in fear, along with your savage minions, from this servant of God, Barbara, who seeks refuge in the fold of the church. I adjure you again, [priest blesses on Barbara's forehead] not by my weakness but by the might of the Holy Spirit, to depart from this servant of God, Barbara, whom almighty God has made in His image . . .

"Depart, then, transgressor. Depart, seducer, full of lies and cunning, foe of virtue, persecutor of the innocent. Give place, abominable creature, give way, you monster, give way to Christ, in whom you found none of your works . . .

"Therefore, I adjure you, profligate dragon, in the name of the spotless [priest blesses] Lamb, who has trodden down the asp and the basilisk, and overcome the lion and the dragon, to depart from this woman [priest again blesses on the forehead] . . .

"The longer you delay, the heavier your punishment shall be; for it is not men you are condemning, but rather Him who rules the living and the dead, who is coming to judge both the living and the dead and the world by fire."

There were more prayers and blessings, then a third exorcism, similar to the second, and with many Old Testament references.

In my experience, the actual exorcism prayers are the points at which things can really explode. In ensuing years, I came to believe that this confrontational, "authoritative" and almost-mocking litany of commands simply stirs up the priest, especially an inexperienced one, and the assistants. This allows the demon, which is actually no such thing in the classical sense, to feed on their negative energy and to gain strength. The resulting antics can freak out the humans, who only put out more energy to be eaten by the "possessing" creature or creatures, who couldn't care less about our religious beliefs.

At this point in Barbara's exorcism, however, there was still no reaction. She did seem more awake, but nothing happened. In later years, I looked back and suspected that it was because we were all quite calm, even me. In retrospect, I think the entity was quiet because it had nothing to feed on.

Then came more prayers, a hymn to the Virgin Mary, and further declarations of Catholic faith and doctrine. The whole thing can take more than an hour.

The ritual includes the realization that it might not work, and the priest is advised to keep reading the actual exorcism prayers until the experiencer is "delivered." If the priest is convinced the entity is gone, he reads the final part of the ritual, which thanks God for the deliverance and asks that the deliverance be permanent. In this case, Fr. Lawrence didn't believe the thing was gone. He didn't repeat the exorcism prayers either. He declared simply: "We must repeat this tomorrow."

Back in her private quarters, Barbara was monitored all night by handpicked female staff members who had the guts to stay in the room. The next day, we were told that a chair twice rose from the floor and hit the ceiling. There was more wall pounding, and several times Barbara's blanket and sheets were torn from the bed by some unseen force. I asked but was told that none of this had been photographed.

On Friday, October 26, Barbara, Fr. Lawrence, the doctor, nurses, and we two assistants returned to the same bare room. Barbara seemed fully awake and calm. But something was different. The air seemed heavy and electric. And I felt the dirty, sterile, alien presence of what I still believed was a demon, a servant of Satan. Fr. Lawrence seemed to sense something different, too, but he said nothing about it. He started the ritual from the beginning.

All remained quiet until the priest reached the part that commanded the creature to announce its name.

". . . Tell me by some sign your name, and the day and hour of your departure . . ."

Fr. Lawrence stopped short. We all stared at Barbara, who was rising quietly out of the chair, and I don't mean by standing up. The nurses both gasped.

"Paul, Leonard," the priest said quietly. "Pull her back down and hold her in the chair by the shoulders."

Barbara was still rising. Leonard and I each had to take hold of a pajama leg. She came down slowly, lightly, and easily. It was like pulling on a bunch of helium balloons. The moment the girl was back in the chair, there was a vibration in the walls and floor. Then a deep but vaguely female voice, certainly not Barbara's, came from nowhere we could place.

"Chall," it uttered.

I was shocked, but not so much so that I believed this thing.

Baloney, I *thought*.

Evidently, it somehow heard me. Fortunately or unfortunately, the doctor's tape recorder was rolling, and this is what it picked up in Chall's deep but oddly female voice: *Saya berada di sana ketika ayahmu membunuh dirinya sendiri. Saya memberitahu dia untuk melakukannya.*

If this had been in English, I would have "lost it," because it was directed straight at me. It took the doctor three days to track down the language and the translation. It turned out to be Malay, and it meant: "I was there when your father killed himself. I told him to do it."

Fr. Lawrence knew my history, and that I'd been present when my father committed suicide. I was seven years old. When the priest told the doctor about this, neither wanted to tell me what Chall said. In a long, prayerful conversation toward the end of that school year, in May 1974, Fr. Lawrence told me. He said he didn't feel right not doing so.

I don't think anything except the suicide itself has ever shaken me to the core as those words did, coming from that unclean alien thing. How could it know? How could it have been there? Had it really seen me standing there in that Connecticut driveway on that cold January day in 1961, a terrified, helpless, traumatized little boy?

"These things happen," Fr. Lawrence said. "If you're going to work in this ministry, pray always for strength. You will need God's strength because anything can happen."

I was a little surprised that he didn't recommend that I cease paranormal studies then and there. Maybe he felt, as I did, that I'd passed the point of no return, that once certain things have happened to you, you can't turn back. Maybe he saw me as the priest-exorcist for my diocese someday.

The rest of Barbara's second exorcism was rocky. Chall made no further attempt to hide. While there was no more poltergeist activity that day, the thing seemed to balk at the lengthy commands from Fr. Lawrence as we proceeded through the third and final exorcism prayer. There were squeaks, squeals, groans, a few verbal outbursts and obscenities, and Barbara floated out of the chair again. Leonard and I just pushed her back down.

Nevertheless, I couldn't shake the nagging suspicion that Chall, if that was its name at all, was just toying with us, pushing our "buttons" and getting stronger. It was feeding off the whole process as we reacted to its antics by pumping out energy through shock, anger, or fear. Whether I was right or wrong, Day 2 brought no resolution. When last heard from just after the third exorcism prayer, Chall was laughing at us through Barbara in a shrill voice none of us had heard before.

Fr. Lawrence was focused and persistent. The next day, Saturday, October 27, we would try again. That morning, we all gathered, Barbara was alert, communicative, and well groomed, for a change. The priest then asked for her agreement to be tied to the chair, and she assented. This involuntary levitation was not only distracting, it could be dangerous to her and us if she should get away from us or fall. The two nurses gently tied her to the wheelchair with rolled-up bedsheets, just enough so that she'd stay grounded.

Fr. Lawrence questioned Barbara at length about what she was experiencing. She summed it all up: "Chall is still here, and I don't want him anymore! I want to be with God."

Wasn't that an interesting way to put it? Did she want Chall to be there in the first place? Barbara said in the beginning that the creature made her feel special. And I remembered her telltale smile when Chall announced himself the previous day and on the day of the pounding outside the window. Fr. Lawrence began to repeat the ritual. The air was still electric, and I felt that we hadn't heard the last of Chall.

The priest was into the second exorcism prayer. "Make no resistance nor delay in departing from this woman, for it has pleased Christ to dwell in man . . ."

At that instant, Barbara's mouth opened, and a deep groan ensued. This was a different, very male, voice we'd never heard before. Except for Fr. Lawrence, we all took a step back. The girl slumped in the wheelchair and would have fallen out had she not been bound.

Fr. Lawrence continued, undaunted: "He has cast you forth into the outer darkness, where everlasting ruin awaits you and your abettors. To what purpose do you insolently resist? To what purpose do you brazenly refuse? For you are guilty before almighty God, whose laws you have transgressed . . ."

Barbara suddenly threw her head back, and it shook back and forth violently. One of the nurses gasped. The room filled with the smell of ozone and what looked almost like white smoke. Then the girl screamed in her own voice and suddenly seemed to wake up, looking calmly around the room at all of us. I had never seen color in her face before.

For the first time, Fr. Lawrence finished the part of the ritual that acknowledged the demon, or demons, as gone, the girl as delivered.

Over the next few weeks, Fr. Lawrence and the doctor followed up with Barbara. I wasn't involved with this aspect of the case, but the priest assured me that she was a new person, had left the hospital, had returned to the church, and had promised never again to have anything to do with the occult. Barbara's mother gave Fr. Lawrence the Ouija board, and he had it burned.

I never saw Barbara again.

Over the course of the next year and a half, until I graduated from Wadhams Hall with a degree in philosophy, in May 1975, I helped Fr. Lawrence as he exorcised seven more SLSH patients, all older than Barbara. There were three men and two women, all in their twenties. There was a woman in her fifties and a man in his seventies. There were fireworks from time to time, but none of these cases were as dramatic as Barbara's, nor did they require the same amount of effort. All patients were "delivered," in Fr. Lawrence's judgment, in one exorcism session.

That's actually a stunning success rate—and very quick. Some exorcisms take weeks or even months, and the medical state of the patient is of prime consideration. Nothing is rushed. Evidently, Fr. Lawrence was a world-class exorcist.

Before we leave St. Lawrence State Hospital, an obvious question arises: How could all this activity be kept quiet? People floating out of chairs in the presence of doctors and hospital staff, floors and walls shaking with unearthly voices, objects flying around on their own . . . How could this possibly be hushed up?

We live in a time when "ghost hunters" and "demonologists" are on television every day. Local groups of paranormal investigators seem to be ubiquitous in our hometown newspapers and radio broadcasts. There are news stories about Roman Catholic leaders being, supposedly, more open about exorcism, training more exorcists, and handling more cases of demonic possession. What's more, everyone wants to be famous. Our Boston/Providence-area radio show, *Behind the Paranormal with Paul & Ben Eno*, is forever being contacted by people who want their cases publicized. They don't say it outright, but it's obvious that they hope for a movie or book deal.

That, however, is now. Back in the early 1970s, the term "paranormal" wasn't even in common use. There were only a few people working publicly in the field of popular ghost and poltergeist research, such as Hans Holzer, Brad Steiger, and the Warrens. And society was much less tolerant of "superstition" among professional people. Even though hospital administrators must have known what we were doing, if word got out that any doctor or nurse was involved in an exorcism, it would have been professional suicide, especially if the media found out. Everyone was afraid of ridicule, at the very least.

That's not to say that the few in-the-know medical personnel who worked with us, all devout Catholics, didn't need counseling because of these wild experiences. This counseling always came directly from Fr. Lawrence, who was, after all, the Catholic chaplain at SLSH. He made it clear that these staffers were to avoid socializing with each other, or with me, even outside work hours, and that the exorcism cases must never be mentioned, either directly or indirectly. I found myself wondering whether this inner circle was brought into the cases because they were devout Catholics, or whether they were devout Catholics because of their involvement in these cases. In the end, there were few worries about anyone saying a word.

The same went for me, needless to say. Roman Catholic seminaries are gossip mills, full of young men who have no young ladies to divert their attention. That I studied the paranormal and was involved with the Warrens was well known. In my second year, Ed and Lorraine even came to the seminary from Connecticut at their own expense to present a program on the paranormal to the faculty and students. I introduced them to Fr. Lawrence, and he and Ed were in private conversation for several hours. I believe my classmates suspected that I was working with Fr. Lawrence, but they knew enough not to ask me about it directly.

Then there were the patients at SLSH who "saw things" or otherwise knew there were exorcisms going on. But we were safe on that score, too. After all, most of the patients were more or less officially crazy, so who was going to listen to them?

These were the years before the 'net, before smart phones and texting, before constant and instant information flow, whether the information is accurate or not. Today, in contrast, I'm sure that wild stories about such cases would be—and are—all over the place.

SLSH closed in 1983. Despite the internet, I've never heard of exorcisms being performed at its successor institution, the St. Lawrence Psychiatric Center, where there are busy outpatient and inpatient residential programs.

The author graduates from Wadhams Hall Seminary College in 1975. He's with his mom, at left, and at the hooding ceremony.

SUSPICIOUS SEMINARIAN

The more experience I gained with the Roman Catholic exorcism process, the more suspicious I became. Don't get me wrong: I had tremendous respect and love for Fr. Lawrence, a true priest with whom I remained in touch for years after I left Ogdensburg. It was the method and the reasoning behind the process that wasn't good enough to explain what I saw and felt in the presence of what everyone else believed were demons in every theological sense of the word.

After every exorcism, once we were back at the seminary, Fr. Lawrence and I would talk about what happened and what I'd learned. When I expressed my doubts, he assured me: "The more experience you gain, the more you'll understand."

Fr. Lawrence was right. The more I experienced, the more I thought I understood, but not in the ways he expected. Henceforth, I kept my thoughts to myself, and here's what those thoughts became in ensuing years. By the time I left Wadhams Hall and SLSH in 1975, one case after another made it clear that the demons we were fighting weren't spirits at all, but perfectly physical, alien life forms that live by feeding off the energy of other life forms—us among them.

In my experience at SLSH, the success of an exorcism was measured by whether overt phenomena ceased, whether the preternatural knowledge disappeared, and whether the subject went back to church. Follow-up was extremely important in all exorcism cases, but that was often left in the hands of parish priests, who were busy with their day-to-day duties. So, my information on the aftermath of the exorcisms at which I assisted was limited. But what I did hear after I left Wadhams Hall wasn't reassuring. Six of the eight "sick people" relapsed into some mental illness or physical disease. Barbara herself died of a drug overdose within three years.

I understand that Fr. Lawrence had to go back and exorcise some of these people all over again. I became more convinced than ever that we were dealing with energy parasites that had been, as the old saying goes, playing Fr. Lawrence and the rest of us "like bass fiddles." As with everything else in the paranormal, I was convinced that exorcism isn't what it appears to be.

WHAT ARE THESE PARASITES?

It's easy to see how these highly intelligent cosmic mosquitos picked up all sorts of theological baggage over the millennia. When it serves their culinary purpose, they're very good at filling the role of demons who wish us harm in order to feed on the energy thus produced, and of doing so under the guise of any religion or folk tradition.

The Roman Catholic Rite of Exorcism is certainly on the right track, as far as it goes:

> God, Creator and defender of the human race, who made man in your own image, look down in pity on this your servant, Barbara, now in the toils of the unclean spirit, now caught up in the fearsome threats of man's ancient enemy, sworn foe of our race, who befuddles and stupefies the human mind, throws it into terror, overwhelms it with fear and panic. Repel, O Lord, the devil's power, break asunder his snares and traps, put the unholy tempter to flight . . .

Do parasites put people through "toils"? Absolutely. It's literally their bread and butter. Are they "unclean"? If you ever feel their immediate presence and threat—sterile, cold, alien—you will see that the word "unclean" fits. Are they "man's ancient enemy, the sworn foe of our race"? Definitely. In fact, they are the most ancient and the most formidable enemies our species has ever known. Do parasites "befuddle and stupefy the human mind, throw it into terror, overwhelm it with fear and panic . . ."? Every chance they get.

However, are they spirits, beings with no physical bodies? I still say, "no way." Under the right conditions, we can see and feel them, and I have. I and my colleague Shane Sirois have even photographed them. Where do they go to and come from? And if we take away the veneer of theology and folklore, what is their true nature?

MEET THE BRANE

This is where we have to deal with the difficult ideas of parallel worlds and membranes, or "branes" as physicists refer to them. My son Ben and I deal with these concepts at greater length in *Behind the Paranormal: Everything You Know is Wrong*. We believe that the strange workings of this "multiverse" of parallel worlds are what is indeed "behind the paranormal." Briefly:

> The paranormal is the open interaction between an enormous number of parallel worlds wherein all possibilities have actual existence. The real mind-blower is when you add Albert Einstein's contentions, in his 1952 book *Relativity*. There is no past; there is no future in any objective sense. Time is just a function of our consciousness. It has no real existence.

So why do we see ghosts of people who have died? For the same reason I sometimes run into ghosts of people who have *not* died. The branes of the multiverse are windows, and sometimes doors, into alternate worlds where "the dear departed" never died at all. In the right places and under the right conditions, we can see them and even interact. If we're correct, they aren't ghosts or spirits, but the actual, physical people.

When I embraced these theories in the late 1970s, it explained just about everything in the paranormal that was confusing me. It answered questions like: Why do we see ghosts wearing clothes, riding horses, driving cars, and carrying on tasks as if going about their daily lives? When we see them as glowing orbs or classic ghost figures, it's probably because the branes are charged with plasma, or electrified air molecules. We see through branes as through an electrically charged curtain.

Oddly enough, I've had many cases where the "ghosts" see us just as we see them, and they're afraid because they think we're ghosts haunting *them*. The multiverse idea also explains the physical nature of many ghosts, people seeing ghosts of themselves or of other living people, ghosts of the same person being seen in different places at the same time, phantom buildings, and many other bizarre phenomena.

In the twenty-first century, this is good physics. Many physicists don't describe it the way we do, but they've never been in the paranormal trenches as we have. Nevertheless, there are few physicists left who deny the existence of the multiverse in some form. The implications of this for our understanding of the paranormal go far beyond ghosts and parasites. The same multiversal reality can explain some of the most fundamental religious and mystical experiences in the human psyche, not to mention UFOs, cryptids, and psychic and mediumistic phenomena in general.

How is it that people can "see the future"? How could Chall know about my father? Because all of us are multiversal creatures. There are versions or facets of ourselves in millions of parallel worlds with alternate outcomes, some of which we would, from here, perceive as our past and others as our future, and still others as completely alien realities. Parasites simply know how to cross these branes, see what alternate realities are there, then use the information to push our buttons and feed on us when conditions are right. That's how they live.

What's more, death itself, the supposed cause of ghosts, or what the Warrens referred to as "the ghost syndrome," literally cannot exist in the multiverse with any finality, and in any way that we understand. How can you die—how can even your body die—when there are so many facets of you across, perhaps, millions of parallel worlds? In the multiverse, real death—even for our bodies—is the only thing that would be impossible.

So, we believe that parasites are simply a part of nature, albeit a part of nature largely undiscovered by our narrow, nineteenth-century-style science, which assumes that reality begins and ends with matter. Parasites are a lot smarter than that. They are among Nature's "mimics," creatures that pretend to be other creatures in order to attract prey. But these aren't insects pretending to be sticks or leaves. They're intelligent, calculating creatures with their imprints in many worlds. They can pretend to be whatever it takes to strike at our weakest points, whether that be our deceased mothers or some great cosmic "spirit guide," like Chall, who make us feel special. It's far more complex than just a material world and a spirit world, and there's far more to it than Satan and his demons collecting human souls.

Humans are carbon-based life forms. But parasites, which we believe are just as physical as we are in their own worlds, seem to be based on plasma (ionized gas or electrified air molecules). Most parasites even look like plasma, at least as they are seen through branes; both in photographs and on the rare occasions I see them with the naked eye. Some species appear smoky, either light or dark. Others look very bright, almost like bolts of lightning. Still other kinds appear as shadowy figures, some nearly solid. Some can be quite disconcertingly solid, though this is rare.

They may appear in these forms not because it's what they actually look like but because, in many cases, their energy is simply reaching into our reality from beyond a brane. They or their "feelers" may simply be "riding," for lack of a better term, the inter-world electrical currents that hold the multiverse together. The more solid parasites appear, the more they may actually be on our side of the brane and "in" our reality.

Beyond this, I've seen indications that many parasites not only are organized but have a social structure, with clear leaders, and perhaps even a culture. There seem to be male and female genders. Most seem extremely long-lived, but I believe parasites can and do "die" in, as we've said, whatever sense death can be possible in a multiverse, where every creature is not only present in myriad worlds but also shares the life of every other creature. Any notion of death for creatures that can consciously move, or at least act, between worlds is especially slippery.

The existence of plasma-based life forms already has been theorized by astrobiologists (scientists who speculate about alien life). That's the kind of fluidity that would help parasites ride, or at least use, electrical currents that happen to cross world boundaries. Because of its ionized state, plasma is extremely conductive, and it can interact dramatically with electromagnetic fields (EMFs), which are associated with parallel-world intersects and paranormal phenomena.

Parasites seem to be very good at finding food sources. As I saw while working with Fr. Lawrence, their livelihood is gained entirely by riding or reaching from world to world to feed upon the likes of us—and probably other creatures we know nothing about. But precisely what are they "eating"? Apparently, some sort of negative energy produced by humans. All I know is that they thrive on whatever energy we put out when we're divided, stressed, frightened, angry, and full of hate. When we're united, calm, happy, and full of love, parasites not only lose their food supply, most seem repelled.

One answer may lie in cognitive neuroscience and the study of those little, oscillating electrical voltages all our brains produce. Of the four types of brain waves (alpha, beta, delta, and theta) measurable on an electroencephalograph (EEG), beta waves are most present during situations of stress and anger. Do beta waves "ring the dinner bell" for parasites? Possibly. And if the hosts don't provide enough sustenance on their own, parasites have ways to prod them into doing so, almost like us squeezing an orange to get every drop. Hence, you get stressed, frightened, and angry when something starts tossing around your fine china, or when you become convinced that Aunt Gertrude is hanging around to punish you for wasting the money she left you or for giving away her goldfish. The more frazzled you and your family get, the more food you produce for your unwanted guests.

It's easy to see that an exorcism would be banquet.

As with humans, parasites are amazingly psychic, but their belief systems haven't denied and buried this crucial survival tool. And why shouldn't parasites be psychic? From our viewpoint, "psychic" means perceiving more than one world at a time, and they obviously can do that. Parasites quickly learn which buttons to push to excite not only more fear and anger in individual hosts, but in whole families. Division—attacking all trends toward what we will soon be calling the Unity—is their greatest hunting tool. If they get strong enough, they can engage in communication, including audible verbal abuse of people, and even physical attacks. This, of course, can turn the parasite into the nasty and far more familiar poltergeist.

Taken to its frozen limit, I've seen hosts actually bond with parasites to the point that the possession phenomenon can occur, with the tacit agreement of the host, which I think takes place in all possession cases. It reminds me of hostages who actually bond with their captors, a phenomenon sometimes seen in terrorist situations and known as the Stockholm Syndrome.

Oddly enough, and barring possession, if the typical parasite host drastically changes daily habits or sleeps in a different room, the parasite sometimes has trouble locating him or her for days or even weeks. While parasites can slip between worlds, their mobility while in ours often seems strictly limited.

Many factors must line up for any human-parasite connection to occur. Along with a food source, there have to be inter-world electrical currents and EMFs that parasites can ride to get here. And these currents, in turn, depend on many factors, including site geology: The more electricity the site can conduct because of high water tables, sandy or clay soils, the presence of high-tension electrical wires, etc., the easier it is for the paranormal to manifest.

Speaking of EMFs, what role today's global "electropollution" plays in enabling parasite activities is an open, and pretty scary, question. Unless we live in the Australian desert, all of us are awash in man-made microwaves and EMFs of many strengths virtually all day, every day. What this is doing to us physically and emotionally is unknown, but what it might be doing to branes and parasite travel capabilities isn't even being discussed.

In folklore, ghosts often are associated with places where murders, suicides, and other highly charged events have occurred. Ben and I have found that many ghostly manifestations in such places are the result of parasite activity. If the factors are right, parasites are definitely attracted, not necessarily to the place but to the violent event, even if it's happening at the site in a part of the multiverse that to us is the past or the future. What's more, many parasites feeding on such an event seem able to operate freely in other worlds that intersect at the same site. I've seen this on many occasions.

THE PRUSSIAN PARASITE

A textbook case of a parasite operating across several branes at once occurred in 2004 in King of Prussia, Pennsylvania, not far from Philadelphia. This critter showcased not only the intelligence and versatility of the typical parasite but, crucially, the case demonstrated our own ability to fight back.

The call came October 6 in an e-mail, and it so happened that I was going to be in Philadelphia for a conference later that month. Once at the site in King of Prussia, I checked the house with my usual preliminary methods, concluding that a parasite was on the hunt. Afterward, here's the story I heard.

"Weird things have been happening to Kate, and the night before I e-mailed you I saw firsthand how weird it is. I've never seen her so afraid," stated the young boyfriend, Chuck.

"It's like somebody sits on my chest and I can't breathe," Kate added. "I can't move or speak."

Kate and her older sister, Carmen, both in their early twenties, had moved into the small, rented house about a year before, and the trouble started about four months later, as is typical: soft footsteps on the floor above. As the girls became more frightened and frustrated, the parasite gained strength, pounding on walls and starting the night attacks. Kate seemed to be the prime target.

"Everything stopped for a few weeks after Kate moved her room upstairs, and she seemed like her old self again. But now it's after her again and she has no energy. She's exhausted all the time," Chuck explained.

There was also some minor poltergeist activity, including a few floating dishes. And there were voices.

"Three nights ago, Carmen and Kate were in the living room, and Carmen saw something whitish and smoky hanging over Kate. Carmen is kind of hard to scare and said, 'What the hell?' Then the damn thing floated over to Carmen and she heard a man's rough voice, 'Don't you f—king move, you bitch!' and something started pounding on the walls!"

> Both girls screamed, and they fled the house then and there. They stayed with friends until I arrived the next day. In my preliminary examination, I sensed only one parasite, but quite a strong one. And there was something else, something in the tiny yard at the back of the house. On that little, empty lawn, an event was happening elsewhere and elsewhen in the multiverse. I could almost hear a woman screaming, and I could practically see the deliberate gunshot that killed her husband. And the parasite could feel it too, indeed was feeding off it. But as it did so, it reached into other accessible worlds, like some sort of electromagnetic octopus from a horror movie. And it found Kate.

Eventually, this case was resolved by the girls learning to understand, rather than fear, what was happening, building up positive energy and compassion, then directing it all toward that event in the yard. Within a few weeks, it worked. Deprived of food, the parasite left for greener pastures.

"We knew there was something weird about the yard," Carmen told me. "But when we started sending love at it, that bad energy would turn off like a light switch!"

There was much more to this case, of course. My point is that, in order to sustain themselves, parasites can communicate, manipulate, and exacerbate in all sorts of ingenious ways. One especially effective, and very common, parasite trick in a household is to mimic the voice of one family member and say obscene or insulting things to another family member, and *vice versa*. From a parasite's point of view, you can imagine the quick results this can have! Sounds like something right out of a "sitcom," but I assure you there's nothing funny about it.

THE MULTIVERSE

The term "multiverse" was coined by American philosopher William James in 1895. But the concept goes much further back than that. As any shaman from an indigenous people will tell you, in so many words, our remote ancestors knew all about parallel worlds, multiversal creatures, and, certainly, parasites. They couched these concepts in terms they could understand, and that come down to us in many forms, one being the Christianized version as reflected in the Rite of Exorcism.

That's why, early on, I gradually came to believe that paranormal experiences are really experiences of the multiverse, which certainly seems to be an ineffably vast system of interactive parallel worlds that swirl over, under, around, and through our conscious world at all times and in all places. Physicists, regardless of how they interpret the idea, refer to it as the multiple worlds interpretation of quantum mechanics or the MWI.

Some physicists suggest a different approach, which we believe is just another way to look at the multiverse, its infinitely varied inhabitants, and our own place in it, whether as predators, bystanders, or prey. This is the Holographic Theory. In this view, reality is a mighty hologram of consciousness, what we might even call a computer simulation, an artificial-intelligence scenario to the nth power. They believe that everything, including ourselves, is an illusion projected within this hologram. Some even say that the whole thing is a virtual experiment in linear time, intended to study us, and whoever or whatever else exists. Studied by whom or what? The term "source consciousness" has been used. God? Certainly not much like the one I was taught about in the seminary—more about that later. But the MWI and the hologram: Six of one, a half dozen of the other, I think.

Hologram or not, and regardless of where or when they come from and how they get here, parasites feature prominently in my entire paranormal experience. Over the years, I've listed nine distinct species so far, and I rank them by their hunting patterns, apparent intelligence, experience, power, and vulnerability.

It's possible that some of them could be younger or older individuals of the same species, with their maturity making a difference in my interpretation. But each group does seem to be unique unto itself. There's reason to believe that parasites do not all come from the same world, though they do seem to interact with each other, sometimes in a hostile manner.

Back in the 1980s, I considered naming them by "class" or something, but that seemed too much like the movie *Ghostbusters* ("Sir, what you had there was...a Class 5 Full-Roaming Vapor, a real nasty one, too!"). So, I decided to stick with species. As I said, there seem to be nine.

THE WISE

The most impressive parasite group is the Wise. I use the term with great relativity, and it implies nothing good when it comes to us humans. These top-shelf parasites come across as very ancient and full of knowledge about the multiverse, their prey in general, and the inhabitants of our world in particular. They give the impression of knowing our species far better than we do. They are conversant in most, if not all, human languages and have great telepathic power. They tend to live and hunt alone.

Like huge, invisible spiders, they often quietly park themselves in a place or time where they have access to a certain house or tract of land for centuries, picking up what knowledge they can and feeding on whoever comes along. I have found them to be arrogant, brilliant, and extremely calculating. At the same time, once they know that you know what they really are, I've found them surprisingly willing to communicate in a smug and not-to-be-trusted manner. They can convince us that they are several entities at once.

THE ELDERS

Like the Wise, the Elders seem to have great knowledge and experience, but they are more likely, though not always, to be found working together and to be leaders among other kinds of parasites. They do not seem as interested in humans and human life as the Wise, except, of course, as food sources: snacks, as it were. I've seen some evidence that they also feed on animals.

THE FARMERS

These parasites seem to work quietly, in groups of four to eight, and will attach themselves to a human family, tribe, or other community for long periods of time, cultivating situations and feeding off the results.

Certain individuals of this species might concentrate on, or be in charge of, particular individuals in the human group. In many cases, the parasites are so unobtrusive that—except for occasional feelings of presences or negativity—the humans have no idea they are being farmed.

THE PACK HUNTERS

This species is highly aggressive, highly provocative, and usually will concentrate on one human at a time. Unlike most parasites, they seem highly mobile. Working in groups of up to six, they can and will follow a person from place to place. There is always a leader. If they get enough to eat, they can become poltergeists. Pack hunters also bond with their hosts to cause the possession phenomenon.

They are particularly good mimics, and many hosts become convinced that they are being paid attention to not by parasites but by benevolent and protective spirits.

THE ROGUES

These loners have many of the tendencies of pack hunters, but they operate on their own. They function freely through Ouija boards and séances, and they too can be responsible for poltergeist phenomena or, if they get enough to eat, possession cases. In fact, I strongly suspect that the entity "possessing" Barbara in 1973 was a Rogue.

One interesting characteristic I've noticed with Rogues is that they are often confined to a certain geographic area of our world, probably at points of multiversal intersect. They can travel short distances away from these spots but are soon drawn or snapped back. Weird as it sounds, I actually had a Rogue in the car with me while I was on the way home from a case in 1998. As soon as we crossed the nearest river, it disappeared, snapping back to its base.

THE PASSIVES

This interesting group seems to be satisfied filling the role of second-stringers, usually to the Elders but sometimes to other, brighter parasites. In paranormal cases, we often find the Passives in subservient positions, dominated, sometimes cruelly, by superior species. They seem to feed on, in a manner of speaking, whatever "crumbs" are left after the Elders are finished.

THE LOST

There's an utterly fascinating tendency among all parasites to forget their own origins, and even their own identities, the longer they spend attached to their hosts or in worlds that are not their own. That becomes especially evident as we approach the lower echelons among the parasite species. And that includes the Lost. They seem to operate alone, concentrating on one person even when there is little or no sustenance to be had from that person.

The Lost often communicate verbally, and they sometimes give the impression that they need sympathy. On rare occasions, they'll even communicate that they're sorry for their vampire-like lifestyle. In one case, in the American Midwest, in 2009, one of the Lost was constantly apologizing to its human host. The host could hear a human-like voice but never saw the parasite. (See section four, chapter two, "What Ghosts Have to Say about God.")

THE TRICKSTERS

The concept of the trickster is common in folklore and in all ancient religions. Indigenous peoples talk about trickster spirits, demons, or gods who are very knowledgeable about humans, but who use this knowledge to play pranks, sometimes cruel ones, or otherwise flaunt accepted moral or social behavior. Often, they use our own human failings and foibles against us.

When it comes to trickster parasites, they often come across as intellectual lightweights, but they're clever at the same time. They will get the energy flowing from their hosts through startling antics and unpleasant surprises. As with all parasites, their abilities to travel among parallel worlds make it seem as though they can manipulate space and time, something that in itself, as the great twentieth-century horror writer H. P. Lovecraft pointed out, strikes terror into the human heart.

I believe that tricksters are sometimes the "enlightened masters," "space brothers," or false spirit guides that have a field day among gullible psychics and mediums.

THE BRATS

Welcome to the bottom shelf of the parasite worlds: the Brats. These creatures act like spoiled, but sometimes frightened, children. In fact, they exhibit many of the same behaviors as maladjusted children.

Brats seem to live and feed alone on a specific human who is also alone. Often, an unhealthy bond will result. While Brats aren't very swift, they are very good at manipulating their hosts, and they're terrified of being separated from these hosts, because they are among the most likely to forget who they are and where they came from.

LOST AND FRIGHTENED

As I've said, I have always found that particular parasite characteristic completely enthralling, and it applies to all parasites to some degree, especially those in the lower ranks: The longer they spend in our corner of the multiverse and/or attached to a human host, the more they tend to forget their own origins. Many are afraid—terrified, in fact—to separate from their hosts because they can't recall where or when they are from, or where or when to return.

As for food sources in addition to our negative vibes, all parasites seem to feed on recognition and attention to some degree. Some become "stuck" in certain places because of the conditions there. Interestingly, we've seen this both near homes and in wilderness areas.

As to the parasite version of family farming, the question arises: All families, and certainly every person, has stress and negative experiences. Why isn't every person obsessed, oppressed, or possessed, and why doesn't every home have its very own parasite/poltergeist?

Good question. Over the years, however, it became apparent that many factors must fall into place for paranormal phenomena to occur at all, never mind engulf a person or family. And it became clear that parasites don't have *carte blanche* to feed wherever and whenever they please. There seem to be rules in the multiverse, probably depending on the laws of physics in a given world. Evidently, Godzilla can't just blunder through a brane and eat San Francisco. In the same way, parasites apparently can't just come through anywhere or anytime and carry us away. Or can they?

COULD DEMON EQUAL ALIEN?

In a word, yes. The parasites I have encountered over the years have been truly alien, truly other. They seem just as capable of mimicking space beings and UFOnauts as they do pretending to be your deceased grandma. This is clear from years of what we call "pan-paranormal" research and "crossover phenomena." Consulting with distinguished UFO researchers such as Kathleen Marden and Denise Stoner, Ben and I have run into cases where reports of UFO sightings and alien abductions have been followed by poltergeist activity and "demonic" phenomena.

This isn't to say that there are no aliens from other planets, no actual encounters with people we think are dead, or no Bigfoot. I'm saying these are easy for parasites to imitate, and can provide more buttons for them to push.

We often hear the question: Could parasites be some kind of remnant of deceased humans? There is absolutely nothing human about them, even if we find interesting examples of the Lost actually apologizing to their hosts, which is a rather human thing to do. As we will see in a few paragraphs, however, parasites, though far from human themselves, might have a very disturbing connection with us.

CAN PLACES BE EXORCISED?

While the concept of a parasite "possessing" a place is slippery, in my opinion, we do run into places where parasite activity is long-term and steady. I believe that places can be exorcised in many cases if one is able to bring in positive energy to displace the negative food source—and perhaps even to close the intersect point. In the Bridgeport poltergeist case of 1974, the Warrens, Fr. William Charbonneau, and I stayed in that house for the better part of three days, waiting for permission from the local bishop for "Fr. Bill" to exorcise the place. It never came. Exorcising the place, at least in the Catholic tradition, would have involved the priest-exorcist, in this case Fr. Bill, celebrating mass in the house.

At least three house blessings, by two different priests, took place in Bridgeport. Blessings of this kind, which are not specifically exorcisms, can help bring in positive energy and ease a negative situation. Things really did calm down for a while after each blessing, but it didn't last.

Most Roman Catholic priests who know anything about the subject believe the explanation behind all paranormal phenomena, including hauntings, is demonic activity. As the exorcist for the Diocese of Providence, Rhode Island, once told me: "I don't believe in ghosts. I believe in demons."

In contrast, we have found parasites active in only about 65 percent of haunted houses and wilderness areas. That percentage tends to be roughly 10 percent higher in "flap areas," regions of unusually high paranormal activity of all kinds, all resulting from high instances of parallel-world overlaps, intersects or overwashes. Parasites take advantage of that. (See section three, chapter one).

DOES EXORCISM REALLY WORK?

In my experience, exorcised or not, parasites that aren't afraid to leave their hosts do so only when they're good and ready, almost always when they've had enough to eat. If it serves their purpose after an exorcism, they will lie low, making the exorcist and others believe they're gone. The same can be true across all traditions, where exorcism tends to be much less institutionalized than in Catholic practice.

Since 2008 or so, the Vatican supposedly has lightened up on information about exorcism and has let it be known that it is training more priest-exorcists because of a glut of demon cases. But, according to people I know at the Vatican, what's really happening is that, with so many people obsessed with the paranormal today, more priests are being trained in how to tell if someone is really possessed, according to their definition of the phenomenon. Actual cases remain relatively uncommon, I'm told.

Elsewhere in Christianity, the Eastern Church (the Orthodox and Oriental Orthodox) have a practice of exorcism that's probably more ancient than it is among the Roman Catholics. However, exorcism is understood differently: more as protective prayer and lifestyle that will repel demons before they ever get a foothold in someone's life. Accordingly, exorcism prayers are common in Orthodox daily practice. They're used whenever someone is baptized, right down to blessings for water, oil, and sacramental vessels. For the Orthodox, an ounce of prevention is worth a pound of cure.

If worse comes to worst, and an Orthodox priest runs into a case like Barbara's, where demonic influence is believed present, the priest may proceed on his own authority. Permission of the local bishop isn't generally required. In fact, I was in touch with an Orthodox priest in Connecticut during the Bridgeport case, and he was willing to come in and perform an exorcism as a last resort, which also never happened.

Exorcism in the Roman Catholic sense is common throughout the most conservative Protestant denominations, where all paranormal phenomena are seen as demonic in origin, meant to win believers away from the Bible. Ministers often perform exorcisms with the same claim of authority over demons that would be reminiscent of Fr. Lawrence's practice.

In many denominations, especially the Evangelicals, any Christian can "cast out demons" simply because the Bible says they can (Mark 16:17).

Judaism has a long and lush tradition of exorcism, with several examples of it in the Hebrew Bible, notably in 1 Samuel and the Book of Tobit. The idea of possession by demons has many interpretations, and exorcism is very non-institutionalized. A Jewish exorcism can be based on anything from music to burning herbs, to reading prayers, to (in the old days, anyway) the execution of false prophets, a practice pretty much guaranteed to cure possession.

The Muslim understanding of exorcism, known as *ruqya*, is part of the broader practice of alternative medicine. Their understanding of the entire phenomenon jives rather well with our understanding of parasites.

Excluding the execution part, similar exorcism practices exist across the other major religions, including Buddhism and Hinduism.

IN MY NAME THEY WILL DRIVE OUT DEMONS

This line from Mark 16:17 empowers Christians to perform exorcisms. Faith gives people power—I get that, and I've certainly seen it. The trouble with just anyone performing an exorcism, formally or informally, is that things can get out of hand whether the subject is really entangled with a parasite or not.

There have been cases around the world where would-be exorcists, of many faith backgrounds, and not just among Christians, have created disasters, up to and including the deaths of the people they're trying to help. This can be true anywhere, especially among the uneducated, where faith and wishful thinking are unrestrained by reason.

There are heartbreaking stories of parents performing brutal exorcism rituals on children because the latter were having tantrums. Other reports have husbands performing exorcisms on wives and inadvertently killing them. The only ones benefiting from these horrors are the parasites.

THE BONDING

Now we come to the scary part. How and why does a parasite bond with a host, making it look like possession?

In multiverse theory, there is a concept that most people find especially difficult to wrap their heads around. This is the idea that in many parallel worlds there are different facets of ourselves, and that it's all "us." We have, in effect, a superlife. Combine this with two other MWI principles: that all possibilities are actually real, somewhere or somewhen, and that the past and future exist all at once, and a very bizarre possibility for the nature of possession becomes evident.

From what I've seen in possession cases, it's clear that parasites and their hosts bond because they literally *are* different facets of each other. At some point in the multiverse, Chall is Barbara and Barbara is Chall. Being an active multiversal creature, Chall knew this, found the point, and exploited the cross-brane circumstances. Because of this bond, Barbara was an easy meal, and so were the rest of us who participated in the exorcism.

THE PETER PAN THEORY

Our method of repelling parasites by bringing in positive energy to displace the negative energy food source really seems to work. When I adopted this approach to parasite cases in the late 1970s, instead of calling in exorcists, I found a simple solution that brought major successes, and without the paranormal drama.

Today, Ben and I call this the "Peter Pan Theory": Think happy thoughts!

From there, though, it got a lot weirder. Read on.

CHAPTER TWO

THE BRISTOL POLTERGEIST

The next inkling I had that all paranormal cases are bigger than they appear came in July 1975, just after I graduated from Wadhams Hall Seminary and arrived back home in Connecticut for the summer. I had just defected from the Roman Catholic Church to the Eastern Orthodox Church, was getting their sometimes quite different theology under my belt, and was about to continue priestly studies at their graduate-level seminary, St. Vladimir's Orthodox Theological Seminary in New York.

I was disheveled enough at that point without having to tangle with another poltergeist. "Too bad," said Fate.

This was to be the first "spirit that thrashes about" I'd ever faced on my own, without help from the likes of Fr. Lawrence Wheeler or Ed and Lorraine Warren. In the wake of the Bridgeport poltergeist circus of eight months before, it would continue my reverse-education in what poltergeists really are, what they want, and how far their influence can reach.

The scene this time was a hilltop housing subdivision in Bristol, Connecticut. Brian Dow, a Connecticut radio and early cable-television personality, put me in touch with the family in question. The difference with this case was that, when I showed up at the home for the initial interview, there was a neighbor there who wanted to talk about what was going on at *her* house. That was because almost every home in this relatively new neighborhood had weird goings-on. Here was a poltergeist that broke the rules as I understood them at the time: It wasn't attached to any particular person, roamed the area at will, and was apparently a threat to the entire neighborhood.

According to the narrow, static theology, poltergeists were demons. According to the frustrated pseudoscience of parapsychology, poltergeists were almost like thought-forms, produced by someone in terrible trauma, including children going through puberty. Thanks to the Ogdensburg exorcisms and the Bridgeport poltergeist, I didn't really believe either of those theories anymore. But, as yet, I had no coherent systems to replace them.

So, ready or not, here I was in this Bristol neighborhood, which occupied the greater part of an old farm. All but a few of the houses were new, with some lots farther up the road still undeveloped. Where a road entered the subdivision, on the south corner, one of the old farm buildings had been turned into a private home long before the newer houses were built. Adjacent to this boxy, brown-painted structure stood a dilapidated outbuilding in the process of being torn down.

Right across the road from there was the ranch house of John and Susan Sanford, both in their late thirties, and their two sons, ten-year-old Alex and twelve-year-old Bob. Built about three years earlier, theirs was the first house in the new subdivision, and the first new human habitation at the site since the 1910s. Most people don't associate hauntings with new houses, but I was about to learn otherwise.

Until 1975, the Sanfords experienced nothing particularly weird in their new home. The couple had a passing interest in the paranormal, and they'd seen me on Brian Dow's TV show in April, talking about the Bridgeport case. So, when the most hellish weeks of their lives began, two months later, they called Brian and got in touch with me.

When I met the Sanfords and their neighbors that hot, mid-July week, I was intrigued to find out that their poltergeist problem might have been prompted by an act of kindness.

The neighbors included someone who wasn't among the group I met that day. This was the middle-aged widow and her teenaged son who lived in the old brown house across the road from the Sanfords. Their name was Hobbes, they kept to themselves, and no one in the subdivision really knew them. When the boy, who was about fourteen, pedaled down the road on his bicycle, the new neighborhood children often taunted him, shouting, among other things, that his mother was a witch.

This upset the kind-hearted Susan. So, one muggy Wednesday in mid-June, when John was at work and the boys were in their last days of school for that year, she decided to walk across the street to invite the mysterious Mrs. Hobbes over for coffee. Susan found a nervous but congenial forty-five-year-old woman whose name turned out to be Sarah, and soon the two women were seated in the Sanford kitchen over coffee and pastry. But the Sanfords' small dachshund, usually friendly, yelped, ran, and hid as soon as Sarah entered the house, and he wouldn't come out until she left.

It was a strange visit, and the guest acted as though she'd never experienced air conditioning before. Sarah seemed shy, and reluctant to talk about herself. By way of making conversation, she did mention that she owned the property where the old cottage was being demolished.

"Funny you should bring that up," Susan said. "I notice the work stopped last week. Those workers seemed in a big hurry to leave in the middle of the morning."

In one of the first photos the author took at the old farm building in Bristol, Connecticut, in 1975, a bearded face seems to appear at the door. There was no glass and what had been the window was boarded up. The building was in the process of being demolished, but workers refused to continue when one of them felt invisible hands around his neck.

Sarah, a little more relaxed now, looked nonchalantly at Susan as though they were talking about the weather. "Oh, the contractor said one of the men felt cold hands around his neck when he was trying to take down the back wall. They all just left. I'm not going to pay them unless they finish!"

Susan didn't know how to react, and Sarah left soon afterward. The next day, however, Sarah invited Susan to the old house for iced tea. So, with John packed off to his real estate office and the boys riding their bikes elsewhere in the neighborhood, Susan took a deep breath and headed across the street. She felt a profound and inexplicable uneasiness as she approached the old house, she told me later.

Susan found the Hobbes home gloomy, stuffy, and hot. There was no sign of the boy. But that wasn't the half of it. She nearly choked on a sip of tea when an ash tray suddenly rose from the coffee table, without a sound, and floated across the room. Sarah, not in the least surprised, declared, "Oh, that's only the ghost."

Susan made a polite but hasty exit.

Sarah's next visit to the Sanford home, a few days later, was her last. That's because, as Susan put it, "She brought the thing with her!"

The conversation was pleasant enough, and Sarah seemed more relaxed. That wasn't the problem.

"As soon as she left, dishes flew off the shelves and smashed on the floor!" Susan told me. "Furniture jumped around and pictures fell off the wall!"

Petrified, she backed up against the kitchen counter, then grabbed the telephone.

"I called John and begged him to come home," Susan said.

Then the kitchen door opened, the activity abruptly stopped, and Bob walked in and glanced around. "Mom, what the hell?"

When Alex arrived a few minutes later, he asked if the house had been broken into. As for John, he was home within fifteen minutes. Before he saw the state of the house for himself, he thought his wife was exaggerating. It took the rest of the day to clean up the mess.

Beginning the next morning at dawn, poltergeist activity erupted again, plaguing the Sanford home off and on throughout the following week, though there wasn't as much destruction as there had been on that first day. Not only did objects move around by themselves, but all four family members heard animal-like growling coming from beneath beds and other furniture. "Terrifying" eyes John described as "flaming red" appeared at windows, and knocks were heard at the doors at all hours of the day and night. Of course, when the doors were opened, no one was there. They put most breakable objects in boxes and secured them in the garage.

Initially, John suspected that someone was playing tricks on them. But he couldn't imagine whom. They were good friends with everyone in the neighborhood except, of course, the Hobbeses. Glancing out the front window at the old brown house across the road, the Sanfords settled on Sarah Hobbes as the only explanation, whatever that explanation could actually be. In addition, Susan was convinced that the whole nightmare was connected with the half-demolished cottage, to which the workers still hadn't returned.

That John and Susan needed help was a "no-brainer." But what kind of help did they need? The kitchen was a shambles, everyone was losing sleep, the boys were terrified, and the dog was a basket case. But, dreading a repeat of the global media circus surrounding the Bridgeport affair, they decided not to call the police. They didn't mention their plight to anyone they knew, not even relatives, for fear of ridicule. Instead, they contacted Brian Dow.

THE CHAOS SPREADS

Meanwhile, the chaos was beginning to spread. Only when a neighbor mentioned that strange things were happening at her house (on a more minor scale) did Susan learn about this and confide in the neighbor about their own problem. As it turned out, four nearby families were hearing strange knocks at all hours, and two families were being scared silly by objects moving on their own.

Everyone hoped this was some kind of seismic anomaly or other weird but explainable phenomenon. But an incident at the very end of that first week shook Susan down to her shoes. In broad daylight, she looked out the front window and saw a huge black form, like a cloud with legs, move through the field across the road and disappear into the wall of the old cottage.

That evening, Brian Dow called them back.

It was a hot, but grim, overcast day when I went to the Sanford house. As I've said, Susan and one of the affected neighbors filled me in on the most recent events. For the moment, all phenomena seemed to have ceased after Susan saw the dark shape in the field.

After that conversation, I walked over to the Hobbes property to look at what was left of the cottage and to take photographs. Nothing unusual happened until I approached the structure. About fifteen feet from the ruins, I was abruptly halted by what I can describe only as a wall of electrical energy—a very strong electro-

An orb or other odd shape seemed to be forming as the author took this shot in the backyard of the Hobbes home.

magnetic field (EMF) for which there was no apparent electrical source. It was the strongest EMF I'd encountered up to that point. It engulfed the cottage and seemed equally strong at all points, so potent that my hair practically stood on end. I snapped a few pictures with my trusty Kodak Instamatic camera, high-tech for the time, and retreated across the street.

Back at the Sanfords', I suggested to Susan that I talk with Sarah Hobbes and her son. I also wanted to return in a few days to go over the derelict property again and talk with more neighbors. Nagging my thoughts was the suspicion that this was a parasite, but what was feeding it? On the surface, the Sanfords seemed to be a well-balanced family, though my instincts told me otherwise. Of course, this was still the period when I was burying my instincts.

With that, I bade farewell for the day and drove away in my 1968 Ford Fairlane. But, while I was willing to call it a day, whatever was plaguing the neighborhood apparently wasn't. As I turned onto the main road, the same blast of energy I'd felt at the cottage enveloped me and the interior of my car. All at once, both doors flew open and a stiff wind tore through, blowing everything (except me, fortunately) out onto the road. My vehicles have never been noted for tidiness, so the debris I had to gather and stuff back inside was considerable. Feeling like a character in a horror movie, I made it home to East Hartford without further incident.

As in the exorcism of Barbara, I'd say in hindsight that I was dealing with a member of the parasite species known as the Rogues.

Back in the days of photographic film, negatives, and darkrooms, it was easier to pin down what was weird in pictures than it is in our current digital age. Two days after that first visit to the Bristol hilltop, I had a photo lab report confirming that some elements in two of my pictures were anomalous, with what were known as "extras." In one, a bearded face seems to look out a boarded-up, glassless window of the old cottage. In the other, two odd, bluish shapes seem to be taking form in the front yard of the Hobbes house. Several friends of mine thought they saw the crouching figure of a stout little boy, looking into a puddle before the ruins in a third photo, but a lab examination proved nothing.

The next evening, I went to a gathering at the Warrens' home that included several psychics, along with a few paranormal researchers, notably my friend Dr. Brian Riley, a British American parapsychologist then based in Connecticut. We sat around the living room and discussed the Sanfords' poltergeist. Brian took the standard route by suggesting that the poltergeist was probably being generated by ten-year-old Alex, who was the same age as the little girl Marcy in the Bridgeport case.

JEREMY

Among the psychics present was another friend, Mary Pascarella, head of the Psychic Research Institute in Hamden, Connecticut. Mary took me into the kitchen, sat me down, and pronounced her judgment. This, not to my surprise, was all about dead people. To my alarm, Mary proceeded to drop into a semi-trance.

"A retarded boy named Jeremy was confined to that old cottage in the late nineteenth or early twentieth centuries. At that time, children like Jeremy were considered a shame rather than an occasion for extra love. Many were locked away by their families and abused," Mary declared.

Sadly, she was right about that last part.

"This was the case with Jeremy, who was probably illegitimate," she continued. "He is earthbound in the old cottage where he suffered so much torment."

Naturally, the photo with the boy-like shape near the puddle came to mind. When I told Mary what happened in my car on the way home, she said Jeremy followed me because he sensed I would understand him. She knew I'd worked with disabled children the previous summer.

At that point, I was already way skeptical about the whole idea of earthbound spirits, and just as much so about Brian Riley's attempt to make the whole scenario acceptable to mainstream science, which it never will be. Well intentioned as they were, the group at the Warrens' that evening wasn't much help. Several, including Mary, offered to help me in the case. I declined politely but firmly.

All this time, my comrade in research and a fellow seminary student, Joseph Letendre, was burrowing through Bristol town records. He found no mention of a Jeremy, but this isn't surprising if he was the kind of child Mary described. But Joseph did find that the old cottage had a questionable reputation: It had been the site of prostitution, bootlegging, and other illegal, negative activities during the 1920s.

What's more, there was a nearby thoroughfare known as Witches Rock Road. I was already learning to pay attention to place names. Roads, hills, streams, or just plain places tagged with witches, ghosts, spirits, the devil, giant birds, or other weird phenomena were given those names by our ancestors for good reason. We found that stories of witchcraft in the area around the Sanford house went back to the eighteenth century. Allegedly, a witch put a curse on a rocky outcrop, and the curse haunts the area to this day. Reported phenomena included uncontrollable horses, strange apparitions, and, yes, poltergeist activity.

That said, I suspected even then that local people might cook up a story to explain already-present phenomena. After all, demons are more understandable than energy parasites. And, certainly, ghost children are more comprehensible than real children encountered when parallel worlds intersect.

If I knew then what I think I know now, I'd have known I was dealing with a "flap area," a region of intense but seemingly unrelated paranormal phenomena. (See section three, chapter one.) I would have looked for UFO sightings and found them, and I'd have known enough to push the geographic envelope for more ghost and parasite reports. There had already been Bigfoot sightings north of this neighborhood. If the theories and methods Ben and I use today are correct, all this is the result of intersects, overlaps, or overwashes of parallel worlds with different laws of physics and different inhabitants, including parasites.

Nevertheless, only a week after my initial interview with the Sanfords and the neighbor, Joseph and I were still trying to start a wider investigation. I spoke on the phone with three other neighbors/experiencers, but the really scary phenomena had ceased for the time being. As is typical with some witnesses, the Sanfords and the neighbors began to rationalize. There had to be a "logical explanation." In other words, there had to be an explanation that fit our narrow paradigm and reassured us that everything we know is *not* wrong.

Here's where I found out that it's easier to get experiencers to cooperate one at a time than in a group. They seem to take strength and security from each other, which is very much a good thing, except for the unfortunate researcher who can't get them to cooperate further. Maybe that's why most parasites target individual victims, and why our encouragement toward group positive thinking on the part of victims actually repels parasites. I inadvertently learned this from the Bristol case.

A "gang's all here" attitude by the Bristolians wasn't the only reason we couldn't proceed much further. As with the Sanfords, the rest of the neighbors knew all about the Bridgeport debacle and my involvement in it, and they were afraid of possible media attention. It was just as difficult to contact Mrs. Hobbes; I never even saw her.

While we heard later that there was another, brief poltergeist outbreak at the Sanfords', I was never again contacted for assistance. And in another lesson for the future when it came to parasites, Brian Dow told me that the personalities of John and Susan Sanford suddenly changed drastically, that the family's finances collapsed, and that divorce was being discussed, all within a few months of the phenomena. Later, we heard that the family moved away. We never found out whether the neighbors had any more trouble.

Still, this was a clue not only to what was feeding the phenomena, but also a lesson in: "Paul, pay attention to your instincts!"

Even though there wasn't a full investigation, whatever might constitute that, I reached several opinions at the time. The Sanfords' troubled marriage, coupled with an extremely powerful "psychic residue" at the old cottage and, very possibly, geotechnic energies conducive to paranormal activity, not to mention a parasite of some kind, all played a role. Mix all this with the introverted personalities of Mrs. Hobbes and her son, and the chemistry likely was just right for the sort of paranormal pyrotechnics the Sanfords and their neighbors described.

Before many more years passed, though, I rejected much of that, especially the "residual haunting" idea, in favor of the mechanics of the multiverse. Even if there had been a Jeremy, he was still alive somewhere in the multiverse. As for Mrs. Hobbes and her son, they later moved away also, and the cottage was torn down without further ado.

When the personalities whose energies apparently fed it were gone, this unusually fierce neighborhood poltergeist certainly seems to have dissipated.

Whether my theories are correct (and I'm the first to admit they might not be) or whether "Jeremy" still broods in some parallel universe, awaiting the understanding he never had in one life or another, we probably will never know.

CHAPTER THREE

DOUBLE TROUBLE

Lucy Cormier was a master at becoming a hot lunch for parasites, and at using her Ouija board as the dinner bell. Lucy was a pretty fifteen-year-old with long blonde hair. She and her family lived in Glastonbury, Connecticut, where the Ouija board was given to her as a present for Christmas 1974.

Merry Christmas.

Ouija boards are dangerous. They're among several sledgehammer techniques to smash through the branes between parallel worlds and let in anything that happens to be there. Probably the most dangerous aspect of Ouija boards is that, if users do communicate with an entity, they tend to believe everything it tells them.

As soon as Lucy got hold of the board, she and a friend spent much of their Christmas vacation using it. Both girls became fascinated by the "spirit world" and with the parasite that claimed to be a "spirit guide" called Arten, communicating through the board. Lucy's older brother, Bill, her only sibling, became interested, too. Their parents, Roman Catholic but not especially religious, thought nothing of it.

In mid-1975, Bill joined the US Navy. Soon after he left for basic training, Lucy and her parents were startled by certain phenomena that began late that year and continued into 1976. While it was nothing like the chaos in the Bridgeport or Bristol cases, minor poltergeist phenomena began to occur. Cabinet doors in the kitchen would open and close on their own, books and other objects in different rooms would fall off shelves, and occasional heavy footsteps would be heard in the attic and on the stairs. Loud banging sounds took place on several occasions.

Interestingly, phenomena seemed to follow Lucy. Four times, various members of the family saw a ghostly figure with long blonde hair, usually leaning over Lucy's bed while the girl was asleep. This even occurred at the family's vacation home on Block Island, Rhode Island, nearly one hundred miles away.

While Lucy was visiting it, bizarre happenings also took place at an eighteenth-century home in nearby Coventry, Connecticut, where her boyfriend's sister lived. An orange glowing ball, what today would be known as an orb, was seen on one of these occasions.

In August that year, I was with Ed and Lorraine Warren when they lectured in Glastonbury. I sat in the back of the hall. The young man who sat down next to me and started chatting, having no idea who I was, happened to be a concerned friend of Lucy's family, and he knew what was going on at the Cormier home. When Ed Warren asked me to stand up and be recognized, as an eyewitness to the still-being-talked-about Bridgeport case, the young man's jaw hit the floor.

The next day, he put me in touch with the Cormiers, and, a few days after that, I interviewed Lucy for the first time. I felt, somehow, that Lucy and I weren't the only ones in the room. In fact, I felt three other presences.

"I'm not afraid at all," the girl told me. "I think it's fascinating, really. I have kind of a boring life, and I'm not very popular. I like the attention I get from Arten. In another life, I could have loved him."

Good grief!

In 1975, this was a little difficult to deal with because I was still trying to get my head around the idea that these parasites weren't spirits, demons in the theological sense, or much else that people thought they were. Looking back, what they were, from the looks of it, were Pack Hunter parasites. Today, the minor phenomena and the doppelganger of Lucy would be true clues.

I also visited the Coventry house, and that made for an interesting day. As Lucy and the other young people were showing me around this lovely, eighteenth-century farmhouse, surrounded by fields and stables, something followed us around the house, turning on lights as we went.

One unique point in this case was that it was the first and last time I ever felt the much-vaunted "psychic cold" that supposedly is ubiquitous in disturbed houses. Just about every paranormal sleuth I know talks about it, but that was the only time I've ever felt it engulf my whole body. Why I've never felt it in other cases, I know not. I felt the cold so clearly in that farmhouse, though, that it made a trail I was able to follow. Whatever-it-was led me into a corner room, then dissipated.

This case was, perhaps deceptively, easy to cure. Joseph Letendre and I read prayers with the Cormier family at their home. Then, in the absence of a priest, I took the liberty of sprinkling holy water around the house. Most importantly, we got Lucy to say that she didn't trust Arten, and would never engage in occult practices again. Hopefully, she meant it. She handed over the Ouija board and we destroyed it.

I was off to my eventual fate at St. Vladimir's Seminary that fall, so I admit that my follow-up with the Cormiers wasn't what it should have been. But as I left them, positive energy seemed to rule, phenomena had ceased, and Lucy seemed happy.

The Pack Hunters, hopefully, moved on.

CHAPTER FOUR

THE BADDEST POLTERGEIST IN NEW ENGLAND

People think the worst poltergeist I ever dealt with was in Bridgeport, Connecticut, in 1974. But the four parasites responsible for that extravaganza were only the second -worst. The irony about the New Haven poltergeist of 1979 was that it was the easiest to get rid of.

In March of that year a frantic phone call came from Steve Cargill, a friend of mine in New Haven, Connecticut.

"Even you won't believe this one!" Steve was yelling. I could hear banging and shouts in the background.

"What?" I shouted back, alarmed.

"The craziest poltergeist you ever saw! I'm there now!"

Fortunately, I was still living in East Hartford, about thirty-five miles to the north, so I wasn't far away. I dropped everything and headed down Interstate 91 to New Haven. Following Steve's hasty directions, I soon found myself at the back door of a good-sized, two-story, "mom and pop" convenience store not far from the city line. It was in an old, mixed commercial-residential neighborhood, and there was an apartment above the store. There was a big "closed" sign at the front door, and the store windows all were curtained. I'd been told to slink around to the rear door as invisibly as I could. I knocked, then jumped back when the door opened immediately.

"Are you Paul?" asked a big, forty-something woman.

"Yes, ma'am," I responded.

Without another word, her arm shot out, grabbed my sleeve and pulled me in. She looked exhausted, but her strength was alarming. The door slammed to the nervous rustle of closed Venetian blinds. Before she hustled me through another door and up a flight of stairs, I had enough time to see that the darkened store was a disaster area. Everything that should have been on the shelves seemed to be on the floor. There was an unpleasant smell, and I could have sworn that I saw a two-liter bottle of soda suspended high in the air over the middle aisle.

My apparent hostess didn't give me time to investigate.

"Up this way. This is where it's worst!" she cried, grabbing me by the arm again and hauling me up the stairs, which were littered with articles of clothing. At the top, a spacious apartment opened out. The place would have been very pleasant had it not been like an accident scene. The floor was covered with debris; there were black scrawls of "death," "die," and a few less mentionable things on the walls; and the place reeked of sulphur or ozone—it was hard to tell which. The electromagnetic field (EMF) was so powerful that it felt like bugs crawling all over my skin.

"This is my home! Do you believe this? *Ahhhhh!*" She shrieked, and my head quickly swung around to look where she was looking. We both ducked just in time as a huge armchair whizzed over our heads and crashed against the opposite wall.

"What now?" came a shout from the bathroom, and Steve stumbled out, still fastening his pants. "Oh, you're here!" He picked his way across the room to shake my hand. Somehow, I felt free to skip my usual "Is this really paranormal?" process. In fact, this case would be the closest I would ever come to what Hollywood gives us in horror movies.

"All right!" I stated with a glance over each shoulder. "What's the story?"

At once something started pounding on the floors right beneath our feet. I'd just turned to run back down the stairs to see what it was when the woman, whose name turned out to be Liz Centracci, shouted over the din: "Don't bother. It's the ghost."

Well, it seems that "the ghost" had been raising the devil at this scene off and on for over a year.

"A year?" I blurted in amazement.

It's unusual for a poltergeist to last more than three months at a stretch, though it might recur. The longest documented case I'm aware of was at Kuokkaniemi in Finland, and that went on for a little less than three years, beginning in 1900. It's also unusual, in my experience anyway, for a poltergeist to keep going flat-out when I arrive. Usually things calm down for a while, seemingly until it gets used to me, and my own electrical field is introduced into its mix.

The thing was quiet long enough for me to hear the whole tale.

Liz had been a widow for about five years. Her husband, a cancer victim, had left her the prosperous little store beneath our feet, and a decent chunk of money. That was good, because Liz had their little girl to bring up. Things had gone pretty well until early 1978, when pounding had started on the floor of the apartment, seeming to move rapidly around underneath. In the store below, the pounding was on the ceiling, and Liz would tell customers hastily that she was having some repair work done.

On the sly, she had the place checked for mice, rats, bats, termites, and every other known physical pest. She sought help from utility companies and even consulted a seismologist from nearby Yale University, all to no avail. Phenomena kept getting worse and, within six months, Liz had to close the store—after something started throwing bottles of soda at customers one day. That's how she met my friend Steve.

"I happened to be in the store about six months ago, and I got beaned by a bottle of ginger ale!" he recalled. "There was nobody else in the store, and Liz seemed real nervous. I 'put two and two together' and told her I knew a guy who worked with 'weird stuff.' I left her my phone number."

Meanwhile, Liz told customers that she was closing the store to start a major remodeling project. She even had her brother-in-law, a contractor, park one of his trucks outside for a few days each week. But if anybody was going to do some remodeling, it was the multiversal beast inside.

CALAMITY JANE OF THE PARANORMAL

By mid-1978, voices had joined the pounding. Liz and her fourteen-year-old daughter, Anna, would hear each other speaking even when both parties weren't present. Not long after that, apparitions began, getting more terrifying by the week: faces bobbing in the air, black shadows creeping across the floor and through the air, both in the store and the apartment, and red eyes seen peering from beneath furniture.

That's when Liz packed the frazzled Anna off to her sister-in-law's in nearby East Haven. But Liz, a sort of Calamity Jane of the paranormal, was determined to fight it out. She would take breathers from time to time, staying with Anna and her sister-in-law for a few days just to get her strength back. Swashbuckling as Liz was, things only got worse when she went back to the apartment and the parasite started sucking her energy again.

After a while, Liz wasn't able to sleep in the apartment at all, and she moved in with her sister-in-law and daughter. But nearly every morning, Liz would be back in her domain to keep watch and battle the poltergeist, almost as though she were going to work. Of course, all she was doing was feeding the thing. Liz told me that it would take the critter or critters a good hour to get revved up after she arrived in the morning. In fact, she was a sort of human cup of coffee for it.

Down in the shuttered store, what was left of the stock wouldn't stay on the shelves, and Liz finally gave up trying to keep it there. About two months before I showed up, the black scrawls started appearing on walls and ceilings in the apartment, and the poltergeist began punching holes in the plaster walls.

The real trouble here was that Liz had done everything wrong from day one, right down to the last detail. She and a friend played with a Ouija board for weeks before the trouble began. Obviously, one or more parasites came through. Later, when phenomena got worse, Liz became convinced that it was a ghost and organized a séance with a local medium and a few trusted friends. This just took what the Ouija board did and made it worse. I later met two of Liz's friends who attended, and they confirmed that "the voice of an angry young woman" came through the medium, claiming she had been murdered in a house on that spot in 1820 and wanted revenge. It was the usual nonsense that parasites dish out to get their hosts stirred up. The spot was the middle of a cornfield in 1820, at least in our corner of the multiverse.

The medium never came back.

Liz's solution was to alternately shout at the poltergeist, then ignore it. She sprinkled holy water or salt, burned incense and sage, and otherwise called upon every folk remedy she could find in books at the local branch of the New Haven Free Public Library.

It's not that these methods don't work, but they work much better when done with faith and a positive spirit than with fear and superstition. That's because they're tools: They have little power in themselves, but they can concentrate and energize the power of our own minds to positively take control our own environment. But the tools must fit the user. Crosses rarely work for non-Christians, for example, but I've seen teddy bears work as protective tools for children. It really does depend on the person. Liz was using her chosen tools in fear and anger.

All this hullabaloo provided more energy for the original parasite—and attracted some of its buddies. In my initial investigation, when I wasn't dodging flying furniture, I felt strongly that there were at least six parasites having a field day, not only in the apartment but also in the store below. Looking back on it, I believe they were Pack Hunters.

In a situation that would have spurred most people to hit the road long before, Liz got more and more determined. But as her anger grew, it too fed the parasites. And as she continued to live off her savings, without income from the store, she got more and more worried, and that fed the parasites as well.

I've seen this circle-the-wagons mentality many times, though not for so long a period. Homeowners and even renters have a certain primal instinct to defend their homes. I've often seen people stick it out even on the rare occasions I've advised them to move. Of course, phenomena at Liz's weren't constant. Poltergeists tend to be active for a few days or a week, then re-energize (on Liz, in this case) before getting active again. So, Liz did have a few days of relative quiet every week or so. But nothing she could do seemed to bring the trouble to an end.

Liz struck me as not only strong but also honest. For example, she was a Roman Catholic, but she hadn't called her priest because she was afraid he'd be upset

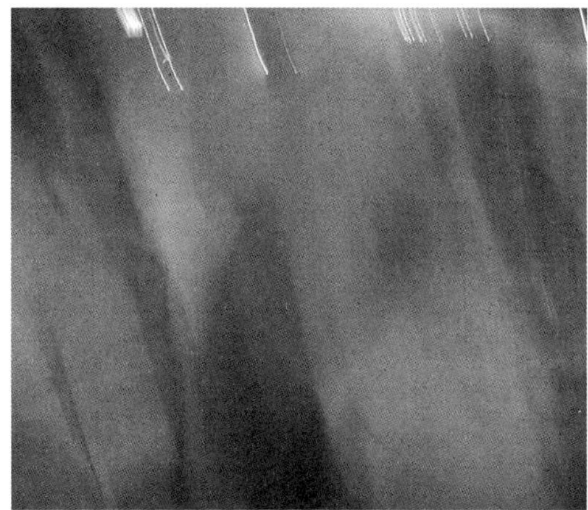

Out of over sixty photographs the author took at the scene in March 1979, this is the only frame on the 35 mm film roll that wasn't completely washed out. It suggests this is a brane or parallel-world boundary.

about her using Ouija boards and doing séances. The idea of simply not telling him the truth evidently hadn't occurred to her. In fact, it probably was just as well that she didn't call in clergy. People often are shocked when I say what I said in chapter one: Few clergy are educated about the paranormal. At times, they can do more harm than good.

A real miracle in this case was that Liz managed to keep the information lid on the situation. I found all sorts of rumors flying around the neighborhood, what with the store closing, Anna leaving, and all sorts of odd noises. The general belief was that Liz had gone a little batty and was holed up above the store. The fact that nobody who saw anything weird in the store or apartment had talked about it, probably for fear of sounding crazy, was a minor miracle in itself. With the Bridgeport poltergeist outbreak only a few years before, reporters would have loved it. If Liz had called the police, one of the first things most poltergeist victims do, the media would have found out for sure.

It was a good thing, too, that poltergeists don't last forever. Sooner or later, they get all the sustenance they can from their victim, and they start to look for sunnier shores. This rat pack got weaker, I'm convinced, simply because even the gallant Liz was starting to wear down. By the time I took over the case, these "noisy spirits" were near the end of their electromagnetic ropes anyway.

I suggested calling in a priest I knew to at least bless the house, actually Fr. Bill Charbonneau, whom I'd worked with in the Bridgeport house, but he wasn't available. Since I realized the parasites were playing themselves out and because I already was starting to form my Peter Pan Theory, I was convinced that Liz, Steve, and I could get rid of them ourselves.

WEAPONIZING THE JOKE BOOK

So that evening, after we'd gotten Liz out of the apartment for a decent meal, we marched straight back in. All was quiet as we stood in the middle of the floor and held hands. We said the Lord's Prayer, and I announced calmly to the parasites that we had their number, the game was up, and Liz wasn't going to be their meal ticket anymore, or words to that effect.

There was a thump under our feet that shook the floor, but I told everyone to remain calm at all costs. That night, I convinced Liz to stay with her sister until we pacified the situation. The next day and the next, Steve, Liz, and I were back. We did everything positive we could think of. We read from the happier parts of the Bible, we shared stories about our families and our happy memories, and we even had a great evening reading from a joke book and singing songs. On the last evening, we had Anna with us, and she seemed completely renewed afterward.

That really did it. I checked with Liz often over the next two months, and Steve stopped by frequently. She and Anna, who moved back home, cleaned up the apartment within the week and had repairs done. Within a month, the store was open again, and it didn't take long for things to get back to normal.

This case really made me think about a question I was asking myself since the Bridgeport poltergeist outbreak: What actually causes the movement of objects? Do the parasites actually toss the chairs, hurl the dishes, and suspend the objects in midair? Or do the electromagnetic or geotechnical conditions at the brane's intersect point create local gravity anomalies? Since I seldom felt the presence of a parasite when objects moved, I tend to favor the latter explanation to this day.

I suppose it's like a table in a hallway with the day's mail piled on it. If we rush down the hallway to answer the door, we might stir up enough of a breeze to blow some of the mail off the table. We don't do so deliberately, but we create conditions that cause the movement.

In any case, after happy night, Liz never had trouble again, as far as I know. Once again, the Peter Pan Theory was the key: Liz kept happy thoughts and that positive spirit, which cut off the last of the food supply to the parasites. With the love of her daughter and her home, she won the victory that anger, or even exorcisms, never could.

CHAPTER FIVE

THE ANGEL OR THE ADMIRAL?

When struggling with parasites, there are times when the experience can turn out to be inspiring, especially when you find unexpected help from some of our neighbors in the multiverse.

That's because nasty parasites aren't the only ones we share the multiverse with. We have friends too, and they might well be the origins of human folklore about angels and other good spirits who help humanity. In fact, I'm convinced that there are far more of what we would consider good entities scattered across the worlds than there are bad ones.

One of the most beautiful examples of this happened to me in 1988, in a moving example of aid from what certainly appeared to be a concerned ancestor. It was during a brief but nasty poltergeist case in Portland, Maine. A mean little parasite had drawn enough strength from its primary host, a fifteen-year-old girl named Deborah, turned into a poltergeist, and was harassing a family of four.

Here's another case ignited by a Ouija board. Deborah and her friends used one in the family's basement, some serious hell broke loose for two weeks, and they called me. All my attempts to get the girl to bring in positive energy, disrupting the parasite's food supply, got nowhere because she was so completely petrified.

I was frustrated, so I did something I'd never done before: I encouraged someone from elsewhen to bring in positive energy. I urged Deborah to call on a beloved ancestor. So, in a conference with Deborah's parents, I asked if there was a forbear the girl had been close to. The standard answer is, "Sure, Great-Grandma Sue or Grandpa Joe."

Not this time.

"Well," replied Dad, scratching his chin, "She really relates to this guy Henry Walke, who fought in the Civil War."

Deborah was a history buff.

It turned out that this Walke, a Union naval officer during some of the campaigns on the Mississippi River, was one of the girl's maternal great-great-great-grandparents. According to Mom, dear old Henry had ended up an admiral, died in 1896, and had three US warships in succession named after him. Deborah was fascinated with his story and even had his picture in her room.

Rear Admiral Henry Walke, USN (1809–1896).

This was going to be interesting.

When I suggested to Deborah that she ask for her ancestor's help, the girl gave me a blank look for a moment, then came the dawn. She was intrigued, even excited. A week later, I received an ecstatic phone call from the family. The girl herself was in tears.

"It was the most wonderful thing I ever saw!" she cried.

As I advised, Deborah for several days projected love toward her great-great-great-granddad and asked for his protection against the parasite. She even slept with Walke's picture under her pillow.

The night before Deborah called me, the parasite had attacked. It, and/or the turbulent intersect points around it, tossed things off shelves in the room and pulled the covers off the girl's bed. Deborah's screams brought the rest of the family just in time to feel what they described as "a warm breeze blowing through the room." Then—and all four said they saw this—what looked like a glowing white rod or sword flashed through the air in front of the girl's bed. There was thumping on the walls for a few seconds, the "sword" vanished, and utter quiet descended.

The parasite was never heard from again. The girl noted with emotion that in some pictures she'd seen of him, Rear Admiral Henry Walke, USN, wore his officer's sword prominently at his side.

ANCESTORS

When I talk with people of Asian descent, they nearly always understand where I'm going when I mention the power of ancestors. That's because ancestors are venerated in Asian cultures, whose people look for the love and guidance of those who bore their blood in past ages.

In the multiverse, however, there is no objective time, so there is no past in any real sense. Those who bear your ancestral blood do not do so in past ages. They do so right now, in parallel worlds where it is still, to us, the past, and where these loved ones never died. If these good people are in worlds where the laws of physics and the norms of society allow them to be aware of us, to love us, and to help us, I believe they do precisely that. They have a connection with us because they *are* us in concrete, real-as-it-gets ways that can be understood only in terms of multiverse living and awareness.

Deborah's case was the first time I used the ancestor approach to get rid of a parasite. The goal was always to replace the negative-energy parasite food supply with positive energy, and bringing in loving ancestors was a new way to do just that, provided I could get by any cultural barriers. Most people of Western Hemisphere descent have little or no idea what I'm talking about when I suggest they call upon their ancestors. Despite the fact that we live in the era of DNA testing and genealogical databases, most Westerners' interest in their blood forbears, especially distant ones, is limited to where they fit in the family tree, whether they were famous, and whether we have long-lost cousins on the other side of town. Except for one or two generations back, thinking of our distant ancestors as family simply doesn't occur to most of us. And to actively love our remoter ancestors, pray for them, and have a certainty that they are by our sides in one form or another can be an alien idea.

Regardless of their own cultural beliefs, people I've worked with over the years have been astounded at how adopting and learning to love their ancestors as family members has changed their lives and attitudes. And when it comes to fighting off parasites, I've seen ancestors come to the rescue time and again. They are truly powerful allies. I should qualify this by saying that all of us have ancestors who are obnoxious, at least in our corner of space-time, but I find that our feelings tend to be drawn to those who are most aware of us and are in a position to help.

This isn't some hokey, New Age, feel-good idea. It's the multiverse at its personal best.

Every family has stories of members who have appeared to loved ones at times of death or crisis to warn or reassure. Traditionally, paranormal researchers refer to these as visitation apparitions. Over the years I've heard a mountain of these stories. Occasionally, they turn out to be parasites mimicking recently passed relatives, but loved ones tend to see through this sooner or later. The real visitation apparition is so positive 99 percent of the time that I've yet to have one turn into a case.

The question might be asked, however: "Was this really the good admiral somehow breaking through a multiversal brane to help his terrified descendant? And a *sword*?

I haven't the slightest idea.

If our theories about parallel worlds are correct, however, there's absolutely no reason why it couldn't have been Henry Walke. If so, he was no spirit, but the actual, on-the-hoof admiral, albeit from a world with different laws of physics, manifesting to defend Deborah because the two are intimate facets of each other and are already completely connected.

If it wasn't Henry, however, who or what was it?

One might think that multiversal neighbors, at least most of them who aren't parasites, would be concerned with their own daily affairs and have better things to do than get involved with the likes of us. Still, there are some neighbors who seem to be located and motivated to help us—and even work with us. Just as parasites are the origin of concepts such as demons and vampires, I'm sure that these positive entities are responsible for our best experiences of angels, guardian spirits, benign Nature spirits, and other good entities. And in their own worlds, they're probably just as physical as we are. Just as many of us try to help our neighbors when they're in trouble, volunteer at food banks, or donate blood, so some multiversal neighbors might look for ways to help.

Whatever cleared Deborah's room didn't identity itself. So, this could have been a multiversal Good Samaritan or, yes, even an angel, whoever or whatever that sort of being really is.

THE BUDDHA WAS RIGHT

Gautama the Buddha, whom Dr. C. S. Shah calls "the sanest man the world has ever seen," taught that we must have compassion for all things. "Truth and Knowledge flowed from his every pore as Compassion, in his austerities and tapas, kindness and humility, and suffering and feelings."

I couldn't agree more with that exhortation. My rule is: pray for everything and everyone, all the time. Ancestors, friends, enemies, people you don't know, animals you don't know . . . the Earth . . . the universes. If you've suffered a miscarriage or had an abortion, pray for your unborn child: He or she is very much alive somewhere or somewhen and loves you—no matter what. I know. My wife and I have one who is active in our lives.

Prayer and "saying prayers" are two very different things. Prayer is a state of being. If you try to live it, you'll learn what I mean: Prayer is the greatest act of love there is, and love is the greatest power in the multiverse.

ANGELS AND GUARDIANS

I'm surprised when I find anyone who doesn't have some story of a lucky coincidence or a miraculous escape. People who don't are pretty rare. To all "primitive" cultures, of course, encounters with angels, guardians, positive Nature spirits, or what have you are normal. These presumably non-human entities seem to be in parallel universes with easy access to us, and many appear to have the best quality we know of in living beings: an utterly selfless desire to help others.

A WARNING

Many people tell me they're convinced that Aunt Ruth is watching over them because every time they go out for the evening, she does the laundry. Don't chuckle, I've actually heard this.

Be careful! Ancestors and guardians will come across as warm, gentle, unobtrusive, and loving presences. Don't try to actively communicate with them. You don't need to. Sure, I meet people who talk to their ancestors or guardians. But I think our lives are full of too many words as it is. Best to commune in silence. Maybe that was the philosophy in the back of my mind when I sat still long enough to communicate with the likes of Gilbert the Canadian train watcher and Bob the crash-victim-turned-Episcopal-priest. You'll meet them in the last chapter of this book.

As the Greeks, Romans, and other ancients knew, respect is the operative word. In my daily rule of prayer at home, I thank all "good and gracious spirits of this place" for their hospitality and protection, adding "may you always be honored by those who live here." I also remember all my ancestors and loved ones, asking for the prayers of those in a position to offer them and praying for those who aren't.

When entering the woods or fields I love so well, I always touch Earth and ask the guardians' permission "to enter with love and respect." But if any entity starts intruding into your life, chances are you're not dealing with anything positive. Let your heart and your common sense—not your imagination or your wishful thinking—be your guide!

CHAPTER SIX

CARMEN'S LOVER

People often ask what kind of cases are the scariest. Certainly, the 1970s exorcisms I was involved with, and two other early cases, are up there. These were among the scariest cases not only because of what happened as they ran their course, but because these earliest encounters completely shattered my cherished belief systems.

That happened in my very first field case, the singular affair of the "Village of Voices," 1970–1972, when the "ghosts" we came head-to-head with gave me more than a hint that they weren't dead people at all, but completely physical, living people going about their daily business in a parallel world.

It also happened in the Bridgeport Poltergeist case of 1974, when I had a very physical struggle with one of four "demons" that were supposed to be spirits. (Both these cases are detailed in *Behind the Paranormal: Everything You Know is Wrong.*)

Then there are the cases that aren't so much viscerally scary as they are profoundly disturbing. Among these are the ones where a parasite develops a deeply personal relationship with its host. For both the host and the researcher who's trying to help, reality can literally become blurred as branes collide and worlds blend. Hosts experience intimate, vampire-like encounters with parasites, with which they often develop codependent or even erotic relationships. It can be the last step before the extreme interaction of personalities commonly thought of as demonic possession.

Frankly, I'd rather have an honest poltergeist throw a television at me, as actually happened in the Bridgeport case, than have to plunge in and try to disentangle one of these sick, supernatural relationships. It's almost always a lengthy process, and the cases themselves are more common than I originally thought.

In my experience, the most frequent host is the weak, vulnerable, insecure person with a history of being abused or otherwise victimized. All too often, this is a woman. I'm reminded quite chillingly of the old vampire stories, with the master recruiting his victim-slaves one by one, then feeding from them until he becomes almost too strong to beat.

The other most frequent parasite prey in these cases is the person who seeks power over others through the occult. In deliberately trying to link up with sometimes hostile forces elsewhere in the multiverse, this sort deliberately invites trouble. In trying to use these entities to control others, he or she usually ends up being controlled, or at least harmed mentally and spiritually. Sometimes self-harm or even suicide can result.

The kind of parasite-host bonding we're talking about can be complicated by the fact that it's often very subtle. Hosts usually don't realize they have a problem until they wind up in psychiatric treatment or worse. Family members, if there are any, seldom even know the signs of trouble, let alone pick up on them.

Fortunately, Carmen Kelly was an exception. She had enough sense to know that something wasn't right, and as the relationship with her parasite developed, she started to realize that there was more to this than there seemed to be. It was Carmen's friend and confidant, Jane Gagnon, who called after reading about me in a New England newspaper.

It was on a sunny October morning, in 1998, that I first visited the house in Burrillville, Rhode Island. Jane and her two children, eight and thirteen years of age, had been renting the nondescript, two-story house for two years. The thirtyish Carmen, the confused victim of a recently failed marriage, had moved in with the family only about two months before.

As usual, I took the grand tour of the house and property before sitting down with the women to hear the whole tale, and it didn't take long for me to start picking up impressions. The home's layout was circular. Entering through the back door, one moved through a small living room, into the kitchen, around to a small family room, then to the bottom of the stairs. All I had to do was start up those stairs and I was awash in a hefty electromagnetic field (EMF). Upstairs, this field was strongest in a bedroom in the northwest corner of the house. To my alarm, I found that this room belonged to Jane's eight-year-old son. Needless to say, I don't want to see paranormal phenomena of a negative kind anywhere near children.

My EMF meter, an engineer's tool I use sparingly but that's overused and misunderstood by most ghost hunters, revealed a fluctuating EM field moving about upstairs but concentrated in the child's room. That was very odd, given that there was no corresponding electrical source moving with it. This had multiverse intersect point written all over it. Nevertheless, all was quiet for the moment, but in the young boy's room, especially at the east wall, I got the very strong impression of an entity with male energies.

What I found really disturbing was that this case wasn't clear to me. Was this a parasite? Ordinarily I could nail them right off the bat. But I couldn't put my finger on this one because it stayed well out of my way.

I examined the basement, but this seemed inactive. I noted with interest that about half of it was much older than the rest of the house. A little research showed that the original structure burned in the 1950s and that the current house stood on the old foundation. And no, nobody was killed in the fire.

The attic, to which neither Jane nor Carmen said they had ever been, was interesting. It was empty and unfinished, but I had no doubt that something was up there. Sure enough, a Polaroid photograph revealed a shimmery substance in the air at one end. I found that this was a hiding place, especially when I was around, for what I eventually concluded was a parasite.

Back on the second floor that day, though, I still wasn't sure whether this was a parasite or some neutral or benign multiversal neighbor, human or otherwise. I gave it the benefit of the doubt.

"Don't fear. All will be well," I said to the not-so-empty air upstairs. Frankly, I wasn't sure about that at all.

Gathered at the kitchen table on that first visit, Jane and Carmen told me their story.

"I've been here for about two years, and I think I've always known there was, you know, somebody else here," Jane said. "But it never really bothered me and the boys. When I first moved in, there seemed to be a lot of activity, but at first I blew it off as old-house sounds."

Still, with all the footsteps she heard late at night, Jane came to call the entity "the walker." All the sounds seemed concentrated at the end of the house where I'd picked up the strongest impressions. As first, Jane said, she thought it was one of her sons on unauthorized absence from bed. But every effort to catch one or another boy walking around the upstairs hallway proved fruitless.

"I thought I was going nuts," she recalled, as do so many people who encounter the paranormal.

Neither Jane nor the boys connected with whatever this was, so it tended to remain in the background. This created doubts in my own mind about whether this was a parasite, which are among the multiverse's most opportunistic creatures. On the few occasions I'd had trouble identifying a parasite and eventually had, it turned out to be one of the Wise, a sly and slippery bunch indeed. As it happened, things really started to heat up when Carmen moved in.

"The sounds picked up, and we felt a strong presence, not only upstairs but in the kitchen. In the living room, it even seemed like 'he' would fool around with the TV and the VCR!" Jane said.

"Aha," I said to myself. "Good old electromagnetic energy: Phenomena are always most obvious in rooms with plumbing and appliances!" This was something I'd noticed in cases as far back as the 1970s.

What's more, there were apparitions of a man of undetermined age, always shadowy, though this was years before my friend Heidi Hollis would coin the term "shadow people." Carmen, especially, reported seeing a man's shadow in the kitchen, upstairs, and at the bottom of the stairs. Something would sit on the edge of her bed when she was in it. What I found most alarming were her reports of waking in the middle of the night with the feeling of being choked by cold fingers.

In response to my long list of questions, I learned that Carmen was under psychiatric treatment for clinical depression and hadn't held a steady job in some time. I could see right away that a sort of love-hate feeling toward the entity, real or imagined, had taken root during her long, brooding days alone in the house. Carmen called it "a conflict." She truly connected with this entity in a way that Jane and the boys never had. Her very state of mind was parasite bait.

Jane seemed to take a naive approach: She wanted to believe this was a "protective spirit." Whatever it was, it seemed to leave the eight-year-old alone, even though I often could feel it in the child's room, which I now felt sure was the intersect point.

I was particularly interested to hear of both women's interest in the paranormal, and to see that First Nations religious articles decorated several rooms. Both claimed they hadn't used Ouija boards or séances in the house, but both also said they relied on the advice of a Tarot card reader.

This is the attic where the parasite hid during the first few visits the author made to the house. Its presence was clear at the far end, where the picture inexplicably blurs.

As a protective measure, Jane was burning sage in the house, a method I've used myself as a way to help dissipate negative energy and cleanse a physical space. In addition, I urged Carmen to use the protective technique of visualizing herself surrounded by a brilliant white light. This really seems to work, and it was one of the few useful things I learned from Ed and Lorraine Warren. And I advised Carmen to communicate compassion and sympathy to the entity, a method I'd found helpful in several early cases, even where certain parasites, notably belonging to the Lost species, were in play.

Given Carmen's clinical situation and the fact that she at first appeared to be the only witness to the most negative phenomena, I was immediately suspicious that she was hallucinating at least some of the phenomena, or perhaps embellishing on a situation with an entity that might not be as threatening as it seemed.

One of the first things I did was to call Carmen's psychiatrist, Dr. Sarah Friedman of Butler Hospital in Providence. Dr. Friedman was very receptive and gave me a general picture without breaching patient confidentiality. Apparently, Carmen had no known condition that would have predisposed her to hallucinations. Later, after reading my book *Faces at the Window: First-Hand Accounts of the Paranormal in Southern New England* (New River Press, 1998), Dr. Friedman commented that I was more skeptical about the paranormal than she.

Later testimony by Jane, her older son, and Jane and Carmen's respective ex-husbands convinced me that Carmen probably wasn't imagining things. Over the next several weeks, with some intensive interviews, site visits, and photographic analysis, here's how the picture would have shaped up if I were a garden-variety ghost hunter:

It looked for all the world as though this entity was some tormented soul who was Carmen's lover in a past life, and that's just what Carmen thought. Frustrated and confused, the poor chap was running around in limbo because he had apparently killed her in that past life and was dripping with guilt. Carmen even wrote a love poem to the thing!

I didn't buy that past-life story in a million years.

As we've discussed in prior chapters, all worlds, all times, all people, all things, all moments are simultaneous in the multiverse. There is no past except as a function of our consciousness; hence there can't be past lives in any objective sense. There are, of course, parallel lives that may be in one time or another, but in none of them do anything but parasites drill into our realm and try to strangle people, at least not in my experience. Carmen's personal history, added to the negative interaction with this entity, said "parasite" to me in flashing neon lights. There were the shadowy apparitions, too, which nearly always mean parasites in my cases.

I found it especially interesting that "the man," as they called it, and Carmen had similar characteristics: frustration, depression, and guilt. Once again, that's common when parasites imitate their hosts, as the Wise and other upper-echelon species sometimes do. Carmen complained of feeling tired and drained, a symptom of depression, yes, but also a clue that a parasite might be in action.

This wasn't as much of an emergency as some parasite cases, as there wasn't a wild poltergeist juggling armchairs. So as Carmen and I worked on the Peter Pan Theory, I had a rare chance to study her antagonist. I would sit for long periods in the child's room, where it seemed to hang out because of the intersect point, literally in or near the east wall. After it got used to me, it would flee to the attic less and less. In that bedroom, each of us knew the other was there. It felt as though we were studying each other, and I got the feeling that it knew it couldn't get anything to eat from me.

I felt sharp, cold intelligence. I felt that it was very old and very alien. And I knew that it was either imitating Carmen's own characteristics or reflecting the personality Carmen was projecting onto it. Either way, it had been able to win her sympathy and build her trust.

On two occasions, I was fascinated to feel the entity in my car with me as I left Carmen and Jane's house and headed the ten miles to my own. As I suspected, however, it wasn't powerful enough to leave the hefty EM fields around its home for long. Even before I got out of Burrillville, the presence dissipated.

I brought in my friend, Joseph Frisella, a prominent hydrologist and soil engineer, who pointed out that the site was very sandy and at the bottom of a hill. Without doing any expensive drilling, he suggested that the water table probably was quite high. Those two circumstances can contribute to a site's EMF conductivity, one of the factors that must be lined up for paranormal phenomena to take place.

The plot thickened later that month. Carmen called me one day to say that she had suddenly gone into a light trance and done what is known in the psychic world as automatic writing, allegedly done under the control of a spirit. What resulted appears to be a conversation between Carmen and the entity. The penmanship in Carmen's part of the dialogue leans right; that of the entity's supposed answers leans left. The picture the entity refers to is the one I took in the attic.

Carmen: What is bothering you?

Parasite: I'm not sure. My back hurts.

Carmen: Did you know that the pain in your back is but a symptom of something much deeper?

Parasite: Yes, I'm aware of that.

Carmen: What are you doing right now?

Parasite: Just sitting here listening and feeling the music.

Carmen: So, what do you think?

Parasite: I like it but sometimes I feel sad. It touches me somehow in a way I'm not familiar with.

Carmen: Are you angry at me?

Parasite: No, but you remind me. Your being here reminds me of my [illegible]. It reminds me of the whole [*sic*] I have here, it's much like yours.

Carmen: So why did you want to choke me?

Parasite: Because you reminded me of her and it never stops hurting. I wander and I walk to try not to feel as that would go but it doesn't go away.

Carmen: Can you tell me about what it looks like where you are?

Parasite: It was sunny at one time. It was bright and filled with laughter but that's gone now. Now its gray and cold and my heart can find no warmth so I walk.

Carmen: What else would you like to talk about? Do you believe I could help you in some way?

Parasite: I don't know what else to say. I don't know how you think you could help. It's been this way for so long. I don't see that I have any other choice. I don't like to talk about it or anything. I just feel so bad and so angry. I have to walk.

Carmen: I understand that sadness, the whole [*sic*] deep inside. I call it the soul. It gets lonely here, too.

Parasite: That's why I get angry because you remind me and I don't want to be reminded. It hurts too deep. I was O.K. for a long time, a very long time but you came and now I remember . . .

Carmen: I keep wanting to ask you what is in the attic?

Parasite: It's the angry place. It's the late place. It's a place where I had to be so long ago but it wasn't there in the way you saw in the picture. It wasn't empty, but it was never not an angry place. I could go there when I got angry. I thought it would be safe for me to be there, so I wouldn't hurt anyone.

Carmen: Now I'm getting scared. O.K. I'll stop. He doesn't want to talk anymore. He's getting angry and I got scared so I walked out. I still sense the anger. I overstepped too far.

I noticed at once that Carmen and her paranormal pen pal made the same spelling and grammatical errors. A handwriting expert later told me that the same person had written the entire piece. Often in automatic writing, if that's what this was, that's not the result of the analysis. I found it curious that Carmen, who at that point still believed this was the spirit of a dead man, never asked the parasite its name or when it claimed to have lived in the house. I also thought the parasite's supposed answers sounded awfully modern.

In its attic reference, it would seem the parasite was peeping at my case pictures. I had, of course, been showing them to Carmen and Jane all along. But here's the thing: Carmen might not have been faking any of this. Remember "The Bonding" from chapter one? Carmen and the parasite might have been starting to blend facets, and I realized that possession might be the next step if the woman hadn't taken my advice.

Throughout this period, Carmen and her ex-husband, Jeff, had an on-again, off-again relationship. Just before she wrote this dialogue, Carmen told me that she'd spent the night with Jeff. Carmen claimed that she'd been very aware of the parasite's jealous presence. Carmen and Jeff had, of course, been intimate, and in the heat of it, Carmen claimed she cried "I died for you!"

Jeff said he'd felt the parasite's presence, too, and "freaked."

In November, Carmen announced that her Tarot card reader would come to the house the following evening, and invited me to meet her. I arrived at about 9 p.m., took a quick turn around the yard to see if the EM field there was as strong as ever (it was), and entered the house.

FRANK WHO?

The card reader, whose name was Keri, wasn't in the living room as I'd expected. She was upstairs in the child's room trying to contact the entity. I flew upstairs to find a young woman with black hair, her hand against the room's east wall. She was very nice but informed me that she was going to talk with the "ghost," whose name was Frank!

I sat at the other end of the room in disgust as the well-intentioned woman asked inane questions like, "What's it like over there? I'd really like to know! Rap once for 'yes,' twice for 'no'!"

Keri certainly was energized. At one point, I watched what appeared to be a bolt of electricity or plasma shoot from her leg as she was in contact with "Frank's" wall.

Finally, Keri, who hadn't received a single answer, urged Frank to "give Carmen her space," and she finally got a rather angry rap "yes."

Even if my multiversal interpretation of these phenomena is all wet, Keri's approach seemed rather air-headed to me. If this really was a human ghost, its mind would have been formed in some previous time, possibly even another century. How was it supposed to know what "give Carmen her space" meant, not to mention the other "I'm okay, you're okay" babble?

In any case, Carmen told me over the next few weeks that Keri's well-meaning efforts hadn't done any good. Surprise.

Then, on Christmas Eve, Jane's ex-husband, Bill, spent the night, sleeping on the living-room couch. He reported waking up in the wee hours to see an "older-looking" man in the adjacent kitchen. Interestingly, Bill reported that the refrigerator was "gone." I never found out for sure if this was Bill's sleepy imagination, dear old Frank, or just a random time slip possible at such a charged intersect site. The absence of the refrigerator is a clue that it probably was a time slip and a "ghost from elsewhen" who had nothing to do with the parasite.

This was a classic example not only of a parallel-world overlap but of one smart parasite playing an award-winning role. My message to Carmen at that point was: "Time to take control and stop being a victim." Because of her personal struggles, however, she wasn't quite able to get a grip on this. Finally, for her own sake and that of Jane and her family, I did something I rarely do. Knowing that the parasite was somehow bound to the site, I urged Carmen to move. And, lo and behold, she took my advice. After a few weeks, she dug in at a much healthier house elsewhere in Burrillville.

Things immediately got better for Carmen. Her personal problems continued, but she got a job and began to put her failed marriage behind her. I was especially pleased to hear that she had no more paranormal trouble. Some months later, Carmen told me that she was going to marry a First Nations elder she knew. I talked to her in 2002, and I'm happy to report that all was well.

One point I hope to make here is that women don't have to put up with domination by parasites any more than they have to put up with it by abusive men. If you can't take control with your own positive power, pull up stakes and get a new start elsewhere. Refuse to be a host and a victim, just as Carmen finally did!

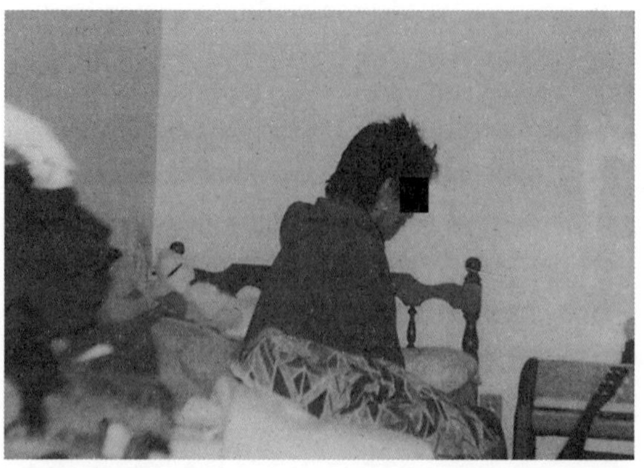

Keri the psychic talks to Frank the ghost.

CHAPTER SEVEN

WAS IT MURDER?

It was a frustrating Sunday evening, and it marked the beginning of one of my most frustrating cases. I had just showered and was looking forward to a comfortable evening, relaxing with my wife, Jackie, and our sons, one of whom, six-year-old Ben, was my future colleague, co-author, and radio co-host. I was just settling down in the family room when the phone rang, and I had to dress and leave the house on an errand I'd forgotten. I'd just donned the jammies and robe a second time when the phone rang again.

"The cops told me to call you," said a thin, slightly gravelly voice.

Was this Edward G. Robinson?

"I got real trouble with a ghost here! Can you come down?"

After a sigh and a few questions, I found out that I was listening to Roger Therrien, a middle-aged man with serious health problems who lived only about a half-mile from me in Woonsocket, Rhode Island. He claimed that the police came to his four-unit apartment house that evening on a noise complaint by a neighbor. Outside, he said, they heard a racket coming from inside. Once inside, they heard and found nothing. This happened several times.

According to Roger, one of the officers went back to his cruiser and refused to come out. The ranking cop, he added, told him to call me and even gave him my phone number. I was never able to fully corroborate this story with the Woonsocket Police, but the chief did invite me to donate a copy of *Faces at the Window* for the department's training room. Indeed, police, clergy, and psychiatrists are the professionals most likely to run into paranormal phenomena when victims first seek help.

Anyway, Roger complained that he and his fellow tenants were being vigorously harassed by a ghost, had seen minor poltergeist activity, were creeped out by feelings of presences, heard strange sounds, and saw the occasional apparition. I took pity, got dressed again, and headed out into this chilly December 1998 night.

Driving down the hill and across the railroad tracks to an area that was in the midst of an urban renewal project, I parked in front of the boxy house to which Roger directed me. My first encounter was with his spastic little poodle, which kept barking at the seemingly empty hallway and at certain corners. The poor thing looked completely bedraggled, and its blood pressure must have been sky high. Later in the case, the poor dog was to die of a heart attack.

Inside one of the two first-floor apartments I found Roger, a thin, friendly man with glasses, and his quiet, white-haired companion, Jan. Both were in their mid-fifties and were very sweet-tempered people. Their apartment was tiny, and I had trouble getting Roger to hold off with his story until I'd had a chance to look around. I moved about the place, snapped some pictures, then followed Roger upstairs to a second apartment he rented for storage purposes. I got a general negative impression throughout the house, but nothing definite. Something—lots of things—had gone on here, but I couldn't quite put my finger on specifics.

Roger Therrien on my first visit. When the picture was developed, the odd, plasma-like band appeared around his legs.

No sooner had we plopped into chairs back at Roger's apartment than there was an indefinite sound across the hallway in the other first-floor unit, which was dark when I arrived. Roger's dog started yipping again, lights came on under the neighbor's door, and a television started blathering.

"She [the neighbor] said she saw a ghost come out of her bedroom wall. She was scared silly and just left," Roger explained in a nervous voice. "Maybe she came back."

We both rapped on the door. No answer.

"Maybe she has her TV and lights on timers," I suggested, realizing that wasn't likely since everything in the apartment seemed to be on.

This was to be one of my most, shall we say, photogenic cases. Anomalies appeared in roughly 40 percent of photos taken at the site, an amazing number. The first batch came from my outside circuit of the building that first night. In several, one can see the energy just pouring out of the windows and doors. Indoor shots show many ball-lightning-like orbs, so familiar in today's pop-paranormal photography.

I was especially riveted by the basement door at the back of the building. Not only did anomalies appear in photos of it, but I was convinced that there was something extremely interesting behind it. Roger, unfortunately, had no key to the basement, something he would remedy in a unique way later.

It turned out that Jan had lived in the apartment for about sixteen years, and Roger moved in some six years before. Things were always a little weird in the house, Jan said, but gradually started to pick up after Roger arrived. It worsened after he became disabled and was stuck in the apartment day in and day out. Roger had ailments that would fill a medical text. With only a modest income, he and Jan saw no immediate prospect of moving.

A self-described devout Roman Catholic, Roger nonetheless believed that he and Jan were very psychic, and he offered a long list of his life experiences in evidence, including "prophetic" dreams and telepathic experiences. At the same time, Roger and Jan both swore they hadn't been involved in occult practices, such as Ouija boards and séances, that would have drawn parasites.

Along with the apparitions and other phenomena, Roger described something that most of my case subjects wouldn't have complained about: the spontaneous appearance of money. I never saw this happen, but Roger and Jan both swore that dollar bills and sometimes loose change would just appear on their bed.

"I'd never believe it if you told me, but we keep finding money on our bed, over $90 so far. We don't dare spend it; we just keep it in a drawer!" he told me.

As if that weren't enough, Roger and Jan said they would hear each other's voices saying some very negative things—even when the other wasn't home. That's a classic parasite ploy, and it really sets off the alarm bells for me.

I dread cases in apartment buildings. I almost never can talk with all the tenants, and the management people usually think I'm either a nut, a potential public-relations nightmare, or both. With all the different kinds of people living in such places, who knows what goes on—or what's going on there in other parts of the multiverse? As the Therrien case began, Roger and Jan were the only tenants left in the house. The apartment above them was vacant, as was the extra one Roger rented. The first-floor neighbor, according to Roger, had run off into the blue. I never even met her.

After several visits and some fruitless attempts at researching the building's history, I concluded—largely from the photographs and my own impressions—that the place harbored intersect points that parasites were using to come and go. In addition, as is common in those situations, there were spontaneous slips in space and time, including "ghosts from elsewhen." I felt all sorts of presences, male and female. The main problem, however, was Roger: He'd evidently made a world-class connection with the house's parasites.

Working with middle-aged to older parasite hosts can be very difficult because of the black-and-white worldview most of them grew up with. Mention to a younger person that the answer to their problem is bringing in positive energy to displace the negative energy, and they usually have a nodding acquaintance with what you're talking about. Older people often have trouble understanding that: They expect people like me simply to "come in and fix it."

For people with loyalties to a church, like Roger and Jan, I consult their clergy whenever possible because prayers and blessings can be vital tools. Used with love, they can help stir victims' faith and confidence to take control of a hostile situation.

Roger mentioned that he had gone to his priest for help, but the good cleric had, not surprisingly, little knowledge about how to deal with such things. He put Roger in touch with a priest in nearby Pawtucket, who sounded to me like the exorcist for the Diocese of Providence, much like Fr. Lawrence Wheeler, the priest I'd worked with at St. Lawrence State Hospital, was for his diocese.

Even though I almost became one, dealing with most priests today is a pain in the neck for me. Even with the few who know anything about the paranormal, they often become hostile, indifferent, or confused when they hear my theories and methods, which don't mesh with church doctrine. The priest I met with in Pawtucket as Roger's case got underway struck me as sincere but insufferably narrow. My ideas apparently went over his head.

"I don't believe in ghosts. I believe in demons," he pronounced.

According to Roger and Jan, money would spontaneously appear on their bed from time to time. They said they didn't dare spend it.

To my surprise, he knew all about Roger and Jan, recognized that they had a paranormal problem but couldn't get by the fact that they lived together without being married.

"They have to straighten out their spiritual lives before I can help them," he said.

I got that—to a point. Certainly, good manners, a well-ordered life, and morals make life better for everyone, especially children. And bravo to straightening out our spiritual lives: Assuming that the spirituality is constructive and positive, it's one of the best ways to start bringing in positive energy and power and to cut off the food supply for parasites.

Roger and Jan struck me as without guile, completely oblivious to the priest's implied claim that they were so steeped in sin that the "demon" couldn't be banished. They were asking for help from their own church, and its representative was refusing to meet them halfway with the compassion necessary for spiritual repairs to begin. If I recall my moral theology courses in the seminary, for something to be a sin, you have to know it's a sin. At least keep in touch with these people, bless their house, and visit once in a while! That keeps channels open. Hurling down moral thunderbolts from on high accomplishes nothing.

Needless to say, the priest was no help.

Meanwhile, Roger became an online pen pal with Shane Sirois, a Blackfoot shaman from New Hampshire. While I've met many a First Nations shaman who has ideas just as preconceived as priests, I find most of them to be sober, spiritually mature, compassionate, and very sensitive to what's going on in my cases. So, when Roger said that Shane was coming to Woonsocket one Saturday a few months after my investigation began, I looked forward to meeting him.

I was more right than I knew. Shane turned out to be a young, capable, sensitive family man with all the qualities I've seen in the best paranormal sleuths. I'm a very solitary person and don't get close to people easily, but Shane and I were brothers from the start. To this day, twenty years later, Shane, Ben, and I work on cases together, and Shane is virtually the only one we will turn cases over to when we can't get to them ourselves. Shane even joins us on open-line *Behind the Paranormal with Paul & Ben Eno* radio shows as our favorite guest co-host.

Of course, when Shane joined Roger's case, it didn't hurt when I mentioned parallel worlds, time slips, and parasites, and Shane knew exactly what I was talking about. Today, he has a stunning success record when it comes to applying multiverse theory to parasite cases.

Back there at the turn of the century, Shane also gave Roger the same advice I did about bringing in positive energy to displace the negative.

"Well, if you both say it, I guess I should try and do it," Roger quipped. That would turn out to be very difficult for him because of his weak physical condition.

A few weekends later, Shane appeared in Woonsocket once again, this time with John, a good friend of his from Massachusetts. The three of us went to see Roger, and it was to be an interesting day: We finally got into the basement.

"It dawned on me that all I had to do was take the bolts out of the hinges!" Roger said.

The basement actually was quite modern and rather clean, but I could see that some of its stone walls dated back at least to the early 1900s. There was some evidence of a fire in an original structure and that the place had been rebuilt. Shane had an infrared video camera, and it got a workout in that basement. The place was filled with orbs, some of which could be seen with the naked eye. On one occasion, my still camera caught an orb racing across the basement, while Shane got the same orb on video.

While they can be solid clues that paranormal conditions exist, I'm still undecided as to exactly what orbs are. Dust, lens effects, geomagnetic phenomena, light angles, EM fields, light leaks (back when we still used photographic film) or defects in digital cameras (which interpret what they see) all can cause orbs or other gadgets people will point to excitedly as paranormal. When we see orbs with the naked eye, sometimes they're just static electricity firing off in our optic nerves.

I certainly can testify that there are orbs for which I can see no explanation but a paranormal one. Heck, I've seen them often enough with the naked eye when investigating cases both indoors and outdoors. I've seen them in several different colors. I've been followed by them, and I've seen them manifest what I can only interpret as consciousness and even intelligence.

When all other possibilities are exhausted, I think that orbs could be living creatures, perhaps plasma-based, from other parts of the multiverse, or at least electrical manifestations of their presence. I suspect that they feed around branes. That could explain why they're so common in paranormal cases, which they might have nothing to do with directly.

What really interests me is that orbs seem much more common than they used to be. When I'd take case photos with old-time film cameras thirty-five or forty years ago, I'd sometimes see little, star-like explosions of light, but not many orbs as digital media record them today. While these light balls would show up in troubled homes now and then, they didn't seem to be a major phenomenon. Today, they're all over the place. Perhaps digital equipment is better at picking up their light spectra. No matter what orbs might be, however, Roger's apartment house was alive with them on some days.

It wasn't long before Shane and I brought in some of my investigatory gang, notably hydrologist Joe Frisella and historian Wendy Reardon. It was the second trip into the basement. Wendy, who also is an expert in the literature of death and dying, brought my attention to the corner of the basement just under Roger's apartment.

"My right ear hurts when I stand here," she pointed out.

So did mine, and so did almost everyone else's. I also got a headache, and I never get headaches. A thorough check revealed no evidence of machinery or electronic devices that could have caused such a reaction. Our only conclusion was that we were picking up and empathizing with a terrible event taking place on this spot somewhere in a parallel world.

We believed that a woman was killed—or would be killed—in this corner of the basement, perhaps accidentally. Such a traumatic event always sends out significant ripples through the multiverse, and in such an electromagnetically charged place as this, those ripples must be tremendous across the branes. I recalled that Woonsocket was once a crowded, rough-and-tumble mill town, a sort of New

What appears to be an orb—or something—streaks across the basement at left center. The author's colleague, Shane Sirois, captured the same object on infrared video.

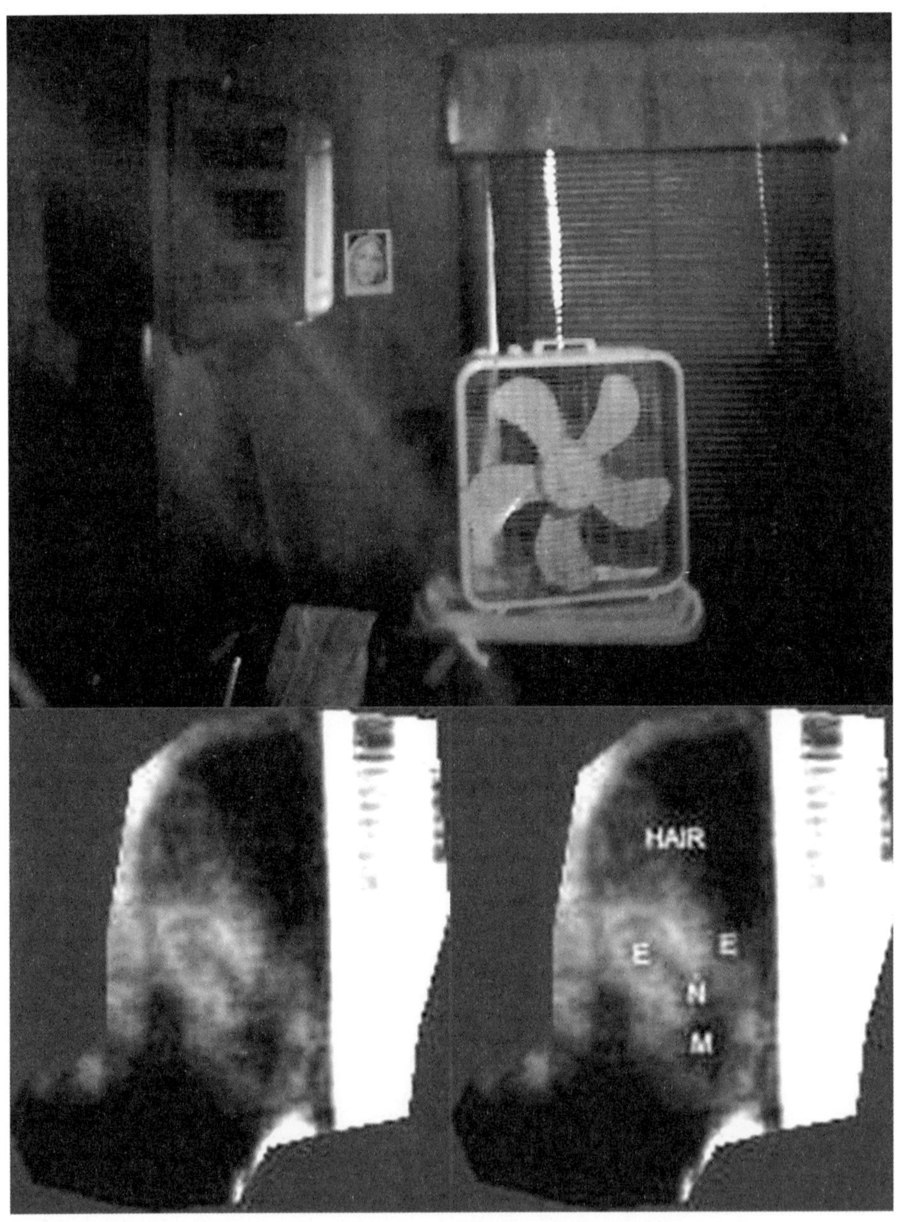

Shane Sirois captured this jarring photo while investigating the case with the author. What both interpret as the primary parasite in the case seems to appear in one of its most common masks, a little girl, complete with hair, eyes, nose, and mouth. Whether this is what the creature looks like in its true physical form is highly doubtful. *Photo copyright 2000 by Shane Sirois.*

England Dodge City, well into the twentieth century. A murder or fatal accident could well have taken place here in those times, and no one would have been the wiser.

Not to sound melodramatic, but it wouldn't surprise me at all if the body was buried in that basement. With its new concrete floor; however, it would take more money than I had in order to find out. Not only would such a terrible event be evident to anyone sensitive enough to pick it up, but it could attract parasites that would be delighted to find an emotional and physical "sitting duck" like Roger.

This scenario was bad enough without the various and sundry time slips and paranormal bric-a-brac going on in this place. I advised Roger and Jan to move, but they assured me they had neither the money nor the inclination to do so.

In ensuing months, we did everything we could to turn Roger into a positive thinker, to disconnect him from the parasites. Shane and I would visit, as would Roger's brother, a positive fellow who also lived in Woonsocket. We deliberately engaged Roger in lively conversations, made him laugh, and urged him to get involved in outside activities. Whenever we did this, phenomena would die down or disappear, often for days.

Roger did take our advice as well as he could, even plunging into a successful campaign to save a historic local church that was destined for the wrecking ball. And by late 2000, we seemed to have made significant progress—for Roger.

"They've [the parasites] been leaving me alone, but now they're after Jan!"

Jan, also in a weakened physical condition by then, had a difficult time and was an off-and-on parasite target over the following months. In early 2001, Roger learned that he had cancer serious enough to endanger his life. That didn't help the positive thinking.

Roger and Jan continued to struggle, both with their unwelcome guests and with illness. In 2002, they finally moved. That made for a more positive environment. On top of that, Roger took our advice and continued his involvement with positive outside activities. He was a major force behind preservation of the historic St. Anne's Church in Woonsocket. I'm pleased to say that he beat the cancer and continued to live many more productive years.

CHAPTER EIGHT

THE DOMINANT PARASITE

The worst of it began when Helen Gadreau and David Lane simply tossed aside an old table that was taking up space in their basement. The one-story duplex house in Burrillville, Rhode Island, had been a little strange for years, but the table incident marked the start of some real paranormal trouble. By the time a friend of theirs heard me lecture, then urged them to call me, Helen and Dave thought they were going crazy.

It was the night of November 1, 1998, and I picked my way along a dark side road in this rural, northern Rhode Island town on the Massachusetts border. When I finally found the house, on a rise set back from the road, I also found a very pleasant family group. Helen was in her early thirties, and Dave was about ten years older. They lived with Helen's lively children, nine-year-old John and seven-year-old Katie, in the house's larger section. In the adjacent in-law apartment lived Helen's friendly mother and stepfather, Art and Sue Major, both in their early sixties. Even the dog seemed well adjusted. But as the old saying goes, all was not as advertised.

In taking my preliminary tour, neither me, my camera, nor my little electromagnetic field (EMF) meter, which I don't pay much attention to anyway, picked up anything that couldn't be considered routine. I did feel something in a corner of young John's room, but it wasn't very strong.

SOUNDING OFF

I was aware even then that creepy feelings don't always have a paranormal cause. Only a few years before this case, Vick Tandy, a computer specialist at Coventry University in the UK, was working late one night. He suddenly broke into a cold sweat, and he was certain that he was being watched by someone or something that was none too friendly. Already taken aback, Vick then saw a sinister, gray form with arms, legs, and a foggy cloud for a head.

Vick had inadvertently discovered VLF (very low frequency) sound, also known as infrasound, as a source of paranormal experiences. When he measured the sound in the lab, the result was 18.98 hertz, exactly the frequency that causes the human eyeball to start resonating, possibly causing optical illusions like the foggy figure. If that frequency was within the range of human hearing, it would have been deafening.

My question is: Does infrasound cause the impression of weird happenings, or does it somehow rattle the multiversal branes enough to cause actual breaches and parallel-world overlaps? Or both?

Back in Burrillville, I checked out the Majors' apartment. Nothing unusual that I could pick up. Then I stepped through a small mud room and out into the pitch-black backyard. Wow! I was immediately awash in an electrical field so powerful that I nearly lost my footing. Something was watching me: I was as certain of that as if we'd been standing face to face. I headed down into the yard toward what seemed to be the center of the electrical field.

I saw it with jolting suddenness, only about ten feet away. It was tall, glowing, and shimmery, like a figure made of plasma. There was only a thin, whitish blankness where a face ought to have been, but I could clearly see its arms. I'm not afraid of these things, and they know it. As I continued to approach, the entity bolted to the right and vanished into the blackness. I chased it for a moment, but where or when it had gone, I obviously couldn't follow. The whole experience lasted about four seconds.

To have such a vivid encounter with the culprit, or one of them, right off the bat like this is unusual. On the rare occasions that I've seen parasites with the naked eye, they'd looked like what I'd just met. And it tipped me off to one thing: Whatever else was going on here, at least one of these miserable beasts was at the buffet table at the expense of this family. My only regret so far was that I hadn't been quicker with my camera. But I'd fix that later in the case, when I nabbed a shot of what I believe was the same creature on the other side of the property.

Back in the house, the children were packed off to bed, and the grown-ups gathered around the table to tell me their story. It was a long one.

During the family's many years in the house, I was told, they sometimes felt presences, and there was the occasional out-of-place footstep or other sound. But whatever it was didn't seem overly intrusive. Most of the experiences happened to Helen.

"Then we moved that table earlier this year, and things went crazy!" Dave said. "We were just trying to clean out the basement!"

Everyone in the family now reported hearing footsteps from time to time when alone in the house. Thinking that another family member had come home, the hearer would go to look and usually find no one. Dave often heard female voices, sometimes calling his name. Often, he was convinced it was Helen's voice. The

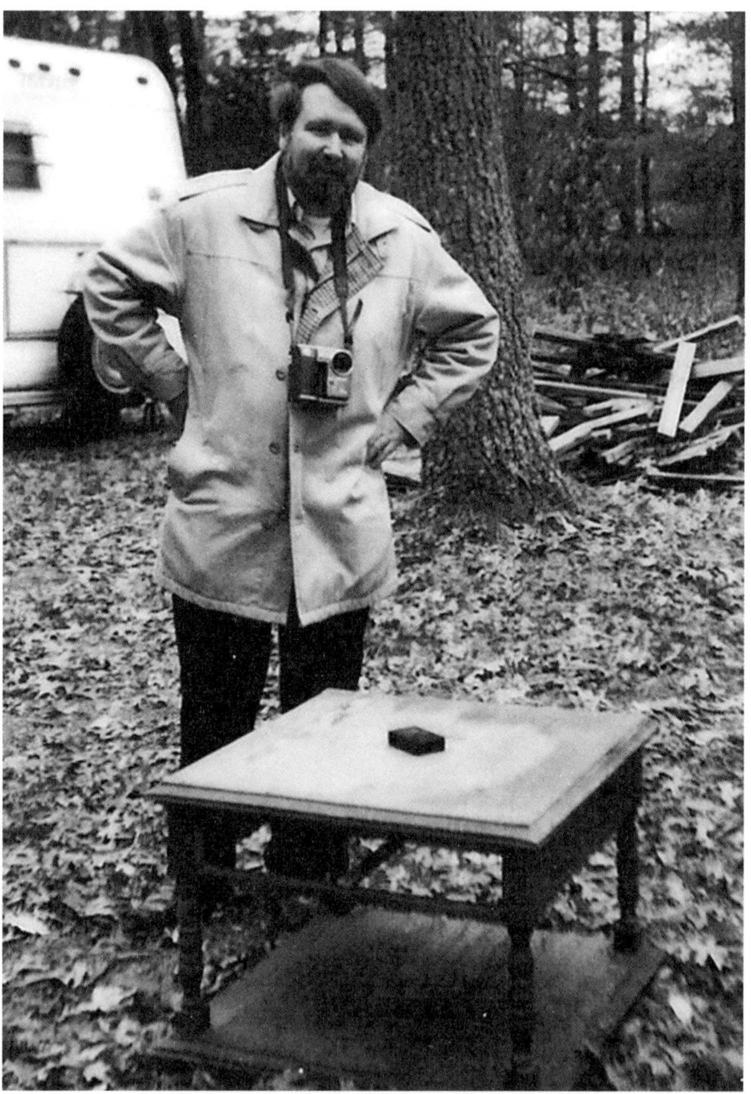

The author meets the table the homeowners originally blamed for their paranormal trouble.

Majors showed me a kitchen cabinet that sometimes would rapidly open and close on its own. Mr. Major even reported being "tucked into bed" by something while he was alone at home one night.

Everyone reported the feeling of being watched through the windows by something outside the house. But it was the child-like Helen who endured the most, even now. She felt vivid temperature changes, numerous presences, and saw the apparition of a small blonde-haired girl with flowers in her hair in the master bedroom and hallway.

Helen and Dave were keeping the children in the dark about the whole thing, something I don't agree with. Children aren't stupid, and they tend to be very sensitive to these phenomena. Better to be forthright, reassuring, and supportive. In any case, John and Katie were starting to report that they, too, were afraid.

How could a table make so much trouble? Well, I'm not so sure it did. As the Gadreau case developed, I tended to think that phenomena increasing after the table moved was just a coincidence. I became convinced that we were dealing with one very strong parasite, probably an Elder, that was dominating at least one lesser parasite, probably a Passive, a Trickster, or both. These creatures were using intersect points that seemed to move around the property, and within the entire rural neighborhood.

The family reported minor time slips here and there, but I had a hunch that the apparition of the little girl was no time slip or glimpse across a random brane. That apparition was a classic archetype used by parasites to encourage potential hosts to lower their guard. After all, what could be less threatening than a little girl with flowers in her hair?

As I listened to the family's stories that first night, I quickly saw that every adult present could be labeled "psychic," which to me means aware of parallel worlds, to one degree or another, but Helen considered herself quite psychic, and I believe she was right: She didn't miss much—seen or unseen—and hadn't throughout her life. In response to my standard question about occult activities, I found that she had read Tarot cards in the house. But Helen and everyone else denied using Ouija boards or doing séances.

Attitudes among these four people were strikingly different and very interesting. Helen, who came across as refreshingly innocent, was terrified, plain and simple. Understandably, Dave was protective, afraid only for Helen. The Majors, to my surprise and alarm, thought the whole situation was rather cool. My whole approach just whizzed right by them. As the case developed—and worsened—the Majors actually expressed sympathy for the parasites, which they considered ghosts. Mrs. Major even referred to them once as "cute"!

Give me a break!

Before I left that first night, I urged the family to "keep it positive" and try to build on their unity. As it turned out, this would be a big problem because there was a serious split between Helen and her parents over Dave, a split that I soon came to realize had more to do with the worsening paranormal situation than any moved table or basement cleaning ever did.

FROM BAD TO WORSE

This case escalated rapidly. After Christmas I returned to the house with Joe Frisella, the hydrologist, who pointed out that the whole lot, well over an acre, was mostly fill and may or may not have been overly conductive for EMFs. We did note, though, that high-tension wires ran past the north end of the property. They were several hundred yards away, but the land between them and the back of the Gadreau house seemed low and wet—an electromagnetic stage that could well lead to some paranormal drama by causing a brane rupture or intersect point.

That's why I wasn't surprised when the only neighbor I was able to interview reported having seen a UFO landing on the property the previous year. As we'll see in a subsequent chapter: When there's a multiversal intersect, overlap or overwash, it's likely that you'll find phenomena going on all over the place, including ghostly phenomena, parasites, poltergeists, UFOs, and cryptids (uncategorized creatures like Bigfoot, lake monsters, upright canine cryptids, and critters that don't even have names yet).

I would come to call these "flap areas," regions of frequent but seemingly unrelated paranormal activity that have the same cause: multiple multiversal intersect points amid which people can and do experience all kinds of bizarre occurrences and encounters. A few years later, in 2005, joined by my son Ben, then thirteen years old, flap areas would become the long-term focus of our research.

Back at the Burrillville case, it was now 1999, and January wasn't very old when I got a call from Helen. She and Dave had started to see shadowy figures "about the size of children."

"It was only last night," Helen told me. "I was in the kitchen, and I actually heard the floor creak. I turned around, and one of those little shadow figures was behind me. When I turned around, it took off into Katie's room!"

The previous week, she said she'd seen another small, shadowy apparition go into John's room and literally pick up a pair of jeans.

"I thought it was John, but he was asleep in the bed!" she told me.

A few nights later I was back, with Joe Frisella and, wonder of wonders, my wife, Jackie. My better half is very psychic, but she's not comfortable with it. In nearly eighteen years of marriage at that point, this was the first time she ever accompanied me on a case. I got her to come along because she has wonderful "people skills," and I thought she could help perk up Helen, who obviously was the parasites' main course.

The more Jackie and I spoke with Helen, the clearer it became that this guileless young lady was the perfect target. She was vulnerable, dependent, and had been at the blunt end of the stick for most of her life. Among other mishaps, Helen, when a child, had discovered the body of a murdered friend. Later, there were family problems and an abusive marriage. She was at something of a plateau now, though, and to all appearances Dave and the children were the lights of her life.

Ironically and sadly, Dave continued to be the focus of tension between Helen and her parents. From what I could see, this was because he and Helen weren't married and because Dave, who wasn't working steadily, was going to school in preparation for a career change. The chemistry here wasn't good, and the parasites were the only ones benefiting from it.

Helen stated that she often felt "something on me." She said she didn't sleep well because of the shadowy apparitions. I believed her. There were too many other witnesses, including me. But I couldn't ignore the impression that she enjoyed being the center of so much attention, something quite common in parasite, especially poltergeist, cases. So, I was on high alert for signs of embellishment.

At the same time, Helen never seemed to develop one of those wildly unhealthy bonds with the parasite, such as I was seeing in the Carmen Kelly case that had begun only a few months before.

Meanwhile, this was the night I was going to capture one of the best paranormal photos of my long career: None other than boss parasite, my acquaintance from

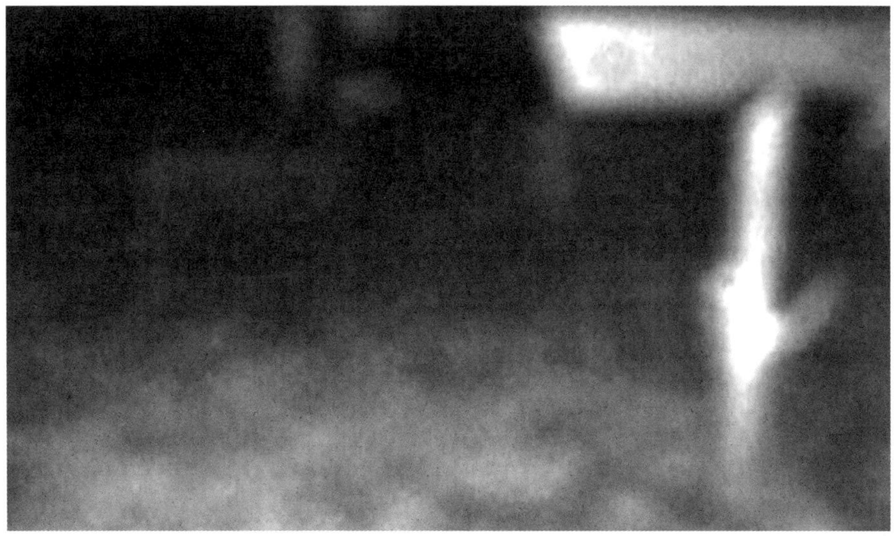

With his first-generation digital camera, the author got this shot of what he believes was the dominant parasite, the same one he saw with the naked eye on his first visit to the scene. The whitish mass above the lightning-like figure is part of a camping trailer.

that first night in the backyard. I was out there because Dave reported walking the dog one night and hearing footsteps coming up behind him. He turned around but could see no one. I was walking slowly through the same part of the yard, and I suddenly felt that strong EM field wash over me. When there was a flash right in front of me, my digital camera was ready.

People often cite the blurriness in photos like these, which involve paranormal entities or UFOs. Especially with digital media, the EM fields at the intersect point can distort the image. That's my opinion based on a military photo background anyway. I'm always amused that, when photos like this are clear, people often cry, "That has to be faked!"

In any case, I don't trust flash photos taken at night. Backflashes that look like orbs or other phenomena can bounce back from anything remotely shiny, even bugs in the air. So, whenever possible, I go back to the same spot in daylight to see if any object there could have created the illusion of an anomaly. Back in the Gadreau yard the next afternoon, I was disappointed to find an old tomato plant stake in the ground near the site that might have reflected. But measurements indicated that the stake would have been well out of the camera's field of vision. It was much shorter than the object in the picture, and it certainly didn't have arms.

On the last evening in January, I was back at the house listening to Helen describe more shadow apparitions. Dave reported seeing the same glowing, lightning-like figure I'd seen, both in the house and in the yard after dark. He also said there was a glowing orb and what looked like white, shiny "eyes." Helen saw the same "streak" entity in the bedroom and, later, a black, dog-like figure.

Meanwhile, the Majors declared they had awakened on a recent night to a shaking bed and a "weight," as though something were sitting on their legs. So much for cute ghosts.

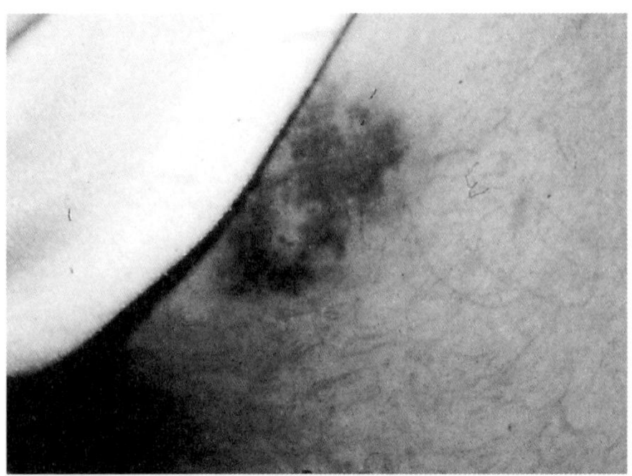

Dave frequently woke up with bruises he believed resulted from parasite attacks. Whatever force did this to him, it never woke him up.

In a particularly nasty turn of events, Dave showed me some bruises he said had appeared on his body while he slept. I'd seen this happen in other cases: Yes, parasites can be jealous! As if that weren't enough, everyone recalled that something had started pounding on the walls just after Christmas. It happened only once, but I saw it as "only the beginning" of a serious poltergeist outbreak unless something was done at once. Of course, some of these incidents may have had mundane explanations. But I wasn't taking any chances. It was time to act.

The first step was to get Helen's permission to have a long talk with the children, who were as jumpy as hens by this time. I told John and Katie they had nothing to be afraid of, and I explained as best I could what was going on. I stressed that what mattered was sticking together as a family, loving each other, and trusting God. I promised to do everything I could to help, and I gave them each an Eastern Orthodox icon of the guardian angel. Helen and Dave already were taking time each night to pray and read the Bible with the children.

Actually, the family wasn't connected with a church, but there was some Roman Catholic background. So, I brought holy water and a medal of the Blessed Virgin Mary. Used properly, both of these "sacramentals" can evoke powerful positive energy. I always find holy water especially powerful. All water is holy, as are all the good things in the multiverse. But water that has been concentrated upon and prayed over by people filled with faith and love makes perfect the holiness that's already there. Just as parasites may draw power from wet, electromagnetic ground, so they can be pushed back by water shot through with positive power.

Dave, Helen, the children, and I went from room to room, and I had Helen sprinkle holy water in each. I meant this to be an empowering experience for her, and by this time I was explaining to her again and again that she had to take control of the situation: Be a victim no more!

All went well until we got into the basement, where I could feel a great deal of energy in and near the furnace room. Dave and I suddenly looked at Helen. She had stopped, her eyes were blank, and some of her hair was standing up. She wasn't putting this on.

"I feel it on me!" she said, her voice nervous but not fearful. Then, suddenly: "He says you'll never find him."

"We've already found him," I replied calmly. Then, to it: "We know what you are, and you will leave this girl alone. You have powers arrayed against you that you can't possibly imagine!"

"He's laughing!" she said. "But he doesn't want you here, and he doesn't want the holy water."

"Enough," I said. "Dave, take Helen's hand!"

The author leads the family in an impromptu "house cleaning." At one point during this exercise, the parasite was "on" Helen. Taking her hand in solidarity made it leave.

I took one hand and Dave the other. Immediately, the thing backed off. I called upon God, Goddess, angels, and every other positive power I could think of to help protect Helen, and to help build love and protection in this house. In another moment, the thing was gone. Helen looked and felt normal again.

It was because of this incident that the light bulb finally went on for Dave.

"After we did that, I can really see what you mean about love driving this thing out!" he said.

It was true. All my preaching to Dave and Helen couldn't have gotten my point across any better than this experience with this nasty Elder. The fact that it backed right off when we held Helen's hands in a simple act of love and solidarity taught the lesson best.

As the case progressed, Dave and I discovered that the parasites often would hide, for lack of a better term, in a small barn on the slope behind the house. I made sure to sprinkle holy water there, too.

But I got an interesting reaction from Helen when I gave her advice that I sometimes give to parasite victims: Call upon your loving ancestors to help.

"I don't want any more ghosts!" she said.

I'd never heard it put that way before.

"These aren't ghosts; they're your extended family and, no matter where or when they are, they love you!"

It turned out that Helen had experienced a "visitation apparition" from a beloved aunt right after the lady had translated. It's very rare to be afraid of such visits from loved ones, but Helen was so gun shy about the paranormal by then that she was scared out of her wits. According to Helen, the aunt just wanted to tell her she was okay, apologized for startling her, and was never heard from again.

After the incident in the basement, though, Helen got steadily stronger. Dave seemed to be her rock. By March, Helen's increased self-confidence and power were keeping the parasite at bay—at least when it came to herself. There were indications that the Elder had given up on her and was trying to go after Katie, but the family was supporting the child, too.

Helen and Dave reported that at least one of the parasites, probably the Passive or Trickster, would get frustrated now that it couldn't get at her. They would hear it literally pacing up and down in the hallway at night. Phenomena like these continued, though to a lesser degree, and the shadow figures faded away. The Majors, still doubtful about my theories, weren't participating in our remedies and became increasingly out of touch with the situation. The tension between the two sides of the house went on, which made beating these critters all the more difficult. Still, the path toward a poltergeist outbreak seemed to have been blocked. But some closure was needed.

On March 21, I was at the house with one of my photography experts at the time, Eric Baillargeon, probably the only member of my gang more skeptical than I was. Eric was there to record what I call the "bell and candle ceremony," a very generic, family-oriented prayer of protection that I made up. It's not an exorcism, and it's very simple.

Dave, at left, and the author track the parasite to an old barn on the property. From this building several years later, the parasite would physically attack Reuben, Helen's husband.

I carried a candle, and we all went from room to room. At each door and window, I would make the figure-eight sign, which represents infinity, and say words to the effect that, "May all that is holy, good, right, and true come into this house and into the hearts of all who live here. And may they be protected forever."

When there are children, as in this case, I have them go ahead of us into each room ringing a little guardian-angel wind chime, which always makes them smile and gives them confidence. The bell or chime is one very ancient method for purifying the energy in a room. John and Katie also carried the angel icons I'd given them.

At one point, in the first-floor hallway, Helen seemed to black out for a moment. Dave and I had to support her, but she quickly recovered. She couldn't pin down quite what happened. Perhaps her old nemesis had made another vain attempt to come through. Still, I later advised Dave to keep track of any future incidents like this for possible medical attention.

This impromptu ceremony stopped the trouble, at least for a while. For much of the rest of 1999, I was pleased to hear that things were fine at *Maison Gadreau*. The parasites, which I knew by then were pretty much spatially limited to the area, always were in the background but were well under control. With critters of that kind, that's about as good a result as I can expect if the person or people who have connected with them are going to stay at the site.

In October, however, the family was having more trouble. Evidently, the entity was making another try for Katie. But Dave and Helen had learned a great deal about keeping things positive, and they knew what to do. I didn't even have to get involved. I talked with Helen again in March 2000. Things were great with her, and, aside from the occasional outdoor sighting, all was well.

In a sad postscript that ended up in a happy ending, Dave translated a few years later after a long battle with cancer. Eventually, Helen met and married Reuben, a full-blooded Aztec from a Mexican family with a long and distinguished shamanic tradition, and they continued to live in the Burrillville house, from which

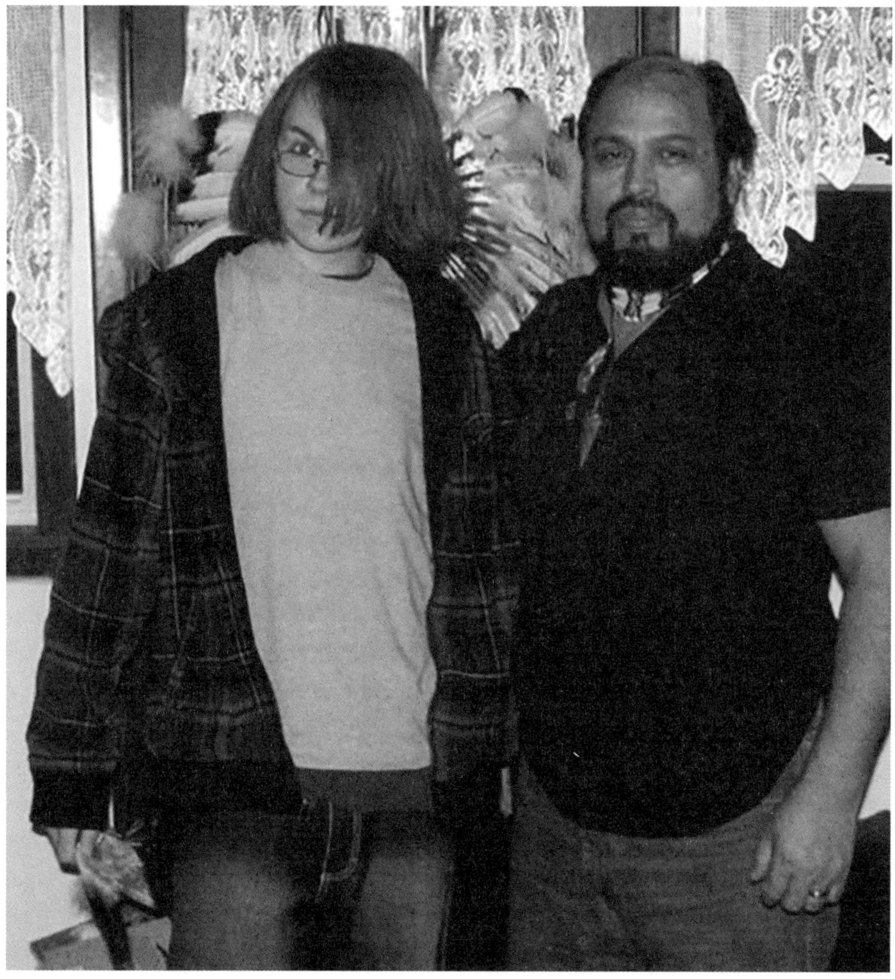

The author's son, colleague, and radio co-host, Ben Eno, at left, with one of his mentors, Reuben, the Aztec shaman, at the house in June 2015.

the Majors had long since departed. The new couple, along with John, Katie, and Reuben's lovely daughter, Maria, made a beautiful family.

THE ELDER ATTACKS

In 2008, after a long hiatus, the parasites tried to make a comeback, but they didn't figure on Reuben. I got to know this amazing man, who knew all about parasites. I was at the house one night that June for a sort of checkup on the case, when we decided to examine the old barn where the creatures would hide in the earlier years of the case.

Sure enough, the Elder was home. As Helen, Maria, and I watched, something dark jumped out of the barn and attacked Reuben. I ordered the women to stay back as the physical struggle continued for nearly a minute. Reuben then collapsed to the ground, panting and in a sweat, as the thing backed off him.

Helen rushed to help Reuben, but I warned her not to touch him. If you touch a shaman during or just after such a contact, nausea and vomiting can result. Meanwhile, the parasite was enraged and went for Maria, who started to tremble and cry. I hugged her as she was amid a swirl of electrical energy, and the thing backed off. I don't have the shaman gene, apparently, so the parasite left me alone, backed off, and fled.

Ben, on the other hand, does seem to have the gene, and that was evident almost from the day of his birth, certainly continuing into his paranormal partnership with me. Reuben took Ben under his wing and, for several years before the family moved out of that never-a-dull-moment Burrillville house to head for North Carolina, mentored my son in the shamanic gifts.

This has stood by us ever since, and we are proud to have known Reuben, Helen, and their great family through this, one of our longest-running cases.

SECTION TWO

THE NEIGHBORS

CHAPTER ONE

THE MISTAKEN MEDIUM

Rumor on the 'net has it that Ben and I think all ghostly phenomena are ultimately caused by parasites. Not so. Sure, parasites are among Nature's great mimics and will pretend to be your dead but angry Uncle Chuck so they can push your buttons and eat, as if you were a walking vending machine. But we believe it's perfectly possible to see, hear, smell, or even interact with the real Uncle Chuck, even if he translated umpteen years ago.

Psychics and mediums say they communicate with the dead every day, but almost all of them think they're talking to spirits—"human discarnates." That raises many questions. If they're actually talking with another being and not just imagining the whole thing, is it a ghost, a parasite, or even a facet of themselves? What's actually happening when you communicate with what we call a ghost? Whether they're spirits or not, can you truly help them, as so many people believe? Can they help you? How do you know you're not really dealing with a parasite? And a critical issue no one seems to address: Without your body and brain, would you still be you?

These and a hundred other questions vexed me as I approached graduation from Wadhams Hall Seminary. It was February 1975, amid a snowy, frigid winter in New York State's North Country. Over the previous two years, I'd assisted Fr. Lawrence Wheeler with clandestine exorcisms on seven people at St. Lawrence State Hospital (see section one, chapter one), endured the Bridgeport poltergeist outbreak, and was about to switch my church loyalty from the Roman Catholics to the Eastern Orthodox, something virtually unheard-of among students for the priesthood.

I will always be grateful to the Wadhams Hall faculty for their patience, tolerance, and support. But during that brutal winter, I couldn't shake the feeling that little of what I'd learned in the seminary, let alone from my priest mentors or from Ed and Lorraine Warren, was good enough to explain the paranormal as I was experiencing it. It was a turbulent time, and it was about to get worse.

A week after the last exorcism I would assist with at St. Lawrence State Hospital, I met Pat. Fifty-six years old, broke, suffering from emphysema, and too young for Medicare, Pat wasn't a psychiatric patient. The hospital would close in

1983, but even with its dwindling resources, it would accept the occasional medical patient who couldn't afford to go anywhere else.

Pat was in what I thought of as the haunted ward, in one of the older buildings of the hospital complex. People didn't hear spectral screams or see apparitions. There were no faces at the window or wall pounding. And it didn't feel parasitical to me. This was different. It was a dominant feeling of heaviness and presence, but from what I could find out, there was no history of this. The hallway "haunting" had existed only for about a year. Patients, most of them elderly, were constantly asking to go home or to be moved. Staff didn't like to work there at all, let alone on the night shift.

In my final days of seminary pastoral work at the hospital, I visited the ward and felt the weirdness. If I ran into that environment today, I'd suspect infrasound (see section one, chapter eight). But whatever the cause, the pall over the ward was almost tangible.

Pat, a slim, soft-spoken, just-going-gray Catholic lady, started talking about the strange atmosphere almost as soon as I introduced myself.

"This part of the hospital is haunted, Paul," Pat pronounced calmly. "Everyone here feels it. I'm a psychic medium."

She was very matter-of-fact.

"You know, Pat, Catholics really aren't supposed to do that," I replied.

Look who was talking.

"Oh, it's fine!" she waved.

I didn't think it was the right time to argue with her.

"You know what's really going on in this hallway, don't you, Paul?"

"Uh . . . no?"

"There's a man who has already passed. His wife is here in the ward. She's going to pass, and he's waiting to take her home."

I'd heard this sort of thing many times, especially from Ed and Lorraine Warren's medium friends.

"Well, even if that's true, the poor man must have been waiting here for a year! That's when the ward started to be haunted," I commented.

"Time in the spirit world is different from here," Pat replied.

I had more questions for her, but I was too interested in what was really going on in this ward.

"If this is a nice fellow waiting for his wife, that's positive, isn't it? Why does it feel so 'heavy,' and how come people don't want to stay here, do you think?"

Pat looked into my eyes, as if trying to read me.

"People don't like the feeling when a spirit is present. It reminds them of their own deaths," she said.

"Pat, which patient here is the wife who's going to pass?" I asked.

"I can't be sure. This is a hospital, after all. People die all the time."

I never did find out who the about-to-die wife was supposed to be.

Back at the seminary, I thought long and hard about this situation. In fact, I was insatiably curious. By the time I returned to the hospital the following week, I'd made a reluctant choice. Since it didn't feel like a parasite, I would do something I'd never dared do before. I would passively open myself up to contact with whatever was haunting that ward. This decision seemed to go against everything I believed, let alone preached. Catholics weren't supposed to contact the dead, and neither were the Orthodox, right?

Maybe I was rationalizing. But at the Village of Voices in 1971 (see *Behind the Paranormal: Everything You Know is Wrong*), I somehow knew the names of the "ghosts" who seemed like they were just going about their daily, physical lives in the 1800s. I seriously doubted that I was dealing with the dead at all. But if it wasn't the dead, who or what was it? And I told myself that I wasn't trying to do the medium thing. Oh, no! I'd simply quiet my mind, make like a radio, and see what I could pick up.

I knew full well how reckless it might be. After all, there was plenty of parasite activity at St. Lawrence State Hospital, and I wasn't arrogant enough to think I could see them all coming. But how to pull this off without arousing suspicion? I realized there was a little room off the hallway that was used as a simple chapel or meditation room. I would simply go in there and meditate. I was a seminarian, after all. How strange would it seem for me to disappear into the chapel for a while?

In the end, the whole process took more than a while.

Classes were over for the day when I drove to the hospital, and the duty nurse looked at me curiously as I walked into the ward.

"You're usually not here on Mondays," she chirped.

These were the years before photo-ID badges, dour security guards, and key codes. People just recognized each other.

"Special visit," I smiled back. Luckily, she was busy and didn't ask any more questions.

Most of the ambulatory patients were watching the television, which babbled mindlessly from the common room. Pat, however, told me that she was indifferent to TV, so I knew I'd find her in her room. I hobnobbed with her for about eighteen seconds, telling her absolutely nothing about what I was planning to do. Then I slipped down the hall to the chapel.

I'm sure it was once a small storage room. It was windowless except for a single skylight, but this did little good, as it was March and the sun still set early. I switched on the light, a bare bulb overhead, and sat down in a rather uncomfortable wooden folding chair. There were several of these, along with a table on which sat a wooden cross and a vase full of plastic flowers.

I relaxed as best I could, then began the basic breathing method to clear body and mind, which I'd learned the previous year from the monks at the Trappist monastery in Spencer, Massachusetts, of all places. I used a simple, heart-united-to-mind technique centered on the word "peace." I also visualized a protective white light around me, the room, and the whole ward. As I've said, this was one of the few things I'd learned from the Warrens that actually worked.

I don't know how long it took to happen, because I always lose track of time during this process, which I use very seldomly. I slowly became aware of something I would come to call the Leinster Effect. Murray Leinster, pseudonym of American author William Fitzgerald Jenkins (1896–1975),wrote masterful science fiction novels about parallel worlds with alternate historical timelines. I would come to believe that his concepts aren't fiction at all. It's a nanosecond of blackness between perception of one world, then another. It's almost like the transition from one image to another with an old slide projector.

MEETING GILBERT

All was silent, and I was drifting. Suddenly: "Hello!" came a male voice right in my left ear. Ordinarily, I would have been startled out of my chair. Somehow, though, I remained utterly calm and kept my eyes closed, as if being addressed by an unseen stranger was completely normal. There was something odd about the way he pronounced the word: He stressed the wrong syllable: "HELLo!"

I hesitated to answer vocally. Surrounded by a largely psychiatric hospital, the last thing I needed was the staff outside hearing me talk to myself. I remembered that parasite a year-and-a-half before during the Barbara case: It had heard my skeptical thought and responded.

"Hello!" I *thought* as enthusiastically as I could. I clearly felt the presence of another person. It wasn't cold and sterile, like a parasite. Whoever this was, he was standing right next to me. I also felt an electrical tingle all over my skin, but it was different from the one caused by parasites. I was slightly dizzy, and I felt like I was floating.

"Do you wait? I wait," came the voice in my ear.

Wait? Dang! Could Pat be right after all?

"Why do you wait?" I asked in thought.

There was a pause, as if my unseen companion was unused to my word order. Then I heard the beginning of a word and…silence. It was as if a bubble burst, or a wall had descended between me and whoever he was. The Leinster Effect.

I looked at my watch. It had stopped. I got up, pulled open the door a crack, and peeped into the corridor. The clock down the hall revealed that over an hour had passed. The shift had changed, and the new nurse on duty, who also knew me, good-naturedly asked what I was doing there.

"Leaving," I replied as pleasantly as I could.

Back in the dormitory at Wadhams, where seniors, fortunately, all had private rooms, I brooded into the night, then found that I couldn't sleep. The next morning, I almost fell asleep during mass, and I was useless in Eastern Philosophy class. But I was determined to see this latest paranormal adventure through.

Tuesday was my usual afternoon and/or evening making pastoral visits at the hospital, so I couldn't wait for classes to end that day. I made it a point to drive to the hospital alone, then managed to slip back to the chapel. The electric tingle was there, and I began to feel heavy and dizzy almost at once. I sat down, did my breathing, and waited. Again, I don't know how long it took. But suddenly, there he was.

"HELLo! You wait?

"I seek," I responded silently.

"Same as wait. Seek who?"

"Well, maybe you!"

"I? I here now."

This was getting frustrating. We were speaking English, but it was as if we each used it as a different language. And sometimes there were other sounds in the background that I couldn't identify. I tried a different tack.

"Name?" I asked.

"Name Gilbert. You name?"

Gilbert? That seemed normal enough.

"I am Paul," I replied.

"You am Paul?" Gilbert seemed as if he'd never heard the name before.

"Where are you?" I was almost afraid to ask.

"Prescott."

What? Prescott was the town right across the St. Lawrence River, in Ontario, Canada.

"Prescott, Ontario?"

"Yes," he replied. "Where you?"

"Ogdensburg! How can we be talking if you are in Prescott? The river is a mile wide!"

As if to bring things back into logical geographical order, that was the last I heard from Gilbert that day. When I got back to the seminary, I was tempted to go straight to Fr. Lawrence and spill the whole kettle of beans. But I had a feeling that

I shouldn't. As I said in an earlier chapter, any hint of the psychic or medium out of me, and I'd be out the door for sure. And all this was too weird! In years of studying paranormal literature, I'd never heard of anything like it.

I slept that night out of sheer exhaustion.

Straining at the bit, and realizing that I was falling behind on homework, I pushed my luck and headed back to the ward after dinner on Wednesday. Now the nurses were getting suspicious. Anticipating that, I was carrying some spiritual reading, the New Testament and Psalms.

"You back again?" the duty nurse commented. "What are you up to?"

I just told her the truth. More or less.

"Well, it'll be exam time soon, and everybody's in a panic back at Wadhams. I love this little chapel, so I'm just coming to pray and read for a while."

"Oh. Well, don't make too much noise." She was hilarious.

Back in the chapel, which I really was growing rather attached to, I heaved a sigh of relief before starting my breathing exercises. As soon as I calmed, there was Gilbert. The more I did this, the easier it seemed. Gilbert acted as if the conversation from the day before had never been interrupted.

"Why probLEM, Paul? You be neighBOR."

It took me a second to get my thought footing.

"Gilbert, what you waiting for?" I was beginning to think like he talked, and sparing the verbs.

"Wife."

Well, that about clinched it. It looked like Pat had nailed it.

"She must be very sick." I was sympathetic.

"No!" Gilbert sounded upset. "No sick! Why say Ellen sick? We be wait [a muffled sound] train from Montreal. You talk odd. From Ogdensburg another way. But we talk. Later wife home I take."

This hit me almost as hard as that parasite in the Bridgeport house about four months before, or that parasite with his Malay. Here I was in a mental hospital, weird-talking to the Invisible Man everybody else thought was a dead guy. And he was telling me that he was across the river, waiting for a train. And when "Ellen" debarked at the station, Gilbert would take her home. Was that what this "haunting" was all about?

"You to neighBOR talk never in your way?" Gilbert's voice shook me out of my shock. Somehow, I got the impression that "way" meant where and when I was. My world, as it were.

"Your way and my way. Different?"

There came a word that sounded like "certain" or "curtain." Then: "Many ways, many neighBORS. We talk to talk with many neighBORS. Many good neighBORS."

I didn't know how to respond. Finally: "Thank you for the talk, Gilbert."

"Paul yes. Must go train comes and many people."

As if this conversation wasn't peculiar enough, I actually heard what sounded like the roar of a diesel locomotive approaching. It was doubly weird because there really was a railroad station in Prescott, and I'd taken the dear old Canadian National from there to Montreal and back on a number of occasions.

Once again, a case shook me to my core, challenging the most common assumptions. It took another four years, until I ran into "The Haunter" of Maine (see the next chapter) for ideas about the multiverse and its immediate presence throughout reality to "click" in my very paranormally confused mind.

Eventually, here was the scenario I worked out when it came to what happened in the haunted ward, which, by the way, completely ceased to be haunted after my final conversation with Gilbert.

Who was Gilbert? He was no discarnate human, he wasn't a parasite, and he didn't seem to be any kind of spirit. I believe he was exactly what he seemed to be: A guy waiting for his wife, who was arriving on a train.

How the hey could he communicate as he did? Perhaps because of the simple fact that non-distilled water conducts electricity. By the mid-1970s, I'd already found that more paranormal events seemed to take place near rivers, streams, and lakes, and where water tables are high. When I later learned about quantum mechanics, it made sense that such areas could more easily energize the electromagnetic (EM) branes, or boundaries, between parallel worlds. Water's properties can include "subtle energy" effects caused by EM radiation from non-standard sources such as human and animal brainwaves and our own planet's magnetic field, along with the EM effects of distant planets and stars.

Think of the multiversal possibilities!

In Gilbert's case, the mile-wide St. Lawrence River was between the hospital and the Canadian town where he said, "I wait." Apparently, we communicated across a brane.

Why couldn't Gilbert speak proper English? Gilbert must have been in a close parallel world. By close, I mean that the laws of physics there were nearly the same as in our world family. Among the things that were different were an alternate historical timeline, in which English grammar developed a little differently. Gilbert spoke a bit like Tarzan did in the 1950s movies I watched as a kid.

Why did the ward seem haunted, and for a whole year? The EM properties of branes can, among other things, affect the human brain much as infrasound can. We get uneasy feelings, sensations of being watched or threatened, and we can even "see things."

The question of duration is very interesting. It seems clear that, in Gilbert's world, the laws of physics were dissimilar enough that time seemed to flow differently. Of course, as Einstein essentially proved in 1952, time doesn't flow. In fact, it has no objective existence at all because it's relative. Our consciousness only experiences time going from past to future, and it seemed to flow much more slowly for me than it did for Gilbert. That's why the brane's intersect point at the hospital seemed to last a year, and why my conversation with Gilbert lasted three days for me and, seemingly, only a few minutes for him. So, as far as she perceived this, Pat was right about time being different on the "other side."

If Gilbert wasn't a spirit, why wasn't he afraid of me, as some neighbors have been in other cases? That's even more interesting. Time and again, I've run into "ghosts" who are afraid of me because they think *I'm* a ghost haunting *them*. That's because, if they see us at all, it can be as we often see them: glowing mists, scary figures with arms and legs, shadow people, even orbs. That's because we're looking through a brane. It's like looking through a tinted or smoked-glass window.

Of course, there are times when we can partially cross the brane, and so can they, but that's another story.

As for my communication with Gilbert, here's the thing: "You to neighBOR talk never in your way?" and "Many ways, many neighBORS. We talk to talk with many neighBORS. Many good neighBORS."

If my eventual conclusions were correct, I would translate that as: "Don't you talk to neighbors in your world? There are many worlds, many neighbors. We talk to many good neighbors."

Evidently, "neighbor" in Gilbert's world didn't just mean the people in the house next door. It also meant the people—or whatever—in the *world* next door. For him, it seemed perfectly normal to stand on a railway platform and yak with me, a neighbor from another world. In fact, he thought it was odd that I didn't think it was normal. This was my first exposure to this mind-wrenching concept.

Why did Pat think Gilbert was a spirit? Pat was sensitive, and she picked up on all the electromagnetic stimuli. But, as with nearly all mediums, she was steeped in the nineteenth-century spiritualist ideas about what the paranormal is all about. While some psychics and mediums use terms that make them sound scientific, actually applying the principles of theoretical physics seems rare. So what else could Gilbert be but a spirit?

Incidentally, the laws of physics in our world would not permit the existence of disembodied spirits with self-contained personalities, minds, memories, etc. There would have to be a physical level to their existence. In fairness to mediums today, however, I think more are beginning to interpret their experiences as I do.

Why didn't other people on the ward communicate with Gilbert? Maybe they did, but it would have depended on their brains' reaction to the intersect point. Some might have heard his voice, and even our chat. Others might have dreamed about him. Still others would have said, "A ghost! Get me out of here!"

In subsequent years, I would see all of the above played out many times, and in a number of different scenarios. I wondered what the multiverse approach did for—or to—not only the old ideas about ghosts, but to concepts like reincarnation, remote viewing, an afterlife, and how it changes the idea of death itself. It certainly has profound implications for religion and our understanding of God (see section four).

The result of this confusing time was a strangely comforting thought: I don't know anything for certain, and it's the first day of school.

CHAPTER TWO

THE BREAKING POINT

Could there be anything more terrifying than a cosmic parasite announcing to me during an exorcism that it had told my father to commit suicide? Or anything weirder than communicating with what everybody thought was a ghost, but who said he was just a guy waiting for his wife at a railroad station across the river, albeit in a parallel reality?

Almost. It happened in a little bungalow in Bridgeport, Connecticut, on the evening of Monday, November 25, 1974. In what was destined to be called "the world's most haunted house," and in the middle of what would become known as "the best documented and most witnessed poltergeist case in history," my paranormal belief system was jarred to its core.

It only took a moment. I was in the house with Gerard and Laura Goodin; their adopted, ten-year-old daughter, Marcia; John Sopko of the *Bridgeport Post*; and a neighbor. Four parasites attacked and, in complete shock, I had a physical shoving match with one as I tried to protect Marcia. This thing that was supposed to be a demon, a disembodied spirit, was very much embodied. I could barely see it, but it was made of some kind of matter. I even felt a skeletal structure, almost birdlike, as it pushed back at me, trying to get to the little girl.

In late 1974, I was still a student at Wadhams Hall Seminary, and I was still assisting Fr. Lawrence Wheeler with exorcism cases to free people from demons. But this one incident in Bridgeport shattered what was left of any belief I still had in that classic paranormal paradigm. Not only was the strict, theological interpretation of possession and exorcism off by miles, I was convinced, but the whole notion of spirits must be wrong, too. And that meant that everything I thought I knew about the paranormal was in question. In case after case between then and late 1978, I was at a loss about just how to interpret what I was seeing, hearing, and feeling. In this period, I truly realized that nothing in the paranormal is what it appears to be. In fact, I wasn't sure if the world around us was what it appeared to be either.

Finally, there came a breaking point, an incident that began to indicate that there was no other way than the multiverse, branes, and the Leinster Effect to explain the paranormal. That point came in October 1978, when I came face to face with what I came to call "The Haunter."

While this case didn't involve possessions, exorcisms, or parasites, it was the first one that vividly illustrated to me the vast multiversal processes that allow parasites, ghosts, psychic phenomena, and the rest of the paranormal to manifest. When I first heard the story, in a phone call from a terrified student who swore that it really happened, I thought: "This sounds like some kind of urban ghost legend."

Urban legends are stories that begin with a single telling, then get repeated, changed, and exaggerated to the point that they join the fabric of modern folklore. Alligators in the sewers, the exotic rat or wombat that gets adopted because some poor sap thinks it's a chihuahua, and the elephant that sits on the Volkswagen are among thousands of popular urban legends. Urban ghost legends include the phantom hitchhiker and the hook-handed guy of Lovers' Lane. Most recently, the internet has proven to be fertile ground for legends like Slenderman, who was deliberately invented and spread through cyberspace. Now people actually report sightings.

The Haunter, however, turned out to be even more bizarre than that—and far from just a legend.

That fall was remarkably warm in southern New England. In the only good luck I had in that period, I was enjoying the weather in a cute, isolated lakeside cottage in my native Connecticut. The rent was only $165 a month. Aside from that, my life was in smithereens. I'd been tossed out of the seminary the previous year, with a year or two to go before ordination to the priesthood, because they

The author's lakeside cottage in 1978, just before The Haunter case.

didn't like my paranormal research. I continued graduate studies at Trinity College in Hartford but soon ran short of cash.

Meanwhile, at the tender age of twenty-three, and after eight years of a voluntarily celibate life in the seminary, I had fallen in love for the first time. This turned into a dog's breakfast because I had no idea how to have a relationship with someone of the contradictory gender.

So here I was at twenty-five, with nothing but my little house, an Irish setter, a cat, and a chicken. I had studied for the priesthood for so long that the only other thing I could do was write, so I was supporting myself by writing, believe it or not, plays and grant proposals for the Connecticut Dance Theater and producer Akiva Talmi, who today is CEO of the Moscow Ballet. It would be another year before I stumbled into journalism.

Then there was the paranormal. There's little or no money in ghosts, unless one is a charlatan, a showman, or both. I was in it because I loved the field, wanted to help people, and was insatiably curious. I needed answers to the deepest questions, but these were stubbornly elusive. While I'd recently made my first television appearance, on Channel 8 in New Haven, as far as the famous (or infamous) "grandparents of ghost hunting" Ed and Lorraine Warren were concerned, I was out. After working with them since 1972, we had parted ways over a nasty haunting in Rhode Island. I suspect that, because I wasn't going to be a priest anymore, I was of no more use to them.

So now I had to find my own cases. Then the Haunter found me.

On one of those paranormally warm days that October, I was ensconced on my back porch, sweating over a ballet scene in which I was supposed to get five dancers, five puppets, and a flock of fake butterflies from one side of the stage to the other. I was gazing out at the lake, picturing the whole mob in a heap at stage center, when I was saved by the telephone, or so I thought.

The female voice on the other end of the line was shaking.

After verifying that I was the guy she'd seen on TV: "I'm sorry to bother you with this, but I know my sister, and she isn't crazy," the caller, Janice, declared. "But I was there, too. If I live to be one hundred, I'll never forget it!"

Here's the story as Jan told it. She and her older sister, Pat, both students at the nearby University of Connecticut, had spent a few days with their boyfriends in southern Maine a few weeks before. There, the four of them had a scare such as I'd never heard the like of.

Bear in mind that, today, you can sit on a street corner anywhere in the Western world, toss a pebble, and you're likely to bean a ghost researcher. But we weren't common in the 1970s, and experiencers were far more cautious about telling their stories for fear of ridicule. So, it took guts for Jan to reach out. She'd contacted the Warrens, who were well known in the media, but they hadn't responded. That left me.

On that first phone call, Jan recounted her experience.

"Pat has always been big on reincarnation, dreams, *déjà vu,* and all that. Every now and then, we'll be someplace and she'll come out with something about this or that being familiar," she explained. "She reads lots of books on this stuff, and people think she's a little weird."

THIS IS MY HOUSE!

Things got truly weird on a back road in what turned out to be York, Maine.

"We were driving down this old road when Pat suddenly screamed. She scared the [fecal matter] out of us! 'Stop! Stop!' she yelled. Joey [Jan's boyfriend] was driving, and he hit the brakes."

Pat was "white as a ghost," Jan said.

"Pat yelled, 'Oh, my God!' and pointed at this house maybe fifty feet back from the road."

Everybody's skin was crawling by this time, according to Jan, who noted that the house was white, only about ten years old, and had a rather neglected yard.

"I know this house! This is my house!" Pat yelled, leaping out of the car.

Terrified, and convinced that her sister had finally gone bye-bye in more ways than one, Jan and the boys tore after her and didn't catch up until she was pounding on the front door. The door opened just as the trio were trying to pull Pat away.

Jan told me that what happened next would be seared into her memory "until the day I die."

The woman who answered the door was in her mid-to-late thirties. She took one look at Pat, screamed, and went stumbling back into the house. A fortyish man then appeared, gaped at the young people on the doorstep, but was unable to speak.

In the meantime, Pat recovered her wits a little, apologized for the intrusion, and blurted that she felt she knew this house. The woman in the doorway "was still shaking like a leaf," Jan recalled, but the man, pale as a sheet, finally found his voice.

"I . . . I wouldn't be surprised if you did know this house," he stammered. "It's you! It's haunted by you! For God's sake, please go!"

Even with that, the man and woman continued to stare at Pat in fascination, seeming almost reluctant to shut the door.

Joey took charge.

"We're sorry to bother you," he said, pulling the others away and down the path to the car. Even as they drove away, the coupled continued to gaze at them from their front door.

"We never found out what it was all about, but it was scary as hell," Jan concluded. "Pat's been depressed and scared ever since."

Needless to say, this case captured my imagination. The first thing I did was interview Pat, who said she'd been dreaming about this house for at least two years. Interestingly, the dreams stopped as soon as she actually encountered the place.

"There were a couple of different dreams about my being in the house," Pat told me. "I had one at least once a week, and they almost always stayed with me."

In one common dream, she would walk down the stairs toward the front door, then stop halfway, startled by something she couldn't identify. In another, she would stand in the living room, gazing out the picture window at children playing in the front yard, a television babbling in the background. In still another scene Pat described, she was in the front yard looking toward the house. It was because of this last sequence that Pat said she recognized the place when she came upon it.

What I found most interesting was that, in the dreams, the house was Pat's. She was adamant about that, and she was very sure that the children she saw from the front window—two boys and a girl—were hers. As a matter of fact, Pat told me that when she first saw this house from the road that fall day, the question "Why aren't there toys in the yard?" flashed through her mind for an instant.

Pat struck me as imaginative and somewhat superstitious but not abnormal. She came across as very sincere. With her permission, I called my old friend and teacher Fr. John Kiley, a Roman Catholic priest and psychologist, who arranged a thorough psychiatric evaluation at the Institute of Living in Hartford, today a facility of Hartford Hospital's mental-health program.

In the meantime, I was determined to track down the couple in Maine who had been struck with abject horror at Pat's very presence. Fortunately, Jan caught a name on the mailbox: Kalinowski. The town they were driving through at the time, she confirmed, was York. In an uncanny stroke of luck, my mother's family had owned a vacation home at nearby York Beach since 1875, and I had vacationed in the area all my life. I knew people in town. Through these handy contacts, I managed to get an address and phone number (which was unlisted) for the only Kalinowskis in the vicinity.

I thought it best to introduce the subject, and myself, by letter rather than by telephone. I wrote on October 22, and I included every professional reference I could think of, so the couple would realize I wasn't some kind of nut. Frankly, I didn't expect an answer before the holidays, if at all. To my amazement and delight, I answered the telephone only three days later to find a deeply shaken Peter Kalinowski at the other end.

"This is very difficult for us, but we have to talk to somebody who won't think we're crazy," Peter told me. The man sounded like a complete wreck. Not knowing who I was, of course, he had called several of the clergy, teachers, and doctors I'd given as references.

"They tell me you're not a publicity hound," he went on.

So the day after Halloween found me turning into the driveway of the house in question, a plain, two-story, 1960s-era home on a back road a few miles from the quaint village of York Harbor. The first thing I noticed was a "For Sale" sign on the front lawn.

Peter opened the door before I'd even stepped out of the car. At the door where Pat had caused such terror, I found a childless couple in early middle age. They were two very frightened people. Inside, Ann Kalinowski offered me some coffee, which I declined (I never touch the stuff). Her hands shook. She looked like she could have used some scotch.

"I really checked you out," were the first words out of Peter's mouth. "We don't want anybody hearing about this, but we just want some answers. We've barely slept since this happened!"

As in so many other cases, the Kalinowskis' first concern was whether they were "going crazy." But the story I heard from this couple made the hair stand up on the back of even my neck. In fascination, I listened to Peter and Ann describe their numerous sightings of a transparent figure they said was "the girl at the door" in exactly the same positions Pat described in her dreams: walking half way down the stairs, looking out the living-room window, and even standing in the front yard looking at the house.

Sometimes they'd witness these apparitions individually, sometimes together. "Pat" would make her appearances at all hours of the day and night, they said. So terrified had Peter and Ann become that, in the weeks before Pat and company had arrived at their door, they'd taken to sticking close to each other while at home. In one of the most fascinating aspects of the case, the apparitions didn't necessarily take place at the same time Pat was having the dreams, which was, of course, only at night.

What's more, the Kalinowskis were convinced that the stairway apparition "seemed to see them." It would look not so much *at* them as *through* them, they said. I immediately recalled Pat's description of her dreams: Walking half way down the stairs and being startled by something she couldn't identify. She reported seeing no people. And, yes. Just as Pat's dreams about the house stopped when she finally encountered the place, so did the apparitions, according to the Kalinowskis.

In the course of long interviews with the couple, first individually and then together, I saw no signs they were anything but very sincere and very frightened.

Meanwhile, Pat was undergoing the Minnesota Multiphasic Personality Inventory test, a modern version of which is still used as a first step in evaluating people's psychopathology. It revealed nothing especially abnormal about her. She was highly imaginative, with a tendency to gloss over problems, but that was about it.

Pat never met the Kalinowskis again, but I kept in touch with both her and the couple throughout 1979. In that time, neither the Kalinowskis nor the girl ever reported another paranormal experience. The Haunter remains one of the most enthralling and mystifying cases I have ever dealt with.

Back in the parapsychological Stone Age of the 1970s, my equipment consisted of a few cameras, some recording gear, a notebook, and a pen. I had no electromagnetic field meter, and I was only just learning about the MWI, the theory in physics that there really are parallel worlds.

So, I fell back on research that my friend, D. Scott Rogo, was conducting on out-of-the-body experiences (OBEs). In his California research, in the 1970s and early 1980s, with his colleague, parapsychologist Keith Harary, Scott cited several cases in which someone reported "astral projecting," and someone else reported seeing that person's "astral body" at the place to which they "projected."

Initially, I considered the Kalinowski case just a variation on this phenomenon. But I was confused by one thing: Pat's insistence that there were children at the house and that they belonged to her. I scratched my head for a while, realized that Scott had noted several cases in which "astral projectors" had ended up in what seemed like quite different worlds, and chalked up Pat's children issue to something like that.

Little did I realize how correct I probably was. Looking back on it from the perspective of the multiverse, I believe that what the Kalinowskis and Pat went through was a mutual experience of the same parallel worlds. According to researchers like Scott, people who experience OBEs often do so while asleep, as in Pat's dreams. But where did Pat project to? Just to that house in York, Maine? I don't think so.

I'm convinced that Pat didn't so much "project her consciousness," as most OBE researchers believe, as connect with that facet of her superlife that already carried on daily life in the Maine house, in a parallel world in which it was her house and those were her children. If I'm right, then how many other ghosts are just shadows of people carrying on their lives somewhere or somewhen else, wondering about those weird and vivid dreams that they can't get out of their minds? And how impossibly rare are those cases in which the "projector" and the percipient actually encounter one another in the same day-to-day reality?

In nearly fifty years of research, this is the only one that I've ever dealt with firsthand. How many more have happened that we know nothing about?

CHAPTER THREE

FACE TO FACE WITH A DRUID

By the mid-1980s, I was convinced that the multiverse really existed, and that it went a long way toward explaining paranormal experiences. What's more, I was seeing that it didn't involve just parallel worlds, but parallel worlds in which time was different. In some, it can be what to us is the past, perhaps the same as our history remembers, or an alternate past. In others, it can be a similar or very alien present. In still others, it's a future time that we might or might not see, and that's why I was running into ghosts (neighbors, more accurately) from elsewhen.

As long as I've been in this field, it's still a shock when paranormal sights and sounds happen suddenly, as they always seem to. I'm more of a ghost "feeler": I'm very good at sensing their presence, and even hearing them, but I rarely see them. What happened to me in the West Country of England was a notable exception.

In 1988 and 1989, I made two busy but delightful trips to the land of my ancestors (most of them, anyway). I was there primarily to research Britain's "big cat" phenomena, particularly the splendidly named Black Beast of Exmoor in the northern part of the county of Devon, in southwest England. My "beast" researches are another story entirely, but I have no wish to torture the reader. So, in brief: Since the early 1980s, farmers in several parts of Britain have reported livestock killed by a mysterious, black, cougar-like creature. Cougars or mountain lions aren't native to Britain; therefore the mystery. The instances I was researching centered in and around Exmoor and Dartmoor, two magnificent national parks and wilderness areas that are like something out of a Thomas Hardy novel. As a matter of fact, Sir Arthur Conan Doyle set the Sherlock Holmes thriller *The Hound of the Baskervilles* on Dartmoor. Magnificently bleak, it's an appropriate setting for mysterious creatures.

For me, there was a personal connection with the area and its sweet-spirited people because mobs of my forbears came from Devon and adjacent Somerset. But I must say that if I never see another sheep it will be too soon. I interviewed farmers and other witnesses, examined sheep kills, and followed huge, feline footprints over rolling moors and into mystifying woodlands where the last of the Druids once hid from Roman soldiers, who didn't take kindly to their annoying habit of human sacrifice.

It was March 1989 and, enraptured by this austere and mystical country, I decided to take an afternoon and visit the 365-square-mile Dartmoor National Park. I ended up in the tiny hamlet of Two Bridges, in South Devon, and stopped for lunch at the quaint Two Bridges Hotel, on the banks of the little West Dart River.

The British love to walk, a healthy habit that almost made up for their unhealthy diet at the time, and the whole United Kingdom is laced with hiking trails—public footpaths, as they're called. So, I asked one of the hotel staff if he could suggest a good walk. He said that a little more than a mile across the moor was a place called Wistman's Wood, only about nine acres, but one of the oldest forests in Britain and supposedly haunted. I later looked up the name "Wistman's" and found that its most common interpretation is "wizard's." The name also might come from the old Saxon word *wisht*, meaning weird or haunted by pixies. Anyone familiar with Old World folklore will know about the "Wild Hunt," a perhaps multiversal phenomenon associated with Wistman's Wood, and involving dogs from hell, known as "Wisht Hounds."

Wistman's Wood in Devon, seen as the author approached from Two Bridges.

Haunted woods and dogs from hell being right up my street, off I went. Crossing the road, I struck a footpath that took me past a lovely old farm and out onto the moor. Having spent the previous week running around North Devon's Exmoor National Park in pursuit of the beast, I was falling in love with these unique expanses of open wilderness that many of my forefathers, including the Earls of Devon, once trod.

Despite the fact that they are only about forty miles apart, Exmoor and Dartmoor have quite different characteristics. But on both, distances can be misleading, and fogs and mists can come up seemingly out of nowhere. Here and there, the walker even comes upon ancient burial mounds (known as "barrows") or circles of prehistoric standing stones, where cameras sometimes won't work and compasses often go wrong. Exmoor's landscape is more hilly and rolling, with deep valleys here and there. On Dartmoor, hills topped with bizarre outcrops of rock, known as "tors," rise up both nearby and on the horizon, lending a further aura of the otherworldly.

Telltale monuments to human prehistory are everywhere, and one of the most striking of these came into view as I crested a little rise above the farm at Two Bridges. From where I stood, it looked almost like a patch of tall and ragged brown grass on the eastern slope of the moor just above the river. But as I approached, I could see that it was indeed a small woodland, remnant of a much larger forest that covered Dartmoor until humans cleared much of it about 5,000 years ago.

I'd never seen a forest like it. The trees—ancient, gnarled, and stunted—are miniature oaks, beaten by centuries of stiff winds and biting winters. The tallest tree I saw was only about twelve feet high. Together they stand in a tangle on the slopes of Longaford Tor, their roots coiling among hundreds of huge granite boulders, known locally as "clitter" and apparently dropped there by glaciers during the last Ice Age.

In almost preposterous contrast, a glance across the West Dart River to the opposite hillside reveals a fence line and signs warning of a military training area with occasional live-fire exercises.

In my fascination with Wistman's Wood, however, I admit that I ignored the signs posted by environmental authorities asking visitors to keep out of the actual woodland. There was an aura of ominous anticipation about the place, as though I were stepping through a brane into an alien time. It wasn't an unfamiliar feeling: That electrical tingle had hit me many times before in hundreds of haunted places and before experiences of the Leinster Effect. The tension seemed heightened by the utter silence of everything but the thin March wind.

I stepped inside . . . and out of the twentieth century. As I moved among the twisted roots and strewn boulders, I soon saw that Wistman's Wood is actually two separate groves with an odd little swath running down the middle. I later learned that this swath traces the subsurface path of a large vein of quartz. From a geomagnetic standpoint, this is a clue to the presence of electromagnetic (EM) fields that can play games with branes and encourage multiversal intersects, which would surely give the place its haunted reputation.

I picked my way around the southern grove, touching tree and rock, and enjoying the atmosphere of total timelessness. There were no birds, no insects, no animals: only the trees, oddly unmoved by a wind that seemed far away. I was surprised, out of the corner of my eye, to catch a movement to my right. As I turned my head, there was just an instant of blackness—like that sliver of blank time in a slide show between one image and another that I've mentioned—and a heightened electrical tingle on my skin. In another instant, my consciousness focused again.

Only about ten feet away, to the north, between me and one of the larger trees, I was startled to see a figure. More specifically, there was *half* a figure. I could see nothing from the waist down, but above that was a man with his right side toward me. Dressed in what appeared to be a combination of brownish furs and a black cloak, with a round fur cap, he was staring intently eastward.

In another instant, he turned with a jerky movement and looked toward me. I don't say *at me* because I was certain that he couldn't see me. A second later, I suddenly experienced that sliver of blackness again and was quite alone once more.

The whole episode lasted about eight seconds, not bad as paranormal experiences go. I stood silent for a while, savoring what to me was a rare and precious encounter. Depending on their own beliefs and backgrounds, friends later told me that I'd had a temporal-lobe experience, seen a classic ghost or simply was punch drunk from chasing fictitious monsters all over the moors for a week.

The attentive reader won't be surprised when I say that I'm partial to the idea that I had a classic multiverse experience: a glimpse around the corner of that self-created wall we know as time, aided by an intersect point where a brane happened to run through the spot, energized by the strange EM fields at Wistman's Wood. Barring that, the temporal-lobe experience comes in a strong second. But isn't it possible that one goes hand in hand with the other? Do neural conditions such as temporal-lobe epilepsy (which there is no medical evidence that I have, by the way) create paranormal experiences within the mind, as is generally believed, or do they open paths for the mind into other times and places? I think the latter possibility deserves serious study rather than shaken heads.

In any case, I believe that I may well have encountered a neighbor from elsewhen in that truly magical place. I call it a precious experience because, for one thing, I am a lover of history, because history is people: People who may live in different worlds but who are one with us in human joys and sorrows.

Who was this man I saw staring so intently eastward? A few overstimulated neurons firing in my brain or a fellow human from the distant past—or future? Was he one of the legendary Druids, perhaps a facet of my own superlife? An escaped prisoner from a far century? A cold hunter out of some dim decade, longing for home? I doubt if I'll ever truly know.

CHAPTER FOUR
THE CRYING GHOST

I certainly didn't have to go to Old England to hobnob with neighbors from elsewhen. There were plenty of them in New England. I met one by courtesy of the Querido family of Auburn, Massachusetts, just outside Worcester and about forty miles west of Boston.

The Queridos, first-generation Portuguese immigrants, heard nothing odd for the first four years they lived in the trim, single-family, 1950s-era house in Auburn. Then it began. In the quiet of the night, even as the family's antique clock ticked reassuringly on the living-room mantle, the sobbing would begin. Little Lori heard it first and then, finally, her skeptical parents, Ann and John.

"I thought I was dreaming, but I was wide awake, and it kept going. The crying, I mean," Ann Querido explained in a phone call to me in January 1991. "It's soft. It even fades in and out sometimes. But we've all heard it. And now I'm really scared because of what I saw in Lori's room!"

That's where I stopped her. In the early nineties, it already was my policy to go and see for myself before hearing the whole story or making any judgments.

I pulled up outside the Querido home on the morning of February 7, a sunny Thursday. Inside the five-room, Cape Cod-style house, I found a worried-looking woman and a husky, curly-haired man, both in their early thirties. Both had taken the day off from work to meet me. Lori, the couple's five-year-old daughter, was at morning kindergarten.

Touring the house and the yard with the couple in tow, I felt that the bathroom, the child's bedroom, part of the backyard, and the basement were indeed "charged." At the same time, I felt that "it" was moving. As a matter of fact, in the course of three hours in this house, I repeatedly followed this electromagnetic (EM) field from the bathroom, down the hall to the child's room, out into the yard, then down to the basement, where it would vanish. All the while, I snapped away with my trusty 35-mm camera, which landed me with just over forty pictures of odd shapes and swirling energy.

I was aware of all the sensations associated with the presence of a parallel-world intersect point or points. One of the most striking impressions I had in the Querido house was an overwhelming feeling of sadness, even depression. Not evil, not

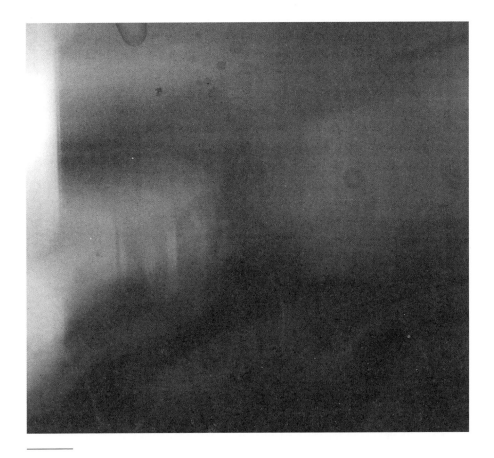

All photos taken in the Querido house were filled with odd shapes and what appeared to be swirling energy.

hostility, not sterility, just sadness. To me, this was already a familiar signature: a distressed person or people whose energy was rippling across a brane.

At the same time, I noted how crowded this semi-urban neighborhood was. The Queridos' house and lot were small. There were many homes, both single-family and multi-family, nearby, and there was a good deal of car and truck traffic: plenty of sources for a sound like crying.

When we finally sat down at the kitchen table that morning and I began my long list of standard questions, I quickly formed the impression that John and Ann were exactly what they appeared to be: an honest, blue-collar couple, faithful Roman Catholics who weren't playing with Ouija boards, séances, or any of the other multiversal dynamite that can blow holes in branes and attract big trouble.

From what I could see, the Queridos' rather normal personal and family problems weren't explosive either. Less chance for a parasite buffet with these folks around, I thought.

Then I listened to their story.

It was June 1986 when the Queridos moved in, truly a day of fulfillment and pride for them. John and Ann had worked and saved for years, and it was their first house. It also would be their first experience with what they believed was a ghost.

LORI'S LAMENT

In the wee hours of a Sunday morning in November 1990, little Lori had climbed out of bed and tramped sleepily into her parents' bedroom.

"Mommy!" she said, shaking Ann, "Somebody's crying."

"What's the matter, honey?" Ann asked groggily, thinking the child was talking about herself.

"I don't know. Somebody's crying. Come on!" the child replied, now tugging at Ann's sleeve.

Ann glanced at the clock as Lori pulled her out of bed: 1:15 a.m. The child led her mother down the short hallway and into her own room. The only sound was the ticking of the old living-room clock and John's heavy breathing back in the master bedroom.

"Lori, there's nothing. Go back to bed," Ann commanded.

It struck me at once that Lori obeyed without complaint. She didn't seem particularly afraid, according to Ann, which meant that perhaps we were dealing with something non-threatening. Children can relate to crying. They do it and see it often. Perhaps all this wasn't paranormal. All sorts of things, from cats to major appliances, can sound like crying. But I couldn't forget the striking impressions I picked up earlier. This could indeed be a neighbor from elsewhen.

Why the four-year wait for phenomena to begin? I find that it often takes people two to four years in a new home to connect electromagnetically with whatever is there. Just as a relationship between two people takes time to develop, so does a relationship between people and their environment. I believe it's that simple.

The next night at 1:30 a.m., Lori was back at Ann and John's bedside. Ann once again heard nothing. And the child was back the night after that. By this time, mom was losing patience.

"This is the last time, Lori!" Ann growled as she heaved out of bed once more.

Then she froze.

"You see, mommy?"

Ann didn't see. She heard. It was indeed a muffled but pathetic sound very much like sobbing. It faded back and forth, as she later described it to me. John was a heavy sleeper, and it took some doing for Ann to shake him awake. When she finally did, he heard it, too.

"I tried to figure out where it was coming from," John told me. "But I just couldn't get around the idea that it was someplace in the house."

Lori crawled into bed with her parents and soon was fast asleep. The sounds died away in about another ten minutes, but John and Ann lay awake for the rest of the night.

The next morning, a fine Saturday with the sun glinting off an inch of new, late-spring snow, John and Ann sat at the kitchen table rationalizing, as most people do after a paranormal experience.

"We told ourselves that it had to be coming from next door someplace, or maybe outside."

That night, with Lori in bed with them again, the sobbing started. Ann heard it first and woke John. It kept going for a few nights, then stopped. The crying was one thing, I thought, but I was just as alarmed as Ann over the apparition.

"There wasn't any crying for a couple of nights; then I just woke up one night, and it was like things were too quiet. I can't explain it!" she told me.

Uneasy, Ann climbed out of bed and glided down the darkened hallway to Lori's room. When she stepped through the doorway, every muscle froze and every hair on the back of her neck stood up. Ann shook as she described the scene.

"It was a ghost! I actually saw a ghost! There was some light from the street and this shimmery thing with like robes and a face—I saw the face clear as day. She was looking at Lori in the bed! That face broke my heart. It was a woman—a sad, sad woman! My God, I was petrified!"

Then Ann's maternal instinct got the better of her terror.

"I started to get mad. What was this thing going to do to my baby?"

Forcing her legs to move, Ann stepped forward. At once, without looking at Ann, the "thing" vanished. She called me the next day.

I pressed Ann with generic questions, and she finally described another common trait of the paranormal experience, one that many people ignore. It was the Leinster Effect once again: That half-second blackout, then a sudden awareness of the paranormal event. It's happened to me often, and I believe it's the slip of a "veil," if I may use that hackneyed term, a brane between one world and another.

There indeed can be interaction with non-parasitical multiversal neighbors at these intersect points. But this can be brief and limited because intersect points can move, depending on energies in the area and among the people at the site. Interaction, however, can be tricky because parasites are tricky. These miserable critters can come across as crying ghosts, jolly old gents, or just about anything else—until they start getting nasty.

On the other hand, I've found that looking into cribs and children's beds seems to be a favorite pastime of distressed humans who find themselves partially in our reality. But I don't believe they see what we see. They're still rooted in their own worlds, and I have every reason to believe that they see things as they would in their niche in the multiverse. Most likely, they get feelings of being watched by us just as we do by them. They walk over and check out noises and feelings just as we do.

Nevertheless, I advised the Queridos to have Lori sleep in their room until we'd gotten to the bottom of this. I was forming tentative conclusions, not just because of the story I'd heard and the impressions of sadness I was getting, but based on past experience. The repetitive path the "ghost" took through the house, into the yard, and down to the basement was a pattern I'd seen before. I didn't tell the Queridos this—yet—but it was my bet there had been a suicide here, not in this house but in another on the same spot in a different world, an act of violence and disorder that echoes across the multiverse in many ways. If it was such an act, it could also be in what to us would be the future. All time is relative and simultaneous, after all.

Past, present, or future, how much suffering must someone endure before they begin fearing life more than death? Suicide. It has been at the root of a number of my cases, and it probably produces more distressed people than any other experience that sends ripples of pain booming through the multiverse. The impressions I get in such places can be heart wrenching. I often feel like crying myself.

I would have bet my breakfast that a woman in a house on this spot somewhere in space-time had lost a child and taken her own life in despair—or would. On the off chance that such a suicide had taken place in our historical time and could be pinned down, I set one of my gang, Mitch Norbock, at the time a student at Worcester's Clark University, to doing some local historical research. He didn't find any suicides traceable to the Queridos' address. But he did find that the houses in that part of Auburn had replaced an older, working-class neighborhood torn down in the 1950s.

Meanwhile, I was determined to hear this spook for myself. I lined up the "crying" dates Ann and John recalled, and it seemed that it happened most often around the time of the full moon. No joke, and no superstition. The full moon affects the Earth's magnetic field—and therefore our EM environments and our own brain functions—just as it does the tides. Ghosts from elsewhen really do tend to be more apparent at times of the full moon because they're electrical, too.

I was a night news editor at the *Providence Journal-Bulletin*, so my day usually ran until 2:30 a.m. anyway. Late hours didn't faze me. I arrived in Auburn just before the chilly midnight of March 29. Very conveniently, it not only was the day before the full moon, it was a Friday, so the Queridos could wait up with me.

Lori was snoozing blissfully in her parents' bed, and Ann, John, and I chatted quietly in the darkened living room. By 12:45, John nodded off and was snoring softly. By 1:00, Ann's head was drooping. I was wide awake, so, with a thrill, I heard it first. Unmistakably, it was the sound of a woman sobbing, but it was difficult to pin down just where it was coming from. The pain of it broke my heart. This was no parasite! I got up very slowly, moving ever so quietly into the hallway. It seemed to be coming from Lori's room. I moved toward it and peered through the door. Was that a slight shimmer by the bed? I couldn't be sure.

All of a sudden, it seemed to be coming from the bathroom. I got there, and it was back in the hallway. This had happened to me frequently in the past. I'd run toward a sound, only to have it pop up again somewhere nearby. Einstein, remember, theorized that space-time is literally curved.

I swung suddenly to look back toward the living room. My heart skipped a beat when I clearly saw a figure there. Just Ann! She and John both were awake, and both heard the sobbing, fading in and out as though from near to far. I had no doubt it was a distance that couldn't be measured in inches, feet, or miles.

YOU ARE LOVED

Back in the living room, I sat the couple down.

"Let's try something before it stops," I whispered. "Let's hold hands, calm down, and quiet our minds as much as we can."

When I felt that my companions had done so, at least as much as they were going to, I spoke up.

"Peace, dear," I said to the darkness. "Peace."

The sobbing stopped immediately. I got the very sharp impression that whoever it was heard and began to listen, uncertain and afraid. I got more confident with what I was doing. I whispered to Ann and John.

"I don't think she can actually hear us. I think she's feeling us. Whatever you do, project love and compassion," I advised.

I spoke toward our neighbor again.

"You are not alone. You are loved. You are not alone!"

Not a peep. But the sense of sadness seemed less.

There was no more activity that night. When I left an excited but groggy Ann and John at about 2:30 a.m., I urged them to build up this feeling of compassion, love, solidarity, and even humor in the house. I advised them to pray fervently and often for this poor woman, whoever she was or would be.

I was wonderfully gratified only a few weeks later when I talked with Ann by phone. She was in tears, but they were the tears of someone who has been deeply touched.

"We did what you said. We prayed and we told her we loved her. My God, Paul! Everything started to feel so wonderful and, like, clean! There was never any more crying. But last night we all woke up at the same time, around midnight, and I swear the whole house smelled like flowers! It was the most beautiful thing I've ever felt!"

Then she let me in on the grand finale.

"John and I came out of the bedroom and into the kitchen this morning. We were all happy. Then, right in the middle of the kitchen floor, we saw this big, beautiful lily! No idea where it came from. Just one lily, biggest one I ever saw!"

I suppose the flower could have gotten there in some other way, but the Queridos saw it as a parting "thank-you" gift from their uninvited guest.

Well, why not?

CHAPTER FIVE

THE FRUSTRATED TEACHER

Probably the only case I've ever had in which the people involved were more terrified of the publicity than they were of the ghost was centered at a large Massachusetts elementary school.

I don't dare tell you where it was, and if you have children you'll understand why. Every school has its ghost stories—95 percent of them silly urban legends, in my opinion. All an authority figure, especially a teacher or parent, has to do is tell a campfire ghost story or make a jocular remark about "the ghost that scared the janitor" or "the kid who died at the end of the hallway." Rest assured that youngsters will repeat it and embellish it for generations. And if children actually see evidence that a story is true, or hear adults saying so, chaos and terror will ensue in the halls of learning.

This actually began to happen at the school in question in June 1993. I first heard about it when I picked up the phone to hear the school's principal. As you can imagine, I've had some pretty odd phone conversations, but this one took the giddy biscuit.

"Is this Paul Eno?"

"Yes, sir. What can I do for you?"

"Is this Paul Eno the...ah...ghost expert."

"As far as I know. What can I do for you?"

"I...ah...really can't begin to explain...."

... And so on for another minute. The man was so embarrassed that I had to lead him to the subject. I thought I'd better scrap my usual just-tell-me-the-bare-minimum-beforehand procedure this once and just hear the story outright, or this case would never get off the ground. When he finally came clean, here's what I got:

Classroom 305 had been strange as long as anyone could remember. The two custodians, who almost always arrived first in the morning and left last at day's end, experienced the most oddities there. When they could be cajoled into talking about it, which was seldom, they would mutter about voices and footsteps heard in the room. They hated to wax the floors because cleaning tools would disappear. And when they rearranged desks, they'd often turn around to find the desks back in their original positions. They didn't even like using the janitors' room next to Classroom 305.

Things didn't just happen off-hours, either.

Teachers never liked to use 305. As each year began, they'd badger the administration to palm it off on some unsuspecting new colleague. Before long, he or she would complain of missing books and papers, odd scrawls on the blackboard first thing in the morning, and even furniture moved about when nobody was looking. Occasionally, there were feelings of an angry presence. There even were complaints that students were rowdier in 305 than in any other room.

Then there were the apparitions. According to the principal, every now and then, if someone happened to be in the building after dark and looked into 305, they might report seeing a "shimmery" female figure moving rapidly back and forth across the front of the room or along the windows. As far as he knew, there had never been any direct interaction with this entity, if entity it was.

"I'm not saying I believe all this," he told me. "But the stories are getting out of hand among the kids. I've even had a parent on the phone about it! This has to be nipped before the press gets hold of it! We heard you don't get the press involved."

They'd heard right but apparently didn't realize the ironic fact that I was a working journalist. Nevertheless, so much for my policy of seeing for myself before hearing the works. Even after the man blurted out the whole story, it wasn't that easy to start an investigation: The superintendent of schools and members of the School Committee wanted to interview me first.

"No cameras," the woman, a School Committee member, declared hands-down as I sat across the table from four big shots that weekend. I'd come all the way up to meet with them, and I'd just explained how I worked.

"But I need photographs to help me find out what's going on. I can't get rid of it if I don't know what it is!"

"No cameras!"

They even made me sign a paper stating that I wouldn't utter a whisper or jot down a letter about the case for five years, and even then, I couldn't name the school or even the town. I felt as though I was dealing with the CIA. They seemed to like the rest of my approach and my theories, however. The superintendent commented merrily that I "didn't seem like a flake." He acted surprised.

At least they took me to dinner after this inquisition.

A few days later, I appeared in the teachers lounge at the school just after classes dismissed for the day. There I interviewed four faculty members and both janitors, who told me much the same things the principal had. The powers that were wouldn't let me interview any students, however.

The superintendent, who hovered annoyingly about during the whole procedure, seemed as nervous as a cat in a room full of rocking chairs. The principal, on the other hand, was starting to get comfortable with all this. He breezed in just as I finished the last interview. By late that day, in fact, he'd apparently appointed himself my assistant. I much prefer working alone on a first visit, but I couldn't get rid of him.

"What do we do first?" he asked after the interviewees and the superintendent left.

"Well, you could show me Classroom 305," I replied.

The room was in a remote part of the rambling school building, at the near end of a long, third-floor hallway. There's nothing quite so lonely as an empty school, and our footsteps echoed like gunshots off the polished brick walls. We stopped at the door marked "305." The principal took a set of what looked like a hundred keys, effortlessly selected one, and opened the door.

It was getting dark outside, and the room was dim. As we entered, I at once felt heavier. There was an immediate sense of depression, to the point that I became almost dizzy. The huge room, about forty-five feet long and maybe thirty feet wide, with a windowed door at each end, seemed clean but uncannily dingy, almost stuffy. I switched on my electromagnetic field meter (EMF) and moved slowly along the back wall, down the long outside wall with its ceiling-high windows, then along the front wall, with its long blackboard. All along that blackboard, readings fluctuated wildly, even into the negative range, which is really the only thing I'm looking for when I use the meter. EM fields are everywhere in the modern world, especially indoors, so fluctuating readings mean very little—as long as they stay in the positive range. When they dive into the negative range, which is very odd, it means the polarity on the EM field has reversed. In my experience, this means an energy exchange is taking place across a brane breach. In old-time paranormal parlance, I suppose you could call it a portal. One way or the other, there was some real multiversal monkey business going on here.

"Now what?" asked the principal in a quiet, nervous voice from the back of the room.

"We wait," I replied, navigating back to his side through a row of desks.

ACTION IN CLASSROOM 305

Even in cases where there are physical phenomena, it often takes hours, days, or even weeks for me to actually document them. But this wasn't to be a problem in

Classroom 305. The principal and I sat quietly at the back of the room for about ten minutes. It was getting dark, and the only light came through the hallway windows at each end of the room. The only sound was the distant roar of traffic through the closed windows.

When it happened, I felt it first. Then the principal looked at me, his eyes wide. He felt it, too: Something had arrived. We both sensed it come through the door at the front of the room and move along the blackboard, then up the wall of windows toward us, then back again. I glanced at my companion, who stared toward the blackboard, sweating.

There came a sharp scrape. A desk chair was moving across the floor at the front of the room. It stopped by the door, and there came a heavy *thrump* like someone pounding once on the backboard. There was even chalk dust in the air!

Fascinated, I got up and moved slowly toward the activity.

"PSSST!" came from behind. The principal gave me a pitiful look as I glanced back. He was terrified! I raised a hand in assurance and made a motion that I hoped told him I had to move forward and that he should stay put. As I moved forward again, another chair scraped, but this time it was the principal making a quick retreat through the back door.

There was another angry *thrump* on the blackboard as I approached, then silence. I was frustrated because of the principal's fear, not a good emotion to be carrying if this turned out to be a parasite. Almost at once, I was engulfed in a swirl of energy, and my skin tingled. This didn't feel like anger. More like frustration. This could be a parasite but, somehow, I didn't think so. I gave it the benefit of the doubt.

"Be at peace. All will be well," I said quietly, trying to clear my mind.

Another *thrump*, this time at the other end of the blackboard, then quick footsteps in front of the windows toward the back of the room. I wasn't getting through.

Then there was a movement by the front door. I glanced that way and froze for an instant as I caught a face staring back at me through the classroom door. It was the principal! He was breaking my concentration again. The presence was gone.

So were we. Back in his office, the man was a wreck. I even had to follow him home in my van after he locked the building. During the next week, I did some research and tried to isolate what I was dealing with. This being had some characteristics of a parasite—negative manifestations such as pounding and chair moving. On the other hand, I've never found parasites operating for long in public places because there's nobody for them to attach to—people in places like that always are coming and going. Besides, I hadn't felt the non-human, cold sterility I always pick up around parasites. In my opinion, the negative emotions pointed toward a distressed human, a multiversal neighbor.

What clinched my diagnosis was some painstaking research at the city library and at the school department. I looked at the history and even the blueprints of the school, which was built in the early 1900s, the history of the area, and even what I could find about its geology. I had no soil engineer working with me in those days, but I knew that the clay soil and high water table the school was built on was a combination that conducts EM fields very well, making it all the easier for paranormal phenomena to occur. From the blueprints, I saw at once that some hefty plumbing and wiring ran past the room's front wall, just behind the blackboard.

All things considered, this room was a good candidate for slips in space-time and neighbors from elsewhen.

I even got into some old personnel records and newspaper archives. I was about to give up on that part of it when I stumbled on the obituary of a teacher who died in 1922 at the age of forty-two in a collision between an automobile and a trolley car. Let's call her Mary Martin. Something "clicked" when I saw Mary's picture, as though I'd met her before. A little more research revealed that she not only taught at the school but reigned for fifteen years over what was today Room 305. The principal, his wits recovered, led me to a retired janitor, then in his eighties, whom he didn't consider a security risk and who had been a student of Mary's the year she died.

"Miss Martin was totally dedicated to the school; it was her whole life. She never got married, and she was a complete nervous wreck," Ted said. "She was always pacing back and forth in front of that blackboard or in front of those windows. And she was never satisfied, with us or with the room! She'd always be telling us we could do better, even if we'd get a B or B+. And she was forever moving desks and chairs around, and sometimes she would pound on the blackboard!"

Well, I saw this as a pretty good place to begin. The personality Ted described could be summed up in one word: frustrated. Then came the breakthrough.

"You know, us kids never really liked that room much after that, and I heard some weird stuff in there when I came back to work at the school years later."

That did it as far as I was concerned. We quite probably had met Mary Martin pacing the room in 1920 or thereabouts.

When I next spoke with the principal, school had dismissed for the year, and I strongly suggested that, starting with the 1993–1994 school year, he put the most positive teacher he could find in Room 305, even if he had to change class assignments. I realized then that it was a good thing the man was with me that night to have the daylights scared out of him—he was all ears to my advice.

The following week, I was back in Classroom 305—alone, this time—quietly expressing compassion and sympathy for Mary. There were no manifestations, and the atmosphere seemed a little lighter.

With other matters competing for my time, school officials gave me the go-ahead to instruct the teachers who were going to use the room about how to project positive energy, especially compassion, there. It worked, from what everyone could see. During the rest of the summer, my follow-up revealed that the janitors had few obvious paranormal experiences in the room. And when school began, things went better, and teachers reported no incidents at all.

School officials were delighted. One of the few who knew the details later asked me why Mary would be "stuck" in the room after she died. Must have been her violent death, right? I patiently explained that, in my opinion, Mary's presence in the room had nothing to do with her bodily death but everything to do with her life. She was still alive in 1920 or thereabouts in any number of parallel worlds, and in many of those she still stalked Classroom 305, fussing over her students and rearranging chairs. Given the EM site conditions, her intense dedication might have manifested across a brane for decades, whether she had translated or not. I have several cases in my files in which the distressed humans manifesting as ghosts actually turned out to be people still living in our corner of the multiverse.

Given the fact that things eventually calmed down in 305, I have absolute conviction that the compassion and positive energy we sent Mary's way did her good, soothed her, and probably made for some very grateful students in one or another corner of our weird reality.

The only question that still bugs me about this case was the movement of objects, such as the classroom chairs. As I've said in previous chapters, I suspect that in poltergeist cases most, if not all, the telekinesis take place because of turbulence at the intersect point, especially the convergence and overwashes of worlds with different laws of physics. That didn't seem to be the case in Classroom 305, where dear old Ms. Martin actually seemed to be moving the furniture. I attribute this to the spatial relationship between the two world families—ours in 1993 and hers in 1920 or so. As these worlds blended at the intersect point, the chairs moving in 1993 might well have been one with their 1920 facets as Mary moved them. Yes, people aren't the only ones with multiversal facets—everything has them.

That's my opinion, anyway.

CHAPTER SIX

KEVIN AND THE LITTLE GIRL

By American standards, New England is a very old place. History really is alive here, and many people live in houses that remember honest Puritan farm families or periwigged gentlemen who offered toasts to King George II.

When I walk through the carved doorway of an old home in our corner of the world, I feel these people around me. And why not? In the multiverse, they are, and we're all part of each other. But their unique personal facets don't always stay behind their own branes, especially if they're in distress. I believe this is a frequent cause of what we consider ghosts, and I believe it was the case at the Marshburn home in Cumberland, Rhode Island, when I got the call in early 2000.

It was my second lecture season after my 1998 book *Faces at the Window* appeared, and I'd recently done a book signing at the Barnes & Noble store in nearby Bellingham, Massachusetts. A friend of the Marshburns came all the way from Leominster, Massachusetts, to be there.

"You've got to talk to this guy!" she told Bonnie Marshburn later.

When I spoke with her on the phone, Bonnie didn't seem especially upset about what was going on in her home. She came across as fascinated and a little concerned.

"It's more interesting than scary," she stated. "But my husband had a real scare!"

That was where I stopped her. "Let me see for myself," I replied.

It was a cloudy day in February when I first visited the Marshburns. To my delight, I found a beautifully restored, eighteenth-century farmhouse surrounded by woods and some newer houses. And since positive people have fewer paranormal problems, I was even more pleased to find a very positive couple in their forties. They had two teenagers, a boy and a girl, whom I didn't meet on that first visit.

I dropped onto a couch in the bright family room, and I was at once joined by the enormous family dog. Bonnie and her husband, John, explained that the place had an intriguing history.

"This house was a stop on the Underground Railroad in the 1850s, and we think one of the escaped slaves must have died here," John declared.

There we went with the standard assumptions about what ghosts must be. The Underground Railroad, of course, had nothing to do with trains. It was a system of smuggling escaped slaves out of the pre-Civil War South, through northern states where slavery was illegal but where they could still be captured and sent back, to Canada, which permitted no slavery at all and where they would literally be home free. Many New England cellars had secret chambers where the escapees could hide while awaiting secret transport to the next "station" on their Underground Railroad journey.

Having been a station is a story that seems to stick to just about every New England house built before 1860 or so. Sometimes it's true, sometimes not, but the Marshburn house isn't mentioned in the town, state, or national historic registers. I've never been able to verify the story. The Marshburns had lived there for about six years. Interestingly, from what I was able to learn later, there was a change of owners every six to eight years as far back as the 1950s.

After my standard, pre-investigation questions, I started, as I always do, with a quiet, self-guided tour. I visited and photographed all the rooms. It was the living room that drew me, particularly the corner with the china hutch. There was something there for sure, and it felt like a young girl.

A PROBLEMATIC PAINTING

My electromagnetic field (EMF) meter registered a weak but alternating magnetic field that could have had several quite ordinary causes. It didn't go into the negative range, indicating a reserve-polarity EM field, a clue to possible cross-brane energy exchanges. It was that clear feeling of being watched by someone shy that made me pay attention. Then there was the painting. Hanging on the living-room wall between the hutch and the front door: It was a lovely, nineteenth-century-style watercolor print of a little blonde girl. It at once reminded me of Renoir's *Girl with a Watering Can*, except that the girl was seated and surrounded by flowers. John said he'd bought the painting on Cape Cod the previous summer.

The portrait of an unknown little girl, which the family purchased on Cape Cod.

"I thought it looked just like our daughter when she was a little younger," he explained. "But I wonder if something came with it."

What John meant was that after the painting arrived, people in the living room started to get the feeling they were—you guessed it—being watched. It wasn't threatening, the Marshburns insisted, but it was obvious. I agreed that it was almost as if someone—a little girl—was hiding behind that hutch.

Then John told me about the apparition, adjacent to the living room and between the first-floor bathroom and the master bedroom.

"I was in the bathroom late one night. When I came out to go back to bed, I saw a young blonde-haired girl standing between me and the bedroom door. I was startled, but I assumed it was Natalie [the daughter]. But then she just disappeared! Actually, she looked like the girl in the painting!"

Here's where some alarm bells started sounding. In a hefty 40 percent of my cases, a little blonde girl, or some other innocent character, pops up at some point, usually in the early stages. More often than not, it turns out to be a parasite, particularly one of the Pack Hunters or Tricksters. Still, it could be the result of an intersect point, with a little neighbor from elsewhen glimpsed now and then across a brane.

If it was a cross-brane view, however, the clarity of the apparition was interesting. I've always found that the clearer and more solid the apparition, the more the percipient is in the neighbor's world and/or vice versa. Otherwise, one would see the other as cloudy or glowing, and generally more ghost-like.

The more fully we physically cross a brane into another world family, the more danger there is of us not coming back. There are reliable reports from people who were present in a group when someone disappeared right in front of them, never to return. At this point in the case, however, the Marshburn family remained intact.

Considering the little girl, both in and out of the painting, it came to mind that ghosts attached to objects are a common theme in folklore, at tourist attractions, and sometimes, in real hauntings. I believe that's because matter is just another form of energy. As our superlife spreads out in vast waves across the multiverse, the objects, thoughts, concepts, talents, ideas, and more that we are attached to in one facet or another are always with us.

If you're a brilliant musician in one or more facets but not in the one in which you're reading this book, the musical talent is still part of your subconscious here. It's always with us, one way or another. When you see a musical instrument, or hear a song or a symphony and feel inexplicably drawn to it, it could be because you're connected with it in that subconscious life. And, if someone else possesses a treasured object of yours in a parallel world, you're with it subconsciously there, too. What's more, on the rare occasions when multiversal conditions are just right, the object can create a link between the two or more facets that possess it. Sometimes this can take the form of one or more ghost experiences.

I really think that's how these kinds of hauntings work. And this could very likely be the case with the Marshburns' painting,

I returned to Cumberland on March 18 with some of my gang. My colleague, Shane Sirois, had breezed down from New Hampshire that morning. Also on hand were hydrologist Joseph Frisella and electrical engineering professor Everett Crisman.

Bonnie and John talked with Shane and me, while Joe and Everett checked the outside of the house and the land around it. The first thing Shane and I always do is try to determine what we're dealing with, and it's the trickiest part of any investigation. We never assume that something is what it looks like because we know that parasites can act just like distressed humans or Grandpa or whomever.

As we progressed in the Marshburn case, however, we became sure that we were dealing with not one but two distressed humans, but no parasites. While Shane and I wrestled with that little issue, Joe and Everett looked at site soil composition and its possibilities for EM conductivity. As stated in previous chapters, we find that most houses with paranormal goings-on are built on moist, sandy, or clay soils with high water tables. Joe noticed right away that the Marshburn lot was most likely one of these.

Shane and I also checked the outside area and found an active EM field, something old-time researchers might refer to as an energy vortex, in the area of the vegetable garden and a large oak tree. Sure enough, family members reported seeing balls of light or orbs in that area from time to time.

Back in the living room, I still felt that little-girl presence, so out came the digital camera. The first shot clearly showed an orb just above the hutch on the upper left. Just to be sure it wasn't a glitch, I took another shot, and there was an orb again, probably the same one, this time on the right.

As I've mentioned previously, I'm not convinced one way or the other what orbs are. I've had them appear in pictures for years, and I've seen them with my own eyes. They've appeared in different colors, and I've even had them act in quite an intelligent manner, interacting—even seeming to play—with each other, and following me, then retreating as I attempted to follow them.

Just when I've convinced myself that orbs must be related to ball lightning or some other electrical phenomenon, they do something maddeningly ghostly, such as showing up with a face in them, somewhere on the floor or up by the ceiling. Even in these instances, I don't think they're some kind of spirits. In tune with multiverse theory, orbs could be something of both—electrical phenomena that tie

The author caught photos of an orb moving around the hutch where the "little girl" was suspected of hiding.

in with our own—or others'—electrical properties and then manifest accordingly. As I've said elsewhere, many of them could be plasma-based creatures that feed around branes.

With orbs, there also might be a connection with the spatial irregularities I've seen in cross-brane phenomena. In the section "Preventing a Suicide" in *Behind the Paranormal: Everything You Know is Wrong*, I talk about a case in which the neighbor I communicated with was in the same room in a parallel world. But in my world at the time, he was up by the ceiling. This odd phenomenon also turns up on a few occasions in section four of this book. So, some orbs could be the visual manifestation of intersect points.

Daughter Natalie Marshburn, apparently the most energy-perceptive member of the family, had seen orbs upstairs. But, orbs or not, what was the connection, if any, with this ghostly little girl? Considering all we've said, the painting might have been a critical ingredient in a mix that stimulated an intersect between the house as it exists in our world and the world of the little girl whose presence manifested in that living room. I'd say she lives in the house in a parallel world that to us would be the past.

As it turned out, the Marshburns consulted a psychic before they called me, and she had a very different idea.

"She told us there is a little girl here," Bonnie reported. "The girl died of a lung illness, maybe pneumonia, and her parents' grief is what's held her on Earth."

Here we were with those dead people again.

"I don't think it quite works that way," I explained. "I think she's very much alive in her world and is simply intersecting with ours. I believe she sees and feels us the same way we see and feel her, at least at times. Sure, she may have died of pneumonia in a million parallel worlds. So have we. But that's not why she's manifesting here. I feel her curiosity, not her pain."

Before the end of that day, however, we seemed to have a double-header on our hands.

THE SECRET CELLAR

"We should show you the 'secret cellar,'" Bonnie said suddenly.

The house had two cellars, and I'd seen only the smaller one on my first visit. Descending into the depths from the only entrance, an outdoor bulkhead, I felt as though I was sliding into a completely different world. It was a larger cellar, lined with rough fieldstones by some long-gone colonial hands. Here was no feeling of childish curiosity. This was the electrical tingle, the pain and depression I'd picked up during some of my worst cases of distressed people.

This was someone other than our little girl, and no one in our group liked this first meeting.

"We believe this is where the escaped slaves hid, and we think one of them died here. We think he's buried in there," John declared, pointing toward another fieldstone wall. Pointing our flashlights through a few large gaps in the stonework, we saw the "secret cellar," a completely bare, dirt floor and yet another wall of fieldstones beyond.

Shane and I took some photos, none of which contained any obvious anomalies. We finally left, knowing that the case had taken on a new depth. Back home, I thought deeply about this new development, and it bothered me that the case seemed unclear.

With all my scientific—some would say pseudoscientific—theories and pronouncements, it may come as a surprise that I very occasionally use a tool that literally dropped into my life many years ago. As a child, I spent a great deal of time with an aunt who was deeply influenced by First Nations spirituality and way of life, at a time when that was very unusual. That's a long story, but suffice it to

Peeping through the stone wall into the "secret cellar."

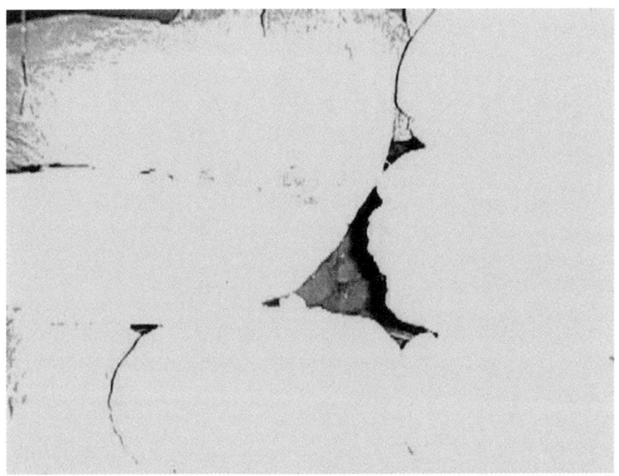

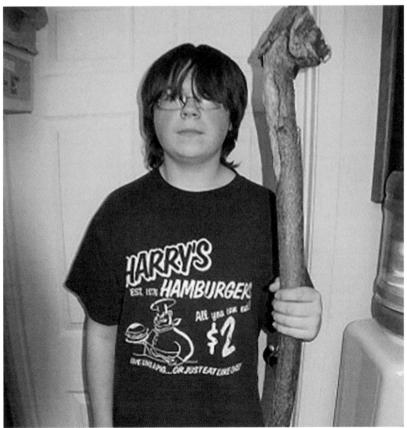

Ben Eno displays the medicine staff in 2004.

say that my own spirituality had a strong indigenous influence long before the New Agers made that trendy.

The tool I refer to is a simple "medicine staff," a long, simple, uncarved piece of wood with a flattened knob at the top. It fell at my feet one day when I was walking behind our old house in Cumberland, the very town in which the Marshburns lived. Presumably, this staff, just short of six feet long, fell from the steep slope above. But who knows? Wherever it came from, I quickly found that if I rested this staff on the ground or floor and placed my forehead against the flattened part, it focused my thoughts and insights. From time to time, I've even been able to grab images from elsewhen that have done people, including neighbors, some good.

As I've made clear, I'm extremely wary about this sort of thing, so I use this staff sparingly. Still, I don't believe I'm contacting spirits. The staff simply seems to be a very personal tool that can concentrate my own powers of connection with intersect points, to gain better insight.

About a week after the secret-cellar visit, I was doing my evening rule of prayer when the medicine staff, which I keep leaning against my home altar, suddenly slid over and hit me gently on the side of the head. That had never happened before. Subtle as a ton of bricks, I thought. I put the staff top to my forehead then and there. The impressions started coming, clear, searing, and immediate: Pain. Suffering. Distressed young man. *Kevin.*

The next day, I was on the phone with Bonnie, and she seemed spellbound as I explained what happened.

"This may seem like a strange question," she said suddenly, "but did you get a name?"

"Kevin," I replied.

"My God! That's what she said his name is!"

"She" turned out to be the family's psychic friend, the one Bonnie consulted before I turned up. Oddly enough, this woman's brother had owned the house at one time, and her sister-in-law had ghost trouble there.

Well, ghosts—at least the ones who aren't parasites—are people, too. And what do we do for people we can't help in any other way? We pray and love.

"He's alive and in trouble somewhere in the multiverse, Bonnie. I don't know if he's an escaped slave or what. That doesn't matter. Pray for him. Have the family pray for him. Think about him with compassion. Send out love for him whenever you're in the house."

As recently as the 1980s, I'd have charged into houses like the Marshburns' with clergy, crosses, and holy water. But that didn't always work. What did work, and works every time as long as the people in the house cooperate, is simply love.

Corny as it may sound, love—the most positive energy of all—can heal the wounds of all those around us, whether our family and friends, or neighbors suffering elsewhere or elsewhen in the multiverse.

Sure enough, I was touched and delighted to hear what Bonnie had to say when I made a follow-up phone call.

"We prayed for Kevin, and we asked all our friends to," she related. "And you know, not long afterward, Natalie came down one morning and told us she'd had the most wonderful dream. She said she'd been gently rocking in a hammock under the tree in the back yard—where you said the vortex was. She looked up and she knew it was Kevin rocking her. She said he had the most beautiful smile and the happiest eyes!"

After that, all seemed well at the Marshburn house. Over the following year, they were working to help the little girl, just in case she needed it, and there were no plans to move.

People who hear about the Marshburn case often ask, "Wouldn't you have to excavate the 'secret cellar,' find Kevin's body, and give it a proper burial?"

"This isn't a TV show," I usually reply. "This is reality!"

It doesn't matter where your body is buried. After all, your superlife has millions of them scattered across the multiverse. What matters is the love and the connection with our fellow creatures of good will. No matter where or when they might be. That's what feeds life and that's what gives peace.

This brings up another interesting point. If all possibilities exist in the multiverse, isn't Kevin still suffering in one or more worlds, no matter what we did to ease his pain? Yes, but here's the idea: If his suffering was so clear to us at that intersect point in the Marshburns' cellar, I believe that means he was suffering in many worlds, making it a dominant factor in his overall superlife. The more loving attention and compassion he receives from us, his neighbors, the more worlds in which his pain is mitigated. The fewer worlds in which Kevin suffers, the less that suffering dominates his superlife, the happier and more harmonious his life becomes overall, and ours, too.

I really believe it's as simple as that. This gives a new depth to the entire concept of "love thy neighbor." So, all the best, Kevin!

SECTION THREE

PARALLEL WORLDS AND THE PARANORMAL ON STEROIDS

CHAPTER ONE

FLAP AREAS

As far back as those mind-wrenching exorcisms at St. Lawrence State Hospital, 1973–1975, I saw evidence that paranormal phenomena never take place in isolation. Barbara, subject of the wildest exorcism I ever witnessed (see section one, chapter one), reported UFO sightings and alien encounters since the age of four. In fact, five of the seven people Fr. Lawrence exorcised at St. Lawrence State Hospital reported such sightings and encounters in the years leading up to their "possessions." These included the classic gray alien figures in their bedrooms at night, along with possible abduction experiences.

Fr. Lawrence said to pay no attention to these stories. In so many words, he told me that either demons or psychiatric illness were responsible for everything weird these people experienced, and because they were psychiatric patients, they were officially bonkers anyway. The priest did make a valid point: There were multiple witnesses to the external phenomena that led him to believe the patients were possessed in the first place, especially poltergeist activity. With the alleged UFO experiences, there were no witnesses. And the aliens weren't talking.

When my friend William J. Hall first contacted me in 2013 to interview me for his excellent book on the Bridgeport poltergeist case of 1974 (*The World's Most Haunted House*, New Page Books, 2014), I suggested that he do what Ed and Lorraine Warren and I should have done in the first place: Talk with surviving people who'd been neighbors of the afflicted Goodin family, check local UFO reports for late 1974, and hunt down other evidence that the area was a paranormal hotspot, a "flap area," as Ben and I came to call it, of which the poltergeist outbreak might have been the proverbial tip of an iceberg.

Sure enough, Bill found plenty: "spillover" phenomena in nearby houses and a spike in sightings of strange lights in the sky. I added some research that indicated geotechnical factors that could have contributed, such as significant natural electromagnetic (EM) fields, sandy soils, and a high water table.

In 2005, when Ben joined my adventures, we decided to specialize in these paranormal flap areas, where the multiverse appears to go haywire. These turned out to be regions as large as 300 square miles or more, where branes are very fluid. These conditions seemed to allow for multiple intersects, overlaps, and overwashes among many parallel worlds at once. Because the laws of physics can vary wildly from world to world, as can the inhabitants, everyday objects might float through the air or crash against a wall. People see bizarre creatures, extinct animals, and people they thought were dead. UFOs and their apparent occupants come and go. Beings and phenomena that don't even have names are manifold.

The hyperactive cores of these flap areas often do seem to form triangles, which can be as small as five square miles.

THE MOTHMAN

Probably the quintessential flap area is in the Ohio Valley of the United States, concentrated around the Ohio River between Wheeling, West Virginia, and the Kentucky border. In 1966 and 1967, this was the domain of the Mothman or, perhaps, more than one. Some say it still is. Hundreds of people reported seeing a terrifying, muscular, man-like being with huge, bat-like wings, either flying or on the ground, usually at night. It or they flew in pursuit of cars at up to 100 miles per hour, looked in people's living-room windows, and had blazing red eyes. Eyewitnesses included police officers, healthcare professionals, and lawyers—and at a time when people dreaded publicity and ridicule over such reports.

The Mothman statue in Point Pleasant is generally considered one of the most accurate likenesses of the being as described by eyewitnesses. *Photo courtesy Jeff Wamsley/Mothman Museum*

There was much more to the scenario than just the main character, dubbed "Mothman" by the media. New York journalist John Keel, who covered the case during numerous visits to Point Pleasant, West Virginia, discovered many other paranormal events taking place in the area simultaneously. These included numerous UFO sightings by many people, reports of alien contacts and poltergeist activity, and visits to witnesses' homes by what we today call "men in black" (MIBs), who warned people not to discuss what they saw.

Thus, Keel became one of the first investigators to suspect that there might be more to the paranormal than the old ideas about dead people, critters that are just really hard to find, and little green men from other planets. He was among the first to realize that, whatever the explanation, these seemingly unrelated phenomena might be related after all. Keel coined the term "window areas" for places like the Ohio Valley.

When I first visited the area in 2003, to speak at the West Virginia Paranormal Conference in Parkersburg, I made it a point to track down surviving witnesses, most of whom were children in the mid-1960s. Not only did I hear about Mothman, UFOs, and MIBs, but there were memories of footsteps on rooftops in the middle of the night, blazing red eyes looking in windows and out from under furniture, poltergeist activity in many different homes, and even an increase in psychic abilities and general knowledge for a number of people.

Mothman was described almost universally as having inspired abject terror in those who saw him, her, or it. Almost. Two witnesses I spoke with had benign Mothman encounters, and one man, a boy at the time, suddenly became a math whiz and a talented artist. He credits Mothman with changing his life for the better.

THE LITCHFIELD TRIANGLE

I wanted to tackle other suspected flap areas, interview witnesses, gather data, and look for commonalities and patterns. But on my own I just couldn't handle cases with such scope. That began to change when Ben joined me, and our first opportunity came in 2005, when a homeowner from Torrington, Connecticut, found our website, Newenglandghosts.com. In her opinion, our multiverse theories were the only explanation for the goofy phenomena taking place in her family's 1793 farmhouse for the previous sixty-two years, and probably long before that.

"My husband, Bob, and I are fourth-generation owners," Donna wrote. "Growing up here, it always felt confusing. I didn't know why, but there seemed to be a constant undercurrent of activity that I didn't understand. It happened so constantly and regularly that it was common to me. Whenever I spent the night at a friend's house, it felt clear."

Donna was surprised many years later when her daughter, Michelle, told her that she "liked to stay at Charlene's house because it was 'clear.'"

"My parents never explained the phenomena to my sister and me because they thought it would scare us, so we just accepted it."

Donna had kept a diary about the phenomena since she was seventeen. When she contacted us, she was fifty-five.

"I recorded every experience I had, along with any and all information pertaining to it. . . . What amazed me when I found your website is that a lot of the musings and thoughts I recorded were related to your theories. I now believe that there is a sort of veil that is between parallel times. In other words, we live in the same space and see each other once in a while . . ."

Among the decades of phenomena witnessed by Donna and her family were many people, including people she knew were ancestors, going about their daily business in the house. There were horses galloping down hallways, strange lights and "orbs" throughout the house, and what could be described as gray aliens seen in bedrooms. On one occasion, the whole family saw human legs dangling from the living-room ceiling and walking as though on a surface that didn't exist in our world.

Donna has many hours of video and audio recordings that contain much evidence for this, in addition to gigglings, groanings, mumblings, and general conversation, all by person or persons unknown. Most interestingly to us, there are nonhuman creatures seen as well, including odd little grayish figures, very tall and thin beings who were cloaked, what could be called "shadow people," and, outdoors, boxy creatures with gangly legs that almost defy description as they bounce by the windows.

Along with the "Haunted Policeman of Vermont," this became the first of two cases that Ben and I worked on together. As we looked beyond Donna and Bob's lovely home and acreage, we found more witnesses and more phenomena than we ever expected. And we still are, as of this writing, thirteen years later. From that old farmhouse, the "Litchfield Triangle" has expanded to nearly 300 square miles and now includes part of the Hudson River Valley in New York State.

The region is a textbook flap area.

For periods of time, particularly in 2009 and 2010, there were nightly UFOs, sometimes witnessed by hundreds of people. We saw several of them ourselves. Things come and go through holes in the sky and air. There is apportation of objects and animals (immediate movement from one place to another, apparently without traversing the space between), sightings of Bigfoot and ultra-bizarre cryptids (some

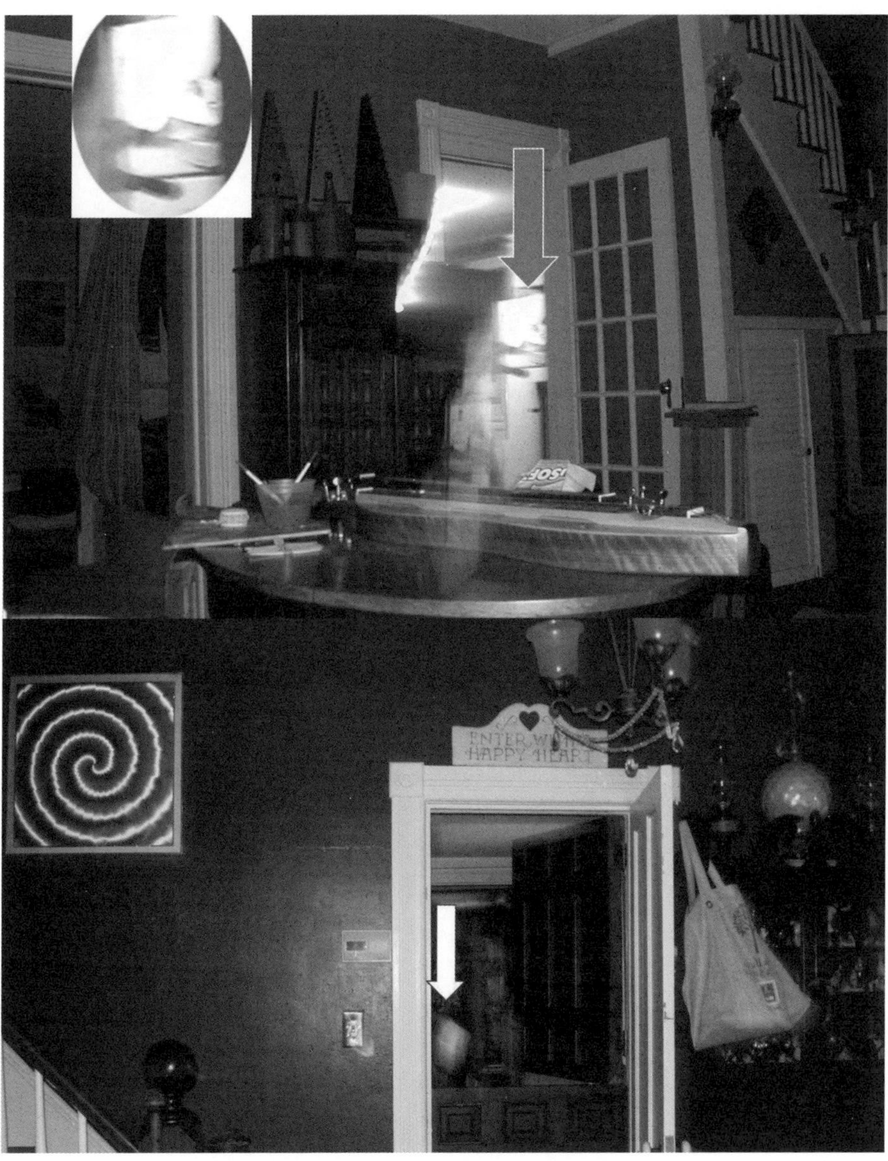

In the Connecticut house that Paul and Ben Eno consider Point One of the Litchfield Triangle, weird doings have been noted for over sixty years. In the upper photo, a luminous brane seems to separate two versions of the same room. In the background, what some consider the face of a gray alien seems to peek in at right. In the bottom photo, a small figure, one of many often seen in the house, seems to look in from the dining room. The author believes that these beings are quite physical, though residents of parallel worlds. The electromagnetic brane between makes them look ghostly to us, and vice versa.

Captured on a home security camera in the Litchfield Triangle area in 2015 was this unidentified being standing in front of the kitchen sink. Nobody was home, but houses in the area were suffering a rash of break-ins, with nothing being stolen.

of which have been photographed), alien encounters, parasite/poltergeist activity, slips in space and time, ghost encounters, and reports of heightened psychic abilities. People tell us they have encountered different versions of themselves or others, sometimes in their own homes.

It's interesting that flap areas often correspond with the sacred lands of indigenous peoples. Were they considered sacred because of the odd happenings there, particularly encounters with beings the people considered supernatural?

ENTER THE MILITARY

One extremely interesting characteristic of flap areas, which we first noticed in the Litchfield case, is the presence of the military, or something that looks like the military. Reports of troop movements and military aircraft in the Torrington, Litchfield, and Goshen areas of Connecticut first started to reach us in 2009. Encounters were sometimes immediate and personal. For example, people would be taking strolls in areas where they had walked for years, only to be turned back politely but firmly by armed troops. In one case, a man was at his favorite fishing spot when a military vehicle pulled up, and soldiers informed him that he couldn't fish there anymore.

The military activity seemed to center on an isolated, abandoned farm in Goshen. There was extensive excavation, along with complete reconstruction of some of the farm buildings, and there was evidence of sensor and ventilator installation. Adjacent property is owned by the US Army and the State of Connecticut. There is little evidence of actual farming. The military presence died down in 2010, but the property is still isolated and hard to access. We have come to call it the "Funny Farm."

About the time the military activity began, there seemed to be mass changes in public behavior. This included a period in 2009 when people suddenly got it into their heads to start driving on the wrong side of the road, in numbers way beyond the statistical probability for the area's population. Of course, this resulted in a number of accidents. When this was noticed in the local press and social media, the behavior changed. People started driving off the road. When this was noticed, that behavior ceased, and a rash of suicides began.

Maybe it's all coincidence. Then again, I don't believe in coincidence.

ACHUAR

One of the oddest incidents in the Litchfield Triangle took place in November 2010 while Ben and I were working with a film crew from New York, making a pilot for a potential TV series on flap areas. Day was done, and the crew had returned to New York City. In Donna's house, however, her four-year-old grandson reported that his invisible friend, pronounced like "Ashwar," was in the tree out front. She and her people lived in trees, the boy declared.

So out the front door Ben and I went. It was pitch dark and freezing cold as I pointed my little infrared camera up into the tree. The resulting video may be seen on the "Behind the Paranormal with Paul & Ben Eno" Facebook page. That bizarre, tadpole-like white thing descending the tree about six seconds into the video: Could that be "Ashwar"?

Five years later, in 2015, our good friend and colleague, Shane Sirois, discovered an obscure reference to the Achuar, South American tree people of the deep Amazon. They are little known, have had almost no contact with the outside world, still live their ancient lifestyle and, as of this writing, there are only about 6,000 left. How could a little boy from Connecticut know about the Achuar, let alone be friends with one of them?

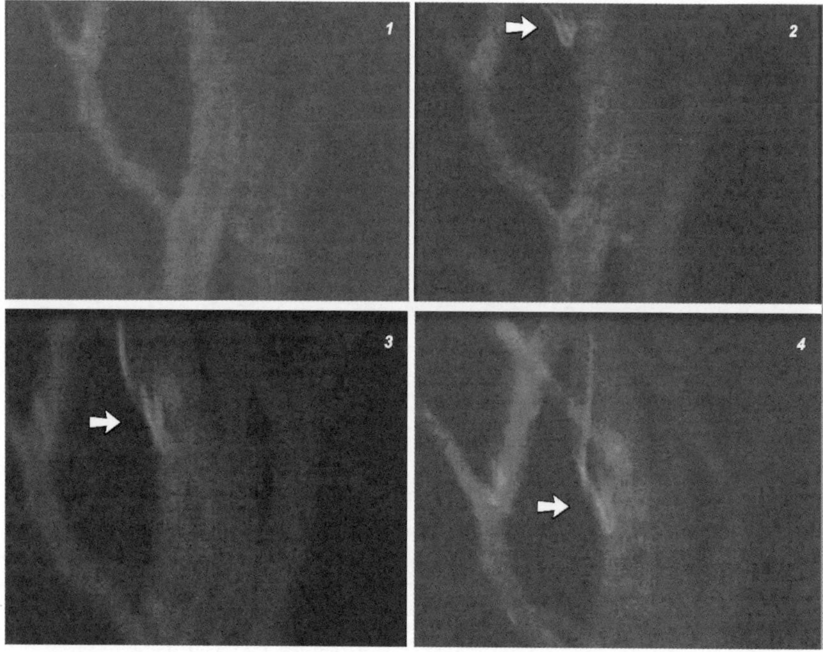

In November 2010, the author captured this video of "something" descending from a tree in the Litchfield Triangle. The four-year-old boy in the adjacent house told Paul and Ben Eno that his invisible friend "Ashwar" was in the tree.

If our multiverse theories are correct, such a relationship is entirely possible. The boy could have been in touch with a facet of himself that *is* one of the Achuar. But why *that* connection? The process may be simple, but the explanations are not, even—or perhaps especially—in flap areas.

To this day, air activity in the Litchfield Triangle continues, mostly involving C-130 cargo aircraft and unmarked black helicopters. Inexplicably, despite determined efforts, we can find neither where these aircraft originate—nor where they go. The information is classified.

BUILDING A SPY NETWORK

When our radio show, *Behind the Paranormal with Paul & Ben Eno*, went on the air in 2008, and especially when CBS Radio put us on the air in Boston, Pittsburgh, Detroit, and Seattle the following year, investigating flap areas became easier. That's because we recruited show reporters in areas we were interested in, got to know them, then worked it from there until we had a network of spies, preferably who didn't know each other. Today, this is how we watch the Funny Farm and other spots we feel are important.

OTHER FLAP AREAS

Ben and I, along with several handpicked colleagues, including Shane, astronomer Marc Dantonio of MUFON, globe-trotting filmmaker and Bigfoot researcher Aleksandar Petakov, producer and behavioral scientist Lori Greer, and UFO researcher and broadcaster Charles Creteau, continue to find, research, and document flap areas. Among these are:

The Pennsylvania Triangle: This region, in the west-central part of the Keystone State, centers near the city of DuBois. The core of the triangle has a bizarre history that includes an apparent meteor strike, about the year 1500, that killed over 160 First Nations people. The region was populated by the Shawnee and Ohio Valley tribes, who apparently considered the lands sacred.

The area is geologically interesting as well, with the Eastern Continental Divide running right down the middle of the flap area's core. Waters to the east flow to Chesapeake Bay, and waters to the west are bound for the Mississippi River.

As of this writing, we are only two years into our work in the Pennsylvania Triangle, but the hallmark seems to be Bigfoot encounters and UFOs. Shane and I have seen both there, and with our own eyes. We already have many odd photographs. We have had three neighborhood meetings, attended by as many as thirty-five local residents, virtually all of whom have seen Bigfoot, UFOs, and other anomalies.

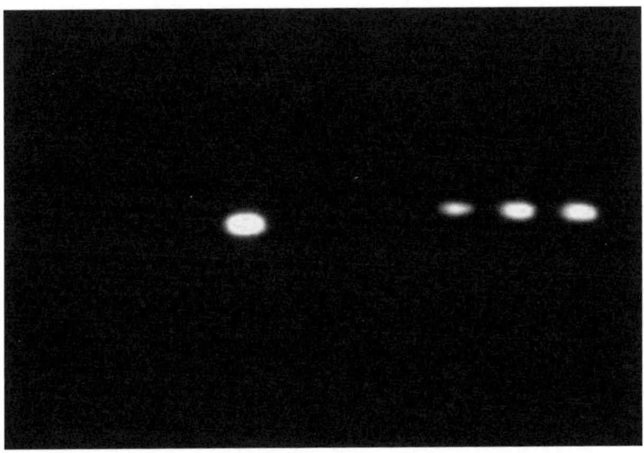

Photographed by the author in July 2017, this string of strange lights was near the ground at the heart of the Pennsylvania Triangle.

By 2018, we were convinced that we had a flap area for the ages. We started formal data gathering on paper, along with on-camera interviews with witnesses, including three generations of one area family. Interviews were conducted by Aleksandar, producer of documentaries on the Lake Champlain Monster in Vermont, along with Bigfoot; and Charles Creteau, creator of *The Galileo Interviews* on YouTube.

Our work in Pennsylvania continues.

Rendlesham Forest: Renowned for the RFI, the Rendlesham Forest Incident of December 1980, this location in England witnessed multiple UFO sightings and, reportedly, landings over several days that month. Being in the Cold War period of tension between the Soviet Union and the Western powers, the RFI drew the attention of British and American security services. This was especially true because Rendlesham Forest sat between two NATO air bases: RAF Bentwaters and RAF Woodbridge. Bentwaters was staffed mostly by Americans. In fact, up to fifty American personnel, including high-ranking officers such as Lt. Col. Charles Halt of the US Air Force, were among the eyewitnesses.

Invited by some local radio listeners, Ben and I headed for the UK, in September 2012, to visit Rendlesham Forest and to hold a town hall meeting in the nearby village of Woodbridge, Suffolk. Even a casual look at the history of the area told us that Rendlesham Forest was almost certainly the heart of a flap area, with weird happenings reported as far back as Saxon times.

Our first visit to the forest was at night, accompanied by several radio listeners, including local researcher Brenda Butler and Larry Warren, a former US Air Force security man present during the RFI.

In our paranormal adventures, Ben operates on a much more experiential level than I do. Strange, almost shamanic, things happen to him. At Rendlesham that night, we didn't get more than twenty feet from the cars when Ben collapsed in a heap. Dogs up and down the road began to howl.

"He does that. Don't touch him. He'll be back in a few minutes," I said when our alarmed companions wanted to haul my son to his feet.

Ben never remembers going into these trances or seizures, but he sometimes remembers multiversal communications with neighbors that take place. At Rendlesham, he spoke with a group of monks who suggested he go with them. Fortunately, he stayed with us. We headed for the former East Gate of RAF Bentwaters, feeling that we were being followed all the way. The photos taken that evening weren't normal either.

In a classic photo taken inside the Pennsylvania Triangle region, the black dog's posterior is transparent. The author interprets this as a quick parallel-world washover. In one world, the dog was present. In the other, he wasn't. And the camera was snapping away in both.

The following evening, we spoke in Woodbridge to a standing-room-only crowd, and it was a long night. After our presentation, and our suggestion that the entire region is a flap area, one local resident after another stood up and talked about what's still happening in Rendlesham Forest: strange lights and UFOs, Yeti (what the British call Bigfoot), sightings of bizarre cryptids and little people, ghosts, odd sounds, out-of-place big cats, spooky black dogs with red eyes, and more. Three people reported feeling that someone or something in the forest was downloading information to their minds when they visited.

So, if these reports are accurate, it's likely that the RFI was only a small slice of what actually goes on in that part of Suffolk. It just happened to be a world-class episode witnessed by the military. Even a casual study of the area reveals events such as these, well known in paranormal literature, within forty miles of Rendlesham Forest.

- The "Green Children of Woolpit," twelfth century—twenty miles;
- The Aldeburgh "Sky Battle" of 1642—thirteen miles;
- The Aldeburgh flying disk with "sailors" looking down, 1916—thirteen miles;
- The disappearing cyclist, Great Yarmouth, 1988—forty miles;
- Numerous big cat sightings, Sudbury area, 1996—twenty-five miles;
- Many "black dog" sightings, ongoing and county-wide.

The Bridgewater Triangle: Located in eastern Massachusetts, less than twenty miles from where I live, this is one of the most active and most studied flap areas in the world. Much has been written about it elsewhere.

It's worth pointing out that this region provides more reports than usual of little people. One creature from Wampanoag folklore is the pukwudgie (probably derived from the Algonquian word *pukwudjij*). They are little humanoids, two to three feet tall, commonly with large noses, ears, and hands. Their skin is usually described as gray, and it sometimes glows.

By 2016, Ben and I had already collected hundreds of reports of odd events in the Bridgewater Triangle and talked with many eyewitnesses to odd events there, two of whom were police officers. Incidents involved Bigfoot, UFOs, giant birds, out-of-place panthers and other big cats, ghost phenomena, time slips . . . and, of course, pukwudgies.

Research in the Bridgewater Triangle is ongoing.

Still other flap areas: As of this writing, we are in various stages of investigating, or helping others investigate, the Leominster, Massachusetts, "Monsterland" area; the East Texas "Big Thicket" region; the Ohio River Valley; the Jefferson County "Square of Weirdness" in Wisconsin; and the Panther Rock area of Kentucky.

THE BOUGUER ANOMALY

While the same or similar phenomena seem present in all flap areas, regions can vary when it comes to which phenomena predominate. For example, Bigfoot is the headliner in the Pennsylvania Triangle. At Rendlesham Forest, weird lights and UFOs are the main fare. In the East Texas flap area, upright canine cryptids have the starring role.

All this probably has to do with the unique physical layout of each flap area. Where the towns, roads, hiking or biking trails, and recreational areas are, that's where the people will be, and that's where the most reports of weird happenings will come from. Still, we look for patterns and commonalities in each flap area. As I've pointed out in previous chapters, we nearly always find high water tables, along with sandy or clay soils, quartz veins, and sometimes, a high presence of lime. This could all be coincidence, but every factor named here has some electrical conductivity and could contribute to brane fluidity and the presence of intersect points, overlaps, or overwashes.

One factor that really spikes our interest, and that's present to some degree in every flap area Ben and I have encountered, is the Bouguer Anomaly. Named for the eighteenth-century French hydrographer Pierre Bouguer (pronounced *boo-zhay*), this is an odd but scientifically recognized gravity phenomenon that is believed to result, at least partially, from the presence of certain geologic factors, such as light-density sedimentary rocks. Other than that, not much is known about the Bouguer anomaly. But it can help geologists find, among other things, oil and gas deposits.

Simply put, when the Bouguer anomaly is present, gravity lessens slightly as you walk downhill, closer to the center of the Earth. What would this have to do with paranormal activity? That could be met with a second question: In addition to the idea that all time is simultaneous and a function of our consciousness, what else did Albert Einstein say in 1952, in his General Theory of Relativity? He pointed out that gravity can bend space and time. Sure, it's a reach. But the Bouguer anomaly is present, sometimes with unusual intensity, in every flap area we have encountered. In the Litchfield Triangle, the strongest Bouguer anomaly in Connecticut is present right at the heart of the flap: Torrington, Litchfield, and Goshen.

We continue to seek information on possible connections between flap areas and the Bouguer anomaly.

WHY ARE THEY ARMED?

Another common factor in our flap-area research: We inevitably run into the military, or something like it. In many areas there really do seem to be underground bases, something that isn't uncommon at all in the military world. But the question is why. What is the military or paramilitary doing in flap areas, and what do they want there?

To us, the most obvious answer is: Wouldn't we just love to weaponize the paranormal? If we could find out not just what UFOs are, but how they move as they do, and if we could know where Bigfoot comes from and goes to, we would have tremendous tactical advantages. If we could learn to control branes and intersect points, we could appear to manipulate space and time in the face of an enemy.

This isn't speculation on my part. Judging from certain military projects in the past, many nations have been trying to militarize the paranormal for at least the last sixty years. The Stargate Project, for example, supposedly ran from 1978 to 1995 and was in response to a similar Soviet project that employed psychics to try to spy on enemies with remote viewing, detonate ordinance remotely, and other applications. I say "supposedly" because many clandestine military projects continue under new names in different locations.

Ben and I are convinced that the secrecy attributed to whatever the government knows about UFOs actually applies to the entire paranormal realm. There's every indication that they know all about the multiverse, and that it is the true secret they're trying to keep.

After all, everyone in the developed world today grew up with Chewbacca, Mr. Spock, and the *Planet of the Apes*. I think most people would be delighted if we discovered the verifiable presence of intelligent, extraterrestrial life, even if it's been visiting us. But here's the caveat: We'd be comfortable as long as this life is based on some faraway planet. If the multiverse is true, and these aliens, along with just about every other creature and scenario you can imagine, are not far away, but right next to us all the time in parallel worlds that can intersect with ours . . . Well, there's the terrifying scenario the government would try to protect us, and mostly itself, from.

There might be yet another layer to the secrecy issue. Let's not forget that, in our society, it's all about the bucks. Think of the cash to be raked in by private industry if multiversal principles can be harnessed for technological purposes. We already believe we might have found evidence of a commercial research presence in the Litchfield Triangle.

Whatever the case might be, and it could be all of the above, somebody doesn't want us to know.

CHAPTER TWO
THE FLASHING NEXUS

Back in August 1972, I was a nineteen-year-old seminary student and thoroughly befuddled. Nothing in my embryonic paranormal research made sense. The denizens of the Village of Voices, whom I'd suspected of languishing in purgatory, showed no sign of being dead at all. And other strange events I was looking into at the behest of friends or relatives seemed, to me at least, to defy the commonly accepted, spiritualistic rules once I looked beyond them to questions no one else seemed to be asking.

Why were ghosts so often seen and heard in very physical circumstances, as at the Village of Voices? How could they have voices at all: No physical body means no vocal chords, right? Why were some seen wearing clothes or even driving cars? How could what were supposed to be disembodied spirits touch people, scratch them, or throw them across rooms?

At this point in my studies for the priesthood, I was learning basic junior college material, English, Latin, French, Spanish, and the rest, with some very basic theology and philosophy included as the root of a classical education. There was nothing as yet about eschatology: the area of theology that deals with "final things," either for the world or for us as individuals.

Then I ran up against something I not only never expected but had never even heard of. I would come to call it the "flashing nexus."

STAN THE MAN

The call came on August 22, a Tuesday, from David, an old friend in Manchester, Connecticut, whose father had just undergone open-heart surgery, a very risky and complex procedure even today.

"Paul, my dad came through the operation okay, but there are some strange things happening," David said. "He won't tell me just what. He wants to talk to you."

A devout Roman Catholic, David's dad, whose name was Stan, considered me, as a seminary student and his son's good friend, the next best thing to a priest, despite my alarming youth. As soon as Stan was discharged, I went to see him at home. He sat on the couch in the living room, looking healthy but tired—and frightened.

He shooed his wife and son from the room.

"Paul, I need your advice. I've never even heard of what's happening!"

I managed to calm him a little.

"What do you mean? How can I help?" I asked, and the story came pouring out.

At several points during and after the operation, Stan had experienced some very odd and frightening shifts of consciousness. And I do mean shifts of consciousness.

"Before they even put me under, it started. The best way I can put it was that all of a sudden I was one of the pre-op nurses. It only lasted three or four seconds, but that's enough time to take things in," Stan said with fear in his eyes.

"Stan, you need to calm down," I advised.

"But you don't understand!" he replied. "I actually *was* the nurse. For those few seconds I had her thoughts, her knowledge, and even her physical sensations!"

I'd never heard of anything like this either. "Are you saying you left your own body and went into hers?"

"I don't know!" Stan replied. "I didn't feel like I left myself at all. I just stopped being myself and started being somebody else!"

Then he launched into the typical experiencer questions about whether he was crazy. Could the medications have damaged his brain or made him delusional, even temporarily? Could the strain of the situation have made him hallucinate?

"Stan, I'm not competent to answer all that, but . . ." I stated calmly.

"But there's a lot more," Stan interrupted. "I was told that I wouldn't remember anything when I was under. That I wouldn't know anything until I woke up. But that didn't happen!"

Between periods of unconsciousness during the operation, Stan experienced the same kind of consciousness shift. He was the chief surgeon for a few seconds.

"Good thing I didn't screw up!" was the closest Stan could come to humor over the experiences.

At another point, Stan said he was a male passerby in the hallway.

"Maybe the weirdest thing was that when I started to wake up in the recovery room, I wasn't me. I was driving a car on the street outside! That lasted for maybe six seconds—I don't know. But it felt like hours!"

I questioned Stan for as long as I felt was prudent, given his need to recuperate. I tried to get him to relax, and promised to research the question. I returned a week later.

"Stan, the closest I could come to any medical information about this is a thing called anesthesia awareness or unintended intra-operative awareness, but that doesn't seem to be what happened to you at all, especially because your experience began before you were anesthetized," I said. "The only other thing is an out-of-the-body experience or OBE."

Stan was clear that at no point did he feel that he left his body. No floating up by the ceiling looking down at himself. No classic OBE profile. Stan experienced what might be called an illusory identity construct or perhaps a version of dissociative identity disorder (multiple personalities).

All I could advise was that he let me know if it ever happened again. Ordinarily I would have recommended a psychiatric evaluation or at least a visit to a real priest. But something inside me said clearly: "Don't do it!" Stan and I watched his case together for the next few weeks before I returned to the seminary for the academic year. But there wasn't much to watch. The consciousness shifts never occurred again.

Over the next decade, I would discover the multiple worlds interpretation of quantum mechanics (MWI) as, at least from what I was seeing, the best explanation for paranormal phenomena. I also had the bizarre experiences related in the next section, involving what I came to call the Leinster Effect. But it wasn't until 1979 that I once again ran into bizarre consciousness shifts such as Stan described. By that time, I was well out of the seminary, and I thought I might have the beginning of an explanation for this ultra-weird phenomenon.

MEDITATION SITUATION

My next encounter with it came from a woman I didn't know, a friend of a friend in Canada. Peggy lived in Ottawa, Ontario, where I was visiting.

"It's happened twice now when I've been meditating," Peggy explained to me one bitter, cold day in the Canadian capital. "I quiet my mind and body, and it's like I just slip away."

Like Stan, Peggy never felt as though she was leaving her body. "I've had OBEs, and this isn't that," she made clear. And the experiences lasted longer, up to fifteen seconds.

Unlike Stan, Peggy wasn't in any kind of physical distress, and she knew she wasn't bonkers. In addition, her consciousness shifts were to people and places she didn't recognize. In one, she was convinced that she wasn't human at all.

"That was the only time I was really shocked," Peggy explained. "Not scared, just shocked. I felt my body and it wasn't human. I don't know what it was. And what I could see was—different. It was like another planet. The sky was green and the vegetation—I think it was vegetation—was purple."

Like Stan, Peggy was convinced that these experiences were genuine shifts in consciousness, not dreams. I stayed in touch with her for several years, and the consciousness shifts kept happening during meditation, though not often. Finally, I shared a theory with her and a name that occurred to me: the "flashing nexus." The concept reaches to the depths of what I now believe we really are as life forms in that elegant, interactive system we call the multiverse.

As I've made clear in previous chapters, my cases at the end of the 1970s really convinced me that we aren't dealing with a spirit world, a material world, and the two-dimensional reality that implies. Instead, as we've touched on throughout this book, I believe we live many parallel lives simultaneously across the multiverse. In some of these lives, we're just slightly different versions of what we are here. In others, we're very different, even alien.

At the risk of oversimplifying, I'm convinced that all those parallel lives make up a superlife. In any one of our other simultaneous lives, our life here is just one of those subconscious lives. And *vice versa*. All the lives—lives where we are wise and lives where we are self-satisfied idiots—form the totality of us. Maybe the totality of all of us in a multiverse where, ultimately, we are all literally each other.

Our superlife has its source at some sort of nexus, a core of superconsciousness that the whole biosphere shares. Perhaps this is akin to Carl Jung's concept of the collective unconscious, but much more. And the lives centered therein seem to be completely interactive. They form a pool of every possibility. They're where we get our talents and our failures, our imagination and ideas, our vision and creativity, even our good and bad habits and attitudes.

If there's a "short circuit," perhaps brought on by physical trauma or just by an awareness so heightened that we aren't ready for it, the nexus can "flash": Our conscious awareness jumps from life to life.

That's how I see it, anyway.

When I shared this idea with Peggy, she shouted two words: "That's it!"

One manifestation of the flashing nexus might be right under our noses: Countless people report being welcomed to their next world by loved ones who have "gone on before."

MORE THAN MOVIES IN THE THEATER ROOM

Probably the weirdest, and most fascinating, example of the flashing nexus came to my attention in October 1999, when I received a frantic e-mail from Meg, a young real estate professional from Hightstown, New Jersey.

"I think I'm going crazy! I need to talk to you!"

I didn't know Meg from Adam, but I offered my support. I happened to be attending a conference in Ocean City, Maryland, that month, and I made arrangements to meet Meg on my way back north to Rhode Island. I found her and Ted, her fiancé, in their snazzy new condominium.

"We just moved in here last month, and the last thing I expected in a brand-new home was anything weird," Meg began. "Every room is fine except our theater room. Whenever I sit in there, it's like I'm going crazy."

Asked to define "crazy," Meg described flashing-nexus experiences such as I'd never heard before.

"First, I feel all tingly, then it's like a black-out for a minute, and I become something else, somewhere else, and sometimes it's even like I'm in another world. What *is* that?"

Instead of just being other people, Meg sometimes had the consciousness of animals, and beings she didn't know how to describe. And this happened for longer periods than I'd ever recorded before.

Meg would share consciousness with several friends, neighbors, and people she didn't know, sometimes in places she didn't recognize. Rather than taking place for a few seconds, Meg said these shifts of space, time, and consciousness sometimes occurred for up to three minutes. As if that weren't enough, Meg had been a horse, some kind of creature flying through the air over a beautiful but utterly bizarre landscape of giant flowers, red mountain peaks, and a purple sky. She'd even been a neighbor's cat.

On one occasion, Meg said she was in the consciousness of an unnaturally tall, thin figure that I immediately recognized as a member of a benign neighbor race Ben would eventually come to call the "clerics" because of their mode of dress.

This began to happen the very first time Meg and Ted used the theater room. Ted felt nothing odd at all but was alarmed when Meg seemed to pass out almost as soon as she sat down. He lifted her out of the chair, intending to place her on the living-room couch, then call 911. But as soon as he took her out of the theater room, Meg woke up.

"I was a woman walking by outside! I had no idea who it was," she told me. "I didn't know what to do with this."

"I was pretty scared," Ted added.

Meg assured me that these experiences never happened to her before this, and never outside the theater room. What's more, they only happened when she sat down.

When I checked the theater room, I definitely felt an electromagnetic field. Sure enough, this was strongest when I sat down in the chair in question. I felt dizzy and light-headed, and convinced that this room was right at a number of multiversal intersect points. I didn't turn into a cat, but I certainly saw what Meg was talking about. She was just more sensitive than me. I asked what to me was an obvious question.

"Meg, if you've had all these consciousness shifts, you must have kept going back into that room. If you were frightened, why did you go there?"

"I was scared but I was fascinated, too. I wanted to see who I'd be and where I'd go!" Meg replied. "I've never done drugs. With this, why would I need to?"

Ted was fascinated, too. "I wanted to be sure Meg was okay, so I stayed in there with her each time. She promised never to go in there when I wasn't here."

Meg and Ted kept count. There had been eighteen different experiences since they moved in.

"Over the past week, the identity changes became weirder and weirder. That's when I got really scared and called you, after I was the cat and then that creepy flying creature," Meg said.

I spent nearly an hour explaining the multiverse, our expansive consciousness within it, and the flashing nexus. To my surprise, Meg and Ted seemed to grasp the concepts well, and they were relieved at the explanations.

"That's so weird, but it makes so much sense!" Ted declared.

What to do? Other than for the bizarre experiences in the theater room, where they had yet to actually watch a movie, the couple loved their new condo. Moving was a last resort, they told me. In several cases, I've found that simply moving a bed or chair can do just what I hoped it would do for Meg and Ted: Break the multiversal connection, or at least help them stay out of its way. So, on a hunch, I suggested they turn the tiny theater room into a walk-in closet and just put their entertainment center in the living room, like most other people. A few days later, Meg called.

"We did it, and so far, so good! We got rid of the chair, so I can sit down and watch a movie and stay 'me,' or at least this me. And I can walk into our new closet with nothing weird happening. We broke the connection!"

Because intersect points can and do move, Meg and Ted kept in touch with me for several years. But their problem never recurred.

I've encountered the flashing nexus only a few times in my nearly fifty years of paranormal work. Oddly, I've never heard of it from drug users or shamans, though that doesn't mean they don't experience it. The message, to me at least, is that we are a lot bigger than we think we are, and our entire concept of ourselves as individuals, as islands totally contained within our own bodies, is now in smithereens. Maybe it's the second day of school.

SECTION FOUR

PARALLEL WORLDS AND GOD

CHAPTER ONE

WHO OR WHAT IS GOD?

There's an eye-catching sculpture at the entrance to the Crystal Palace, an indoor amusement park in Dieppe, New Brunswick, Canada: *The Homunculus*. It shows what we would look like if our body parts actually appeared the way our brains perceive them. The head and hands are huge; the mouth, eyes, and nose enormous. The whole thing looks like some self-centered troglodyte from a Gary Larson *Far Side* cartoon.

Grown-ups raise their eyebrows when they see it. Children laugh. But if you think about it, the artist is right: It's very much the way we can appear to ourselves on the most visceral level. It shows how distorted our whole self-image can be. While the Bible's Book of Genesis says that God made us in his image, whatever that means, I think that most people make God in *their* own image—the image glorified by that statue. Most people think of He, She, It, or Them much as the ancient Greeks thought of Zeus: a giant, human-like figure with a long beard and a hot temper, a giant version of ourselves.

Regardless of what our religions teach, we tend to see God not only in our own ways, but in terms of our individual needs, wants, prejudices, backgrounds, and points of view. And this reflects the same narrow, human-centered way we see the paranormal.

THE FLAVORS OF BELIEF

According to a 2004 survey conducted for the British Broadcasting Corporation, belief in some form of Supreme Being is very high throughout the world, especially in Nigeria (100 percent) and the United States (91 percent).

There are exceptions, of course. An estimated 50 percent of Swedes are atheists (professed non-believers in God), and the Deity gets no public attention in officially atheistic societies like those in China, Vietnam, and North Korea. But since atheists can't prove there is no God any more than believers can prove that there is, atheism is a matter of faith just as much as belief is, so I consider it a religion, too. There also are millions of agnostics throughout the world: People who aren't sure whether there's a God or not.

The Homunculus at the Crystal Palace, Moncton, New Brunswick, Canada.
Photo courtesy The Crystal Palace/Palais Crystal.

What God do believers believe in? And how, if at all, can this belief—and God—relate to the multiverse? I've conducted my own informal survey on this question for years, and the answers seem to have little to do with what organized religion, if any, the answerers associate themselves with. When it comes to God: The more educated the person, the more abstract the answers are likely to be . . . and the more likely the light bulb will go on when "quantum theology," as I call it, is proposed as a basis for understanding God's blueprint for the multiverse.

In the early 2000s, I was thinking very hard about all this. One of the more educated people around at the time was Sister Rita Larivee SSA, a Roman Catholic theologian and publisher of the *National Catholic Reporter*. She started using the term quantum theology before I did.

"Everything is connected. Everything has an effect on everything else. Nothing is in isolation. If I touch a flower that is springing from the Earth, I am at the same time touching a star in the heavens above," Sister Rita wrote in 2004. "Quantum theology emphasizes the experience of the divine as told by the myriad of members making up the human experience, regardless of creed. It dismantles exclusivity so as to affirm that we are all connected."

From other believers with advanced academic degrees, I've had everything from "God is the supreme but unknowable creator and guide of the universe" to "all-knowing, all-loving father . . . or is it mother?" One physicist told me merrily that God is "coexistent with all time and conterminous with all space."

Okay. The multiverse makes that work!

Most garden-variety believers, however, have no such grand visions. They generally adhere to religions, or at least religious traditions, because that's what their parents did. Many are the "salt of the Earth" and have great faith. Some approach God with love, others with fear. Myriad people seem to regard God as a sort of cosmic vending machine. If they go to the mosque on Friday, the temple on Saturday, or the church on Sunday, things will go better for them in life, and they'll have a kind of insurance policy for an afterlife. Amid the latter group, I've encountered people who think that God really is like Jupiter or Zeus: an old man with a white beard, something of a celestial Santa Claus.

Then there are those who profess belief but don't belong to any particular religious group. These folks include many sincere believers in God who are disgruntled because of child abuse by priests, dislike of a pastor or rabbi, or disillusion with a radical imam. Sometimes they don't feel that a particular religion meets their own needs, or that it contains doctrines they can't accept intellectually. Others just have better things to do than go and listen to sermons.

The numbers of those who strike off on their own like this is growing by leaps and bounds in the early twenty-first century.

THE FLAVORS OF UNBELIEF

What God do atheists not believe in? When I question them, a few will describe some goofy, stereotypical God that I don't believe in either. Many will try to broadside me with something like "no Supreme Being, not nobody, not nohow!"

When I point out that there's a logical inconsistency there—that, by the simple laws of Newtonian physics, some force, personal or impersonal, started the clock running and keeps the cycles of Nature moving, they will use terms like "blind chance" and fall back on dear old Charles Darwin (1809–1882), who came up with the original version of the Theory of Evolution.

In return, I cite something like Sir Isaac Newton's laws of motion (indicating that there has to be a force behind all movement) and the fact that, statistically speaking, the Earth hasn't existed long enough for evolution's original ideas to explain all the variations in Nature, let alone the existence of human beings. In the end, his or her faith put to the test, nearly all atheists I know usually will laugh nervously, bluster in frustration, or perhaps admit that further reflection on the subject may be required. Most also argue that religion has been responsible for most of humanity's blood-soaked history. They say that ridding ourselves of religion and other "superstitions" will make the world a much more peaceful place by eliminating differences in belief. This might be a tempting argument, but it ignores three things:

First, and many clergy would protest this, God and religion are two entirely different things. Religion, for better or for worse, is a human response to God. Just because a religion is imperfect, harmful, or even evil, doesn't mean that God is. In fact, most religions might have very little to do with God at all.

Second, if people don't have religions, they'll find some other excuse to kill each other.

Third, just because religions can cause political and social divisions—and not all do—doesn't mean there's no God. Because God—the real God—is all about what we're going to call the Unity.

This is a concept we should already be familiar with through the paranormal cases we've looked at in this book, and the multiversal superlife and interconnectedness they demonstrate.

Fourth, believing in, worshipping, and loving God are as natural to people as eating and sleeping, and nothing is going to change that.

The vast majority of atheists I know seem to have axes to grind with the religions they grew up in, but I believe most are kind and compassionate people. I think they want to believe but can't get past the sorrow in the world. They can't find a God worthy of their belief because the only Gods they know are through this or that religion.

The most honest moments for most people are when they are on their deathbeds. All pretense, all intellectual arrogance, and certainly all bovine fecal matter fall away. I've stood at the deathbeds of four atheists, one of whom was a doctor. Each of them was utterly terrified. All four of them were lucid, held my hand, and asked me about God.

"Just say 'thank you,' and you will never have to be afraid again," I told them. I have always believed in salvation through gratitude. That said, atheists might have a point that will resonate with many believers and unbelievers alike: If God is good, why is there evil? Ben and I suggest a new answer to that question, from the multiverse perspective, in *Behind the Paranormal: Everything You Know is Wrong.*

CITY MOUSE, COUNTRY MOUSE

Educated or not, there are fascinating differences in the way people perceive God from country to country. In poorer nations, where people see death frequently and generally have less control over their own lives, they tend to live in tightly knit communities, be closer to the Earth, and belong to churches, mosques, temples, or whatever. Some may have a close, even intimate, relationship with the divine. It's almost as if they see their need for God more.

In developed nations, where people are more prosperous, rarely see death, and live in artificial environments that make them feel secure and in control, it's almost as if they think God needs them. People in these affluent, more urbanized settings tend to be more fragmented and less likely to belong to an organized religious group. They probably will believe in God, but sometimes as a faraway concept that has little to do with their own lives, even if they do belong to a religion.

This is where we encounter an interesting and, I believe, very important phenomenon that began in the late twentieth century: the rise of New Age thinking and neopaganism. The New Age movement is, on the surface, a highly individual search for self-fulfillment and spiritual growth outside traditional religion, and it tends to be strong in affluent nations where lack of commonality among the populace, separation from the Earth, and social disaffection are most pronounced. New Agers have no central organization, but this diverse movement has inspired fresh interest in things spiritual, some novel philosophical speculation, and even a new genre in music.

Neopaganism is an outgrowth of the New Age movement and is an individual effort to return to one's own ancient pagan roots, or what people perceive as such. It's often driven by one's ethnic background. For example, neopagans of Scandinavian descent often try to rediscover that region's ancient worship of Odin. Neopagans of Chinese descent frequently try to revive traditional ways to honor their ancestors. Whether these revivals are historically and theologically accurate is beside the point: "If it works for you, do it!" is the view. What matters is spiritual self-fulfillment.

No matter where they're from, people who adhere to an organized religion usually feel quite comfortable in it. At the same time, the average member of an organized religious group often will know little about the history, theology, beliefs, traditions (or at least the reasons behind them), and policies of their own religion. They might say they know, but their "knowledge" is frequently off by miles.

One example was my friend Pat, the psychic medium I ran into at St. Lawrence State Hospital when I was a seminary student in 1975. She said she was a devout Catholic and dismissed my comment that Catholics aren't supposed to practice mediumship. I think people remake their religions in their own images and feel perfectly comfortable doing so.

REMEMBERING MOTHER

There is a particularly beautiful carved relief of the Goddess (of Love and Beauty) Hathor at her ancient temple in Dendera, Egypt. Muslim women who want children are sometimes seen at this image, leaving a vegetable offering and praying for the kindness of Hathor as "the mother of all children." This also occurs at several sites where there are images of the chief Egyptian Goddess, Isis, who was beloved throughout the ancient Mediterranean world. Isis is still worshipped today, here and there in one form or another.

Hathor in her temple at Dendera, Egypt. *Photograph by Cristophe Capelli/Shutterstock.*

Islam is a strictly monotheistic religion: Muslims believe in one God, and it's not Hathor. Are these Muslim women in Egypt simply ignorant about their own religion? Why would they risk official censure or worse to pray to an ancient pagan Goddess?

"I don't know who she is, but she is a good lady," is a typical answer. And they will tell you that the prayers work.

DO ALL RELIGIONS WORSHIP THE SAME GOD?

What about the religions themselves, as opposed to the people who belong to them? In the pluralistic societies of the developed world, especially in Europe and North America, a common belief among rank-and-file members of most religious groups is that "down deep, all religions are the same" or "all religions worship the same God."

In a way, that may be true when it comes to most ordinary believers. But when it comes to official religions, it's not true at all. Probably the most glaring rift between personal belief and official religious belief is the *believe it or not* belief. While a large majority of people on the planet believe in a personal God, some of their religions don't. That's right—several major religions don't officially believe in God as the creator or ruler of the universe.

Buddhism, at an estimated 375 million adherents the world's sixth-largest religion, doesn't acknowledge God either as creator or guide of the universe. It's almost entirely concerned with personal salvation through overcoming the failures of the world, especially human passions. Some ancient Buddhist philosophers, especially in the Mahayana tradition, actually condemned God-worship. In fact, non-belief in God as creator or ruler goes all the way back to the sixth century BCE in the old, but little, religion of Jainism, centered in India, with only about a million adherents.

Hinduism, the fourth-largest religion, with nearly a billion adherents, is actually a collection of polytheistic (worshipping more than one God) sects. Some will talk about "God" and some won't. There are myriad small religions and tribal faiths around the planet as well, most of them polytheistic. The thing about polytheism, though, is that in some forms it's actually monotheistic: The various gods are just different faces of the one God.

THE BIG THREE

Christians, Jews, and Muslims: They worship the same God, right? Maybe and maybe not. Theologically it can be argued that they don't. While Muslims honor Jesus as a prophet, they certainly don't acknowledge him as literally God, as orthodox Christians do. Many Jews would balk at the idea that their God and the Muslims' Allah are one and the same. And there are Jewish and Muslim scholars who would say that the Christians' worship of the Holy Trinity—Jesus, as well as God the Father and God the Holy Spirit —makes them polytheists and pagans.

Even within Christianity itself there have, at times, been theological debates about whether the vengeful God of the Old Testament is the same as the loving God of the New Testament.

So, we have a certain fuzzy, but deep-seated, unity of belief across humanity, regardless of official religious doctrine. Still, we seem no closer to an answer to who or what God really is.

Perhaps the path to the answers lies in changing our point of view. Maybe if we turn away from the distorted, self-centered vision expressed in that funny Canadian sculpture, and that seems to typify humanity's overall picture of God, maybe we can get somewhere. Maybe we can ask the right questions, and maybe the multiverse, and even the paranormal, can help us.

If we can find our way into the remote past, return to our common point of origin—the beginning, the alpha point—of humanity and our mutual experience, things might become clearer. Maybe we can discover the original God. But who says there *was* a common point of origin, or an original God? Didn't humanity start out grunting at each other in caves, and end up talking on smart phones in condos? Didn't we have all kinds of superstitions and worship hundreds of little gods?

The idea that we started out primitive and got more sophisticated until we became the geniuses we are today is a variation on the linear theory of history. On the contrary, there's plenty of evidence that the cyclical theory of history is more accurate. Things might start simple and get more complicated, but it all happens in fits and starts—and again and again. There are forward steps and backward steps. What goes around comes around. There's even archaeological and folklore evidence, controversial to be sure, that we have advanced from stone tools to power tools as many as four times in our long, virtually unknown prehistory, each time to be sent back to "square one" by a global natural disaster, a worldwide pandemic, or even war. After all, modern humans have been around for nearly two million years, and our known history goes back only about 12,000 at best. That's an awful lot of empty time—time enough for a thousand civilizations to rise and fall.

In the words of British journalist and author Graham Hancock (1951–), who believes history is indeed cyclical, humans are "a species with amnesia." I believe that, too. It's not that we can't recall; we've simply accumulated so much baggage that we don't consciously remember. Our subconscious minds, on the other hand, remember everything, mainly because we're still there in one world or another in our multiversal superlife. But I think those memories also are embedded in our genes, our basic instincts, and our deepest dreams, loves, hates, and fears.

It's in the subconscious that our original God might abide.

THE UNITY

Driving through the West Country of England on a mellow March evening in 1989, I happened upon a scene I'll never forget. The narrow country road curved around the bottom of a hill, where an old man and a young boy were driving a herd of cows through a break in a low hedgerow. Beyond the gate was a dirt road leading toward a rambling house and some simple farm buildings. Behind it all, the most glorious of sunsets was ablaze. It was like an old painting, awash with peace.

I pulled off the road and got out to take in the scene. The boy looked at me curiously. The old man smiled and put his hand to his cap in greeting.

"What a beautiful sunset!" I called across the sea of cows.

"Aye," he replied. "Not a bad sunset for such a little farm as this!"

I chuckled at such a cute quip, of course. But as the years passed, it became a symbol to me of how people see the world. While *The Homunculus* illustrates our distorted view of ourselves and God, that little exchange on an English byway has been a symbol to me of our limited view of the world and the multiverse.

For decades, scientists looked back into the deeps of space and time, about fourteen billion years to be precise, to the moment of what they called the "Big Bang." Today, there's some debate about whether that actually happened, whether our universe has always existed, and/or whether it will eventually collapse back into the cosmic "singularity" whence it came. But none of that really makes any difference because, in the multiverse, it happened in all possible ways somewhere or somewhen anyway. Besides, even if this or that universe had no specific point of creation, is it not *being created* from moment to moment?

That singularity (a point in space that has infinitely small mass but infinitely large density) is the perfect signpost on our search for the original God. The singularity is a literal and absolute Unity. And I believe that the entire motivation behind everything Nature does, and everything that we and all our fellow creatures do, is a single-minded quest to get back to that primal Unity.

Even in the Holographic Theory, a variation on the multiverse idea as expressed in quantum physics, theoretical physicists expect the "matrices" projected by Whoever or Whatever is doing the projecting, all to collapse back into the great Unity at some point. If any of these scenarios are true, we will see the countless worlds in the multiverse blending until they are one. Maybe that's what we already see in the paranormal, especially in flap areas.

At first glance, the contention that Nature is tending toward ultimate Unity seems counter-intuitive. The whole point of Nature appears to be the proliferation of infinite variety and unending individuality, not to mention unceasing warfare for the survival of each. Over time, species change and diversify. Only rarely can members of different species mate and produce offspring, and, even then, their DNA must be very similar. The purpose of each creature seems to be the spread of its own genes, as rapidly as possible, at the expense of the genes of others. To this end on the human level, individuals, species, tribes, nations, and empires battle to the death. The spilling of blood and the exaltation of the self seem to be far stronger than any primal desire for Unity.

If we look deeper, however, a different picture emerges.

THE PARADOX

Life in the multiverse is full of paradoxes: things that seem contradictory but are actually true. The greatest paradox of all may be this: The quest for Unity is the ultimate motivation for things that seem to destroy Unity. Take any day anywhere in Nature, and we seem to see Darwin's principle of survival of the fittest played out. Plants struggle against each other for space, soil, and sunlight. Insects, birds, and animals compete for food and sometimes devour each other. They vie for mates, and most struggle to protect their young. As Darwin contended, the strongest survive. But the paradox is here: By battling to survive, the individual—even the weakest one—serves the whole. Cruel as it may sound, when the weak are devoured, they become part of the strong. They die so the strong may prevail, and that strengthens an entire species because it helps the strongest genes survive. And because every species is an integral part of the biosphere (the entire interdependent community of life), the whole is strengthened.

There's one ingredient that Darwin never suspected: It's not just one world, but many. Death is an illusion, the only thing in the multiverse that's impossible. That's because, just as there are countless facets of ourselves, there are countless facets of every life form. And, as I believe we see even in the dismal world of possession and exorcism, every being shares the life of every other being.

SEE IT OR NOT

Tribal shamans (priests and healers) know this, as do the spiritually adept of many faiths and traditions. Legitimate mediums and psychics may not know the Unity as such or understand it, but many of them use it and live with it. When any of us has a paranormal experience, and we all have them regularly in one way or another, whether we know it or not, we are living it as well.

Some of us ordinary folks have begun to discover the Unity, too, but we're not sure what to do about it, how to embrace it, what to do with it. We know that something is happening in the early twenty-first century, something the words "miraculous," "uplifting," or "joyful" just can't capture. In spite of us, or because of us, I think our original God is returning from the shadows of the past. But we won't see this God unless we realize the multiverse's greatest paradox of all: Our sense of self is an illusion whose true goal is to serve the whole. Until you achieve that realization, you will continue to see only yourself, and one version of yourself, at that. This will color your whole vision of God, making it narrow, limited, and selfish.

The realization that the sense of self is an illusion does not destroy our own uniqueness. In another crucial paradox, this realization defines and fulfills our uniqueness. Realizing that we each are integral to the Unity fulfills our individuality. Each of us is a unique expression of all of us.

THE NEW AGE

Wherever you found this book, it may well have been listed or shelved in the New Age section. The New Age movement began in the late twentieth century in response to the environmental crisis. With all its faults, it does promote respect for the Earth, spiritual and emotional growth, and human harmony.

One of the stimuli for this movement was the Gaia Theory, advanced by James E. Lovelock (1919–), a distinguished British physician, philosopher, and author considered by many as the spiritual father of the environmental movement. Whether he knew it or not, Lovelock was to become a major proponent for recapturing the Unity.

Named for an early Earth goddess who personified the planet as mother of all life, the theory, originally known as the Gaia Hypothesis, puts forth Earth as a unified system of interdependent life—the biosphere. While Lovelock stopped short of calling the planet and the biosphere a living superorganism, many believe the Gaia Theory amounts to this.

At the far edge of our knowledge there is evidence that, because the multiverse is an interactive system, the biosphere embraces not just Earth but all worlds and all versions of worlds. In this vision, matter, energy, and consciousness flow more or less freely across the branes. What we call paranormal phenomena or "exceptional human experiences" are not only clues that the multiverse is there, but that it really is an open system and that this universal flow indicates a deep, underlying Unity not only in all things but in all possibilities.

I believe that Ben and I see this in action all the time in our paranormal work.

What's more, everything we do echoes across the worlds through our superlife. When we embrace the ferocious self-centeredness that modern society seems to encourage, we break the Unity of the entire biosphere. When we break the Unity, we mar our own nature, and we destabilize the multiverse for every facet of ourselves—and for every other creature and thing within our sphere.

MITOCHONDRIAL EVE

It didn't begin that way. There was, as we've said, a common beginning and a common purpose. There's little genetic doubt that all humans alive today descend from one woman who lived in Africa about 150,000 years ago. We know about what scientists playfully dub "Mitochondrial Eve" through the microscopic mitochondria in our bodies, which are passed only from mother to daughter, in this case over 1,500 centuries. That's about the time the DNA and fossil records indicate that the human race nearly died out from some disaster, perhaps a pandemic, or possibly an asteroid impact or the eruption of a super-volcano. Either of the latter would have filled the atmosphere with pulverized debris and blocked sunlight for years. This would have obliterated most life on Earth.

Not only do we have a common ancestor, it appears that we really do have a common God. Before the mid-twentieth century, anthropologists and scholars of religion assumed that humans started out as polytheists. As nomadic bands of hunter-gatherers gave way to settled farming villages and large civilizations, it was believed that people became more sophisticated, with most finally working their way up to a belief in one God. By the mid-twentieth century, however, it began to appear that it happened the other way around. The picture changed thanks to the discovery of religious writings from the Sumerians, the earliest known civilization.

When the Sumerians' cuneiform, at about 6,000 years old the earliest known form of writing, was first deciphered in 1835, it revealed a world of gods, goddesses, greater and lesser demons, and all sorts of spirits. All these beings seemed to engage in constant and terrible warfare—with humankind in the middle. But as earlier and earlier cuneiform tablets came to light, and the ability to translate them got better, an entirely different picture emerged. Instead of the unbridled polytheism of the later tablets, there appeared a rather elegant hierarchy of beings presided over by one God.

In 1931, near the end of his career, the eminent archaeologist and cuneiform scholar Stephen H. Langdon (1876–1937) of Oxford University was almost reluctant to publish these hard-to-believe findings.

"I may fail to carry conviction in concluding that both in Sumerian and Semitic (early Middle Eastern pagan) religions, monotheism preceded polytheism. . . . The evidence and reasons for this conclusion, so contrary to accepted and current views, have been set down with care and with the perception of adverse criticism."

Langdon eventually became convinced that the journey from monotheism to polytheism represented a steady deterioration in the human experience.

"In my opinion, the history of the oldest civilization of man (the Sumerians) is a rapid decline from monotheism to extreme polytheism and widespread belief in evil spirits. It is in a very true sense the history of the fall of man."

Remember this point. It's crucial.

The most ancient texts we have from the Semitic nations indicate the same trend at about the same times—between 8,000 and 10,000 years ago. These nations included the Assyrians, Babylonians, Canaanites, Chaldeans, and other ancestors of the Jews and Arabs.

From the shadowy origins of Sumerian religion to about 3500 BCE, the number of gods in the Near East went from what appear to be three, headed by the Sky God Enlil, to some 5,000 entities of every ilk and attitude. Nevertheless, as more discoveries came to light, the more Langdon appeared to be right. The distinguished University of Chicago anthropologist Henri Frankfort (1897–1954) wrote during his Iraq excavations of the 1930s:

> We have obtained, to the best of our knowledge for the first time, religious material complete in its social setting. . . . For instance, we discover that the representations on cylinder seals, which are usually connected with various gods, can all be fitted into a consistent picture in which a single God worshiped in this temple forms the central figure. It seems, therefore, that at this early period His various aspects were not considered separate deities . . . .
>
> This raises . . . the possibility that polytheism (arose) . . . because the attributes of a single God were differently emphasized by different people until those people in later years came to forget that they were speaking of the same Person. Thus, attributes of a single deity became a plurality of deities. It is not

> merely that single individuals laid emphasis upon different aspects of God's nature, but whole families and tribes seemed to have developed certain shared views about what was important in life and what was not, and therefore, not unnaturally, came to attribute to their god and to put special emphasis upon those characteristics that seemed to them of greatest significance.

Other scholars have traced evidence of monotheism to polytheism in ancient religions elsewhere, including Egypt, India, Asia, Africa, Australia, the Pacific islands, and North America. Oral histories from Aborigine, Aka, Aztec, Berber, Carib, Dogon, Eskimo, Khwe, Masai, and Zulu all tell essentially the same Creation story.

WHO SHATTERED GOD?

Any student of folklore will tell you that every tale or belief, no matter how outlandish to us or no matter how much baggage it has picked up over the millennia, began with some human experience, some shared event, some grain of truth. Rather than being enjoyable, but untrue, yarns we repeat around the campfire, folklore and myth carry ancient lessons and truths—even historical truths—through the ages.

Folklore and myth are the vessels of the collective memory of the human race. So, the long-vanished Sumerians and their myths aren't our only clues about our original God. There exists today a few dwindling populations descended in unbroken line from the remote past—and in which prehistoric folklore remains a living thing. These include the San and Khoisan Bushmen of southern Africa, who still live a hunter-gatherer lifestyle, and whose genetics have been reliably traced directly back some 60,000 years at least. Their Y chromosomes, the part of DNA that's passed from father to son, has been followed to about 150,000 years ago, right to the time of Mitochondrial Eve and the last mass-extinction event. Not far behind the Bushmen are the isolated natives of the Andaman and Nicobar Islands in the Indian Ocean, whose genetics go back about 70,000 years. Then there are the Australian Aborigines, with a continuous tribal life and oral tradition reaching back 30,000 years and probably much further. Their very name means "from the origin."

We get a glimpse of our common beginning by looking at these three primal peoples, located in different parts of the world, whose religious beliefs predate those of the Sumerians by many millennia. And when we look, we find a personal God, perhaps a bit misty, certainly with some animistic (surrounded by spirits) and anthropomorphic (given some human characteristics) baggage picked up over the ages, but a clear God nonetheless.

Whether called Huve, Paluga, or Baiame, the Supreme Being walks serenely behind the prehistoric legends of these peoples. Usually thought of as having a wife and son, He presides over the Dream Time—the Time before Time—the era of Creation in which the Unity had not yet been forgotten. It was a time when all things were known to be conscious, and all living things could converse with each other. You could have talked with the trees and communed with the rocks.

What's more, it's a time still present in the many worlds of "dream" accessible by shamans, who can access these realms to help solve the hurts of our world and to learn from those who live in other worlds. And here we see the multiverse and even the Gaia Theory in their original glory. It's a multiverse whose meaning is simply and beautifully expressed in primal human belief systems such as the Africans' principle of Ubuntu: Everything I do affects you. Everything you do affects me. And everything we do affects the whole world. Indeed, it affects all the worlds.

What these "primitive" peoples and their prehistoric legends describe is the multiverse as an open and unified system and as our original God's blueprint for, and map of, reality. It describes the Unity as the guide on how to live life and the path to truth and fulfillment. Life for these elder peoples takes unimaginably varied forms—us, insects, animals, trees, ancestors, spirits, gods, goddesses, godlings, demons, ghosts, spirit guardians, monsters, and it flows freely among a myriad of worlds. It's all a vast, interdependent reality full of friends, enemies, and answers: the neighbors we've referred to throughout this book. It's a multiverse where the paranormal is entirely normal. It's an infinite diversity that forms the perfect Unity.

This appears to have been our common world at the beginning.

In this primal world where Unity still rules, God is the Unifier, the Teacher, the Starting Point, and the Goal. God is the One Who shows the way and personifies things as they should be. God is not the result of the Unity; God is the Unity. God is Reality. But God also is the two primary forces of life—the male and female principles, in balance and fertile with new life. In these primal religions, God is Father (represented by the sky) and Mother (represented by the Earth). Their love produces a Child (us or a god representing us). To these children of the human dawn, God is not just a symbol for the powers of Nature. God is Nature; God is a Person intimately close to us—closer to us than we are to ourselves.

Since the family is the basic unit of human society, indeed human existence and survival, these original people seem to have seen our families as simple and beautiful mirrors of God. They realized that we really are made in God's image.

And behind all their beliefs is a prophecy that somehow, somewhen, the Dream Time, the Unity would someday return.

The name we rather arrogantly give our species, *Homo sapiens* (the man who knows that he knows), is a misnomer because we hardly "know" anything, let alone ourselves. Much more accurately, we are *Homo adorans* (worshipping man). God is in our genes. Down deep, even our modern religions remember the existence of many worlds and the ultimate goal of existence: the return to the Unity.

From the *Bhagavad-Gita* (Song of God) of the Hindus:

> I instructed the imperishable science of uniting the individual consciousness with the Ultimate Consciousness . . . (chapter 4:1).
>
> . . . With your consciousness absorbed in Me, taking complete shelter in Me, executing the science of uniting the individual consciousness with the Ultimate Consciousness, you will be able to know Me completely, free from doubt (chapter 7:1).
>
> . . . there are many worlds of the living and the dead. Pierce them all through love at the last moment when the great transition (death) comes, be only in Me (The Bhagavad Gita and Inner Transformation).

And the disturbing:

> I am become Death, the destroyer of worlds . . . (chapter 11:32).

From the Jewish Torah and Christian Old Testament (claimed by Daniel M. Berry of the University of Waterloo to be the correct translation):

> In a beginning, God created the heavens and the Earth . . .

From the Christian New Testament:

> But in this the final age He has spoken to us in his Son...and through Him He created the worlds (Hebrews 1:2).

FATHER, MOTHER, AND . . .

Sometimes the primal faith is remembered in the most unlikely places, including two of the most ferociously male-oriented religions in history: Judaism and Christianity. Just as in the primordial Bushmen religion, with Huve having a wife and son, Yahweh had a female counterpart in ancient Judaism. She was known as the Shekinah. Even the prophet Isaiah refers to the Shekinah with feminine pronouns (Isaiah 51:9–10). And us? We are all "sons of God," according to the Torah.

In Christianity, the notion of the Holy Trinity (Father, Son, and Holy Spirit) is not unique. It's a reflection of the primal divine family as experienced in many other and far-older religions. Theologically, the Holy Spirit has feminine characteristics and is personified in the Bible as *Chokma* and *Sophia*, Hebrew and Greek, respectively, for Wisdom. Both are feminine words. This is all through the Bible, especially in Proverbs (8 and 9) and even in the New Testament (Matthew 11:19, Luke 7:35, and much more). And us? Jesus, who theologically is fully God and fully man, is the "Son of Man" in the New Testament. He, too, is us.

In modern times, the break from our original God, and thus from the Unity, has had deadly consequences for our vision, our society, our lives, and our planet. And some scientists, philosophers, and theologians have known it.

A man we've mentioned previously, Pierre Teilhard de Chardin (1881–1955), was all of the above and a controversial Roman Catholic priest to boot; he may have been a little shaky on the multiverse thing, but he saw the break with the Unity as a break with God and with what humans are meant to be. A French member of the Jesuit order of priests, Teilhard was a paleontologist, biologist, philosopher, mystic, and one of the greatest visionaries of the twentieth century. His lifelong motivation was to reconcile natural science (especially the Theory of Evolution) with religion, specifically Christianity. His studies led him directly to the idea of humans as creatures of endless possibility whose ultimate destination is the "Omega Point": a total reuniting of all things in the consciousness of God.

Decades before the environmental movement or the Gaia Theory, Teilhard saw this ultimate Unity as the whole point of life and the Earth, which he characterized as having its own personality and spirit. He clearly equated our modern separation from the Earth as a symptom of separation from God and the dis-Unity of all things.

"We have reached a crossroads in human evolution where the only road which leads forward is towards a common passion . . . . To continue to place our hopes in a social order achieved by external violence would simply amount to our giving up all hope of carrying the Spirit of the Earth to its limits."

THE PROBLEM OF EVIL

Teilhard's words are all very nice, especially if you're not poor, hungry, sick, or abused. But with all this wonderful Unity and a loving God, why is there evil in the world?

Parasites. Remember them? It's to these multiversal troublemakers that we can look for why the original God shattered into gods. Notice that from the ancient Near East, Asia and the Americas come the oldest tales of vampires: stories not of blood-sucking guys in capes, but of "life-sucking ghosts." While that term is known today mostly in video games, paranormal investigators meet the real thing all the time, whether they realize it or not.

THE GOD CONNECTION

What does all this have to do with God? Everything. What one or more parasites can do in a family, why couldn't they do with a tribe or village, especially when those tribesmen or villagers already had some realization of the multiverse and its interdependent life? Can you imagine the sustenance—the power—a parasite, or even an organized troop of them, could gain by manipulating and communicating with a group of humans until the people thought they were hearing from a super being: a god or gods? Imagine the negative energy—the "food"—generated by human fear on a tribal or national scale. Think of the impact across the worlds of the barbarism we fell into as our God split into god after god, many of which, according to both folklore and archaeology, demanded human blood. Consider the negative power of torture, of human sacrifice. Consider the power of war.

I'm the last one to claim absolution or even temporary insanity, either for individuals or our whole species, because we may have been duped by parasites. And I would never advocate the surrender of responsibility, personal or communal, because of any influence by these wretched cosmic beasts. As we were suckered out of the primal, multiversal Unity of the Dream Time, and we lurched headlong into a world of division and death, we knew exactly what we were doing. The "buttons" of ignorance, greed, lust, and individualism were used against us. With their own keen intelligence, parasites used and still use our worst tendencies to break the Unity, drive us apart, and line us up as hot dinners so they can get even stronger. As we said earlier, we as humans were and are literally being farmed.

As Frankfort stated more aptly than he realized, the history of our estrangement from the Unity; of the splintering of our lives, world views, and societies; of the division of our original God into many gods, "is in a very true sense the history of the fall of man." What could be more evil than that? Folklore or not, parasites have truly earned their reputation as demons.

GODLY ART

In adjoining galleries at the British Museum in London, you can get a vivid picture of our descent into polytheism. In one gallery are the gods, goddesses, demons, and monsters from after-the-fall cultures that generally were closer to the Earth and had to face the fickleness of life head-on, without the protections of what we call civilization.

It's understandable that people would develop images representing their fears as well as their joys. But looking upon the most ugly, petty, and unlovable of these entities, I can't help but be convinced that parasites were in action somewhere along the line. That's especially true with the little tribal gods and back-door deities that had to be satisfied with blood, or one horror or another. More often than not, they were honored by warlike peoples, who undoubtedly fed them well. Who would deliberately choose such loveless gods, unless they'd be duped into thinking they had no choice?

In nearby galleries, however, there are some far more dignified and inspiring figures. In the Egyptian exhibit are the noble faces of Isis and her consort Osiris, Mother and Father of the world. From ancient Greece comes the graceful figure of Aphrodite, as carved 2,400 years ago by the sculptor Praxiteles. As though gazing from a temple in Asia is the serene face of the Buddha.

It's hard to believe that these deities represent "life-sucking ghosts." So, as we enter historic times, we see a gradual drift back toward more positive, and fewer, gods, which we discuss in detail in *Behind the Paranormal: Everything You Know is Wrong*. But we remain a far cry from the Unity, which certainly keeps the table set for parasites.

There is, however, a twist to this tale. There are among modern people, as part of their beliefs about God, certain assumptions about death. One of these is that, after you die, you know everything. You can even become some kind of superbeing, lovingly protecting your family or hatefully wreaking havoc among living people you don't like. I think all these assumptions are naïve and, in fact, nonsense. But the question remains: What can those who are not parasites but are "no longer with us"—or were never with us at all—tell us about God?

CHAPTER TWO

WHAT GHOSTS HAVE TO SAY ABOUT GOD

WELCOME TO PURGATORY

In March 2007, I received an e-mail from a man in Wisconsin who heard me on the radio the night before. It has haunted me ever since.

> . . . 28 years ago my friend killed himself. On the day of his funeral he came to me in a dream and told me that he was going to have to spend a long time in purgatory because God was mad at him. He and I were not Catholic. This really shook me up. So I called a minister that I new [*sic*] and told him what happened. He said that strangely a woman had just called him with the same story about the same person. I am now a Catholic. Remember that the only truth is Christ Jesus . . .

This note came to me like a groping hand out of my own past because of the suicide of my father when I was seven years old. It was the defining event in my childhood, perhaps my life. Had I investigated that purring, smoke-filled car in our Connecticut garage on that cold Sunday afternoon in January 1961, instead of turning away to head for a friend's house, I might have saved my father. Or, in his tortured state of mind that day, he might have pulled me in with him.

From the day of my father's death, my mind was filled with haunting suspicions and tortured questions about God and the dead. Dad, a Massachusetts Yankee with multiple roots aboard the Mayflower, was a non-practicing, garden-variety Protestant. But my mother, my brother, and I were strict Roman Catholics. Mom was of mixed Irish, French Canadian, and Yankee descent and grew up under the heavy hand of an old-time, no-dancing, no-movies Methodist grandmother from New Hampshire. So, one way or the other, Christianity meant business in the Eno household.

When my father translated, I was in the second grade at the local Catholic school. In those days, before the Second Vatican Council (a huge meeting between the pope and bishops from around the world that began in 1962) started to lighten things up in the Catholic Church, the nuns were already programming us to feel lucky that we were Catholics because we could go to heaven. They also petrified us with thoughts of going to hell because of things like eating meat on Fridays, deliberately missing mass on Sundays, masturbation—or suicide. Had my father gone to hell? Had this gentle, kind man who suffered so long with heart problems been cast into eternal fire? Had this good man, who never raised hand or voice to me in anger, been damned forever because of a mistake made during a time of mental torment?

While I strongly suspected that many of the women in black at my school would have been serial killers had they not been nuns, there were some true saints among them. Fortunately, one of these was my second-grade teacher, Sister Mary Joel. I got through that surreal time largely because of her love and support and her assurances that God really does understand and forgive human failings, and might just be bigger than we think.

Contrary to the standard, pop-paranormal scenario for places where suicides occur, things remained peaceful at home. There were no strange footsteps, no feelings of being watched or threatened, no ghosts. After the funeral, my brother, more than sixteen years my senior, went back to Washington, DC, and the seminary where he was studying for the priesthood. About to turn eight years old, I dusted myself off and took up life in a single-parent household in an era when such a thing was very rare. Six years later, in 1967, at the tender age of fourteen, I entered the seminary myself. I soon had an idea that was quite in line with that e-mail I was to receive in 2007: What people think are ghosts might actually be souls in purgatory.

The age-old, worldwide belief in earthbound spirits in one form or another . . . souls trapped between Earth and some spirit world, unable to cross over, refusing to believe they're dead, doomed to relive critical moments in their lives, or the very moments of their deaths: It all fit, so I thought, the Roman Catholic definition of purgatory: ". . . an intermediate state of purification between death and heaven that provides for the removal of personal obstacles to the full enjoyment of eternal union with God." In other words, if you die but aren't quite good enough to go to heaven but not quite bad enough to go to hell, you go to purgatory for as long as it takes to qualify for heaven.

Catholic belief seems to indicate that you have to be a Catholic in order to get this bonus chance at heaven. The universality of ghost stories, however, made me wonder if God is, perhaps, a bit more inclusive, maybe enough to include my father. But I couldn't find anything in church doctrine, let alone the Bible, that said what the nature of purgatory might be. In my entire, ten-year seminary experience, I can't recall any course that studied purgatory. In fact, by the early 1970s, Roman Catholic theology, especially in North America and Western Europe, was liberalizing. Purgatory, along with a number of other holdovers from the old catechism books, was something of an embarrassment.

That was a strange time in the church. The Second Vatican Council had, as Pope John XXIII put it, "opened the window to let in some fresh air." Ecumenism and outreaches to other religions were born. Previously unaskable questions began to be asked. Shouldn't God's love be emphasized rather than his punishment? Shouldn't the church work harder for social justice (whatever that was)? Shouldn't priests be allowed to marry?

In the seminaries at the time, there was a certain amount of confusion. Previously strict, almost military, rules of discipline were relaxed. Those of us in the early years of priestly training no longer had to wear black suits or cassocks (those long, black robes), except on special occasions. Amidst all this new "dialogue"—some would say chaos—came deeper questions that, for many of us, shook our spirituality to the core. Why were so few priests talking about Satan now? Had the nature of our battle against evil changed? And what about dying? What was all this "fresh air" going to do to our understanding of death and its aftermath? Did we even believe in purgatory or hell anymore?

My personal questions came out of all this confusion. What was the connection of these traditional doctrines with the paranormal? Could ghosts indeed be souls in purgatory? And deepest of all: Where was my father?

I found one lonely book on ghosts in the seminary library. Today considered a classic of paranormal literature, *Ghosts and Poltergeists* by Fr. Herbert Thurston, a respected British Jesuit priest, is a rare Roman Catholic treatment of the subject, published in 1953. Despite the title, the book is essentially a collection of poltergeist cases, almost none of which Thurston witnessed for himself.

Meanwhile, without spilling the beans about my having started investigating ghosts, I made some inquiries. When I asked my priest-professors about the nature of purgatory, I got some odd looks and answers that ranged from "a temporary hell" to "we can't be sure."

By this time, my older brother, now Rev. Robert B. Eno (1936–1997), was not only a priest but also a doctor of theology, an author, and a professor at Catholic University of America (CUA) in Washington, DC. Though we saw each other only a few times a year and rarely talked about our dad, I suspect that similar questions were running through Bob's mind. He later took time off to actually study the doctrine of purgatory, such as it is, for a book he was writing about early Christian beliefs, about which he was considered one of the world's leading experts. But even

Bob couldn't help much. He could tell me the history of belief in purgatory, and the history of the history, but that was about it.

"But what is it?" I implored.

"Traditionally, it's considered a place of punishment, but temporary. A 'consuming fire' that cleanses . . . unlike hell, which just punishes," Bob replied.

"But what does *that* mean?" I pressed.

Bob had a unique, rather comical, way of shrugging. He did so.

In any case, what was all this punishment for finite beings committing finite sins? What a horrifying picture! Who or what were we worshipping?

Another priest I cornered on the subject was a lifelong friend of Bob's and a second big brother to me, Fr. Richard P. McBrien (1936–2015), a brilliant scholar and author, and later author/editor of *The Encyclopedia of Catholicism* (HarperCollins, 1995), from which I took the above quote about purgatory. If you're old enough, you might have seen him interviewed from time to time on network television in the 1980s and 1990s, whenever something big was going on in the Catholic world.

"Why do you want to know about that?" Fr. Richard asked, his always-cheerful tone implying that any seminary student in the early 1970s ought to have better things to do. I came clean about my interest in paranormal research. He looked at me with a twinkle in his eye. "Better not tell [a long list of faculty members from my seminary] about that!"

As it turned out, truer words were never spoken. Nevertheless, ". . . that approach to purgatory [ghosts] is an interesting idea," admitted Fr. Richard, who later headed the Department of Theology at Notre Dame University for many years.

The fact is that, when it comes to ghosts, the Roman Catholic Church has even less to say than it does about purgatory. There's no specific teaching on the subject, but there is official mistrust when it comes to all paranormal phenomena. There's an especially deep suspicion of all things psychic, and outright condemnation of any attempt to communicate with the dear departed, something my friend Pat, from section one, chapter one, completely failed to appreciate.

There are, of course, miracles. But unless these are right out of the Bible, they have to be officially approved by church authorities in Rome before Catholics are allowed to believe in them. Among those approved are the famous apparitions of the Blessed Virgin Mary at Lourdes in France (1858) and Fatima in Portugal (1917). More recent apparitions of Mary at Međugorje, in western Herzegovina, were under the papal microscope as of this writing.

Aside from approved miracles, any manifestation that will even be acknowledged as paranormal is often, but not always, considered to be caused by demons.

In my seminary days, there was a certain unofficial feeling that non-demonic, once-human ghosts might be possible, but nobody was much interested in looking into it. A rare exception was one of my early mentors, mentioned in section one, chapter one, a Jesuit priest in Washington, DC, whom I met through my brother. Fr. John J. Nicola (1929–2003) had the deliberately anonymous job of assistant director of the National Shrine of the Immaculate Conception, an enormous basilica—the largest Roman Catholic church building in North America—right across the street from where my brother lived on the CUA campus. Fr. John was technical advisor for the infamous film *The Exorcist* in 1972–1973, and he authored the 1974 book *Diabolical Possession and Exorcism* (Tan Books, 1974).

As we also saw in that chapter, students for the priesthood are not routinely trained in how to deal with the paranormal, or even the church's narrow definition of it. In recent years, the Vatican supposedly is more open about it. Back in the 1970s, however, Fr. John was not only one of the chosen few, he was the most respected American authority on possession and exorcism. He thought the purgatory-ghost theory made sense.

In those years, I also corresponded with that great pioneer of parapsychology, Dr. Louisa Rhine (1891–1983), wife of Dr. Joseph B. Rhine. The Rhines, based at Duke University in Durham, North Carolina, had worked in the paranormal field since the 1930s, when they began studying precognition (knowing about something before it happens) and extra-sensory perception (ESP), a term they coined. Not surprisingly, Louisa didn't think much of my purgatory theory, and encouraged me to study abnormal psychology, which I did on both the undergraduate and graduate levels.

Ed (1926–2006) and Lorraine (1927–) Warren, on the other hand, thought the purgatory thing was right on the money. Always controversial, Ed and Lorraine were two 1940s and 1950s artists who became the grandfather and grandmother of modern "ghost hunting." Throughout their long career, they developed a huge popular following, were highlighted in at least ten books, and were featured in several feature films and television documentaries. Their fame became universal after the 2013 film *The Conjuring*. They also drew heaps of criticism from many parapsychologists, who questioned their theories, methods, and even honesty. The fact that the surname "Warren" was a *nom de plume* adopted during their days as artists didn't help their credibility.

In 1972, Lorraine read something I wrote about my purgatory theory, and she invited me to dinner. Arriving at their Monroe, Connecticut, home one evening that summer, I found two gracious people who were to become dear friends and wonderful supporters of my own work. In some ways, Ed was to become the father I didn't have—for a few years anyway.

Ed told me that he'd made a vow to the Blessed Virgin Mary that he would "fight the devil on his own terms." I was never quite sure what that meant. And we didn't always see eye to eye. While the Warrens considered themselves ultra-conservative Roman Catholics and thought the purgatory theory was brilliant, actual theology was not their *forté*. In fact, they had little academic background in anything. Many of their practices were questionable. For example, Lorraine was a psychic-medium who routinely led séances, and Ed cultivated friendships and connections among many renegade clergy who rebelled against the liberalism following the Second Vatican Council, and were no longer recognized as practicing priests, let alone bishops, by the Roman Catholic Church.

Despite being taken under the wing of people like these, it quickly became clear, at least to me (and sometimes fellow seminarians who came with me), that the ghosts we encountered were not in any state I could recognize as purgatory. As set out in the case histories earlier in this book, these people didn't seem to be dead at all. Most appeared to be going about their daily lives somewhere or somewhen else, and were mostly, but not always, oblivious to us.

Along with the assumptions I questioned in those early days was the Island Theory: Each of us is totally self-contained. In its ferocious individualism, it says that our thoughts, memories, imaginations, talents, and desires are all inside our own brains. Further, it professes the assumption, rather odd in the history of human spirituality, that once I am born, I am uniquely me, that I will still be me after I die, and that I will remain me forever.

What did this mean for the whole idea of an afterlife? What really happens when we die? As we've seen in previous chapters, I came to this simple but sobering conclusion: Everything we think we know is wrong, and that includes much of what we think we know about God. But do our multiversal neighbors have the same issues? What do those who are supposedly dead think? What do they all have to say about God?

GOD HATES ME!

In November 1976, I was astounded to meet a "ghost" who was convinced that God hated him. And that was only the beginning.

I was twenty-three years old, and I'd converted from the Roman Catholic to the Eastern Orthodox Church the year before, to the everlasting shock of my strict Catholic and Protestant relatives and friends, including the Warrens. In the fall of 1975, I moved right into graduate-level studies at St. Vladimir Orthodox Theological Seminary near New York City. I was confident that I would be an Orthodox priest within four years. Of course, I would have to find a wife before ordination, since Orthodox parish priests are nearly all married. That was a far different scenario from what I was used to.

So, here I was in my second and—as yet unbeknownst to me—final year at "St. Vlad's." On weekends, most of the seminary students would fan out over the New York/New Jersey area to visit various churches, nursing homes, and hospitals to sing at divine services, counsel people, teach classes, or otherwise gain some personal experience for their future ministries as priests.

One Sunday that November, I found myself teaching a church school class at a suburban parish outside New York. After the class, I got talking with some of the parents. Suddenly, I noticed another seminarian pointing toward me, and a frazzled-looking, middle-aged lady came scurrying over. She turned out to have the good old Russian name of Luba.

"That nice young man said you know about ghosts," Luba chirped.

I could have pasted my classmate right then and there. My paranormal interests had already pushed me onto thin ice at St. Vlad's, and I tried to keep a low profile because of it. Apparently, it wasn't low enough.

Meanwhile, Luba was having what might be called a classic ghost problem: footsteps and what sounded like moaning in her attic. A few evenings later, I managed to find the two-story, single-family house on a dark backstreet in Yonkers. In my initial interview with the fiftyish Luba and her husband, Jack, I found they were the parents of a grown son and daughter but were recent empty-nesters. And, as I've found in nearly all such cases, they had their own theory about what was going on in the attic.

"The guy that lived in this house before us killed himself out in the garage," Jack declared. The mention of suicide didn't bring up the best memories in me. "We didn't find that out until five years after we moved in," Jack continued, in an accent like the late, great Yogi Berra. "It's gotta be him!"

There they were. The unshakable assumptions. Dead people become spirits, tormented spirits if they commit suicide, and they proceed to haunt the place where they did it.

"Anything else going on that makes you think that?" I asked.

"Isn't that enough? You gotta do an exorcism!" the man replied. I resisted the temptation to roll my eyes.

Certainly, there could be a connection with the suicide, if there had actually been one. After all, I think many stories get started out of people's need to explain phenomena in ways they can grasp. But even in those early days, I'd learned to take nothing in the paranormal at face value.

I spent that first evening checking the attic, and indeed the whole house, for squeaky boards, loose windows, and anything else that could account for the sounds, which "come and go without warning," I was told. Because I assumed nothing about this situation, all sorts of interesting possibilities opened up. Despite the story of a previous suicide, an act that's often a magnet for parasites, there wasn't anything about this case, this place, or these people that felt negative.

Had I taken the commonly accepted psychic-mediumistic approach, I probably would have assumed that the spirit of the suicide victim was active in the house, earthbound and unable to cross over. This would be either an "intelligent haunting"—the actual guy's spirit—or a "residual haunting"—some kind of recording on the environment from the suicide event. I would have tried to contact this spirit by any means available. As for the spirit, he would be completely aware of me, and I would have sought to guide him toward "the light," which I would have assumed was heaven or some equivalent.

By 1976, I didn't believe any of that. I was convinced that, if whoever this was saw such a light at all, it would almost certainly be the electromagnetic (EM) boundary, or brane, of a parallel world. If he, she, or it could hear me, and decided to approach and cross the brane, the resulting destination could be anywhere or anywhen in the multiverse, possibly a much worse place or state than when I first bumbled onto the scene. But because the people in the haunted house never heard from this being again, I and they would rejoice and think he or she had crossed into the light and was now at peace. In fact, I could have convinced the "ghost" to cross the boundary into a hell world.

Had I taken this approach at that house in Yonkers, I'd have been in more danger than the alleged spirit. Any kind of mediumistic activity is definitely no-go, just as much for the Orthodox as for the Roman Catholics, at least officially. Some rank-and-file church members do it anyway, but no seminarian could get away with it for long, if word got back to his superiors.

Nevertheless, I would do something I've never considered mediumistic in the classic sense. I would do what I did in that chapel at St. Lawrence State Hospital a year and a half before. So, I ended up spending hours sitting in a meditative state in that Yonkers attic because, from the start, I felt an energy that I was already beginning to associate with moving branes. I would be quiet and see if I encountered any neighbors, in a place where their worlds intersected ours. If we communicated, so be it. To be perfectly honest, I also wanted to see if this would work again.

Telling Jack and Luba that I was going to visit their dusty, cluttered attic to see if I could hear anything, which was entirely true, I settled down on an old pillow between two big boxes of Christmas ornaments. I switched off the light and sat there for the better part of six hours over four nights. My eyes adjusted quickly to the dark. There were slits of streetlight from outside, the occasional sound of a passing car or police siren, but that was it. I did feel the familiar electrical tingle, but it seemed far away.

On the second night, I was about to give up. It was exactly 8:12 p.m. All at once, the electrical tingle became so powerful that I could feel hairs standing up all over my body. Almost immediately, there was a loud shout right above my head. I couldn't make out what it said, but I was surprisingly unstartled, probably because of the quiet and compassionate state I'd cultivated. Still, the sound was so loud that I wondered if the people downstairs heard it.

"Hello. Peace," I thought.

Nothing for a moment.

"Greetings in peace," I thought again.

Then it came, this time farther away, upward and to my left. "Who . . . who are you?" It was a man's voice, and he was very frightened.

"I am Paul."

The voice replied, sounding even more frightened. But it alternately got softer and louder. Sometimes it was so soft that I had trouble making it out.

"What are you? Are you a ghost?"

This took me by surprise. He thought *I* was a ghost? What was that about?

"No," I thought. "I'm just a guy!"

"You look like a ghost! You look like you're inside a fog."

How should I respond to that? I decided to change the subject.

"Um. I'm Paul. I'm in Yonkers, New York. What's your name?"

The voice was more distant. "I'm Bob…." There was another word that I couldn't make out. Then, more alarmed: "How . . . Yonkers, New York?"

"I don't know, Bob. But sometimes I can talk to people, uh, far away. I don't really know how. Where are you?"

"I'm in Virginia. I don't know what town and I . . . got here."

"You don't know how you got there?" I speculated.

"No," Bob responded. Then, suddenly: "What year is it, Paul?"

"What year is it? It's 1976!"

Silence. Then, "Yes, that's what I remember."

I was entirely fascinated. This looked like another parallel world "ghost," like Gilbert (section two, chapter one).

"What do you remember, Bob?"

That was it. I thought I heard some sound, like a chair scraping across a stone floor. Then silence. The intersect, apparently, was broken. I was frustrated and disappointed. When I climbed down the flimsy ladder from the attic at about 9 o'clock, Jack and Luba heard me, and they came rushing up the stairs.

"So, did you get rid of it?" Jack asked excitedly.

"I'm still trying to find out what it is, but it's not the guy from the garage, and it's no danger to you," I stated.

That seemed to satisfy them, but not much.

The next evening at 7:30, I was back in the attic. After only about ten minutes, there was Bob. This time, his voice was right in front of me. He was unintelligible, until: ". . . remember."

"Hello, Bob. Sorry I lost you yesterday."

Silence, then, "I feel lost but not by you . . . ."

In a laborious exchange over the next half hour, I learned several things. First, our entire conversation was continuous to Bob. He hadn't experienced any break in our connection the previous evening, again just like Gilbert back in Ogdensburg. Second, he didn't know how he got to the church in Virginia where he claimed he was.

"Bob, where were you before the church?" I asked.

As he answered, his voice seemed to move, but not to the right or left. It moved slowly upward as if the slanting attic ceiling wasn't even there.

"I remember . . . plane . . . in an airplane."

"Maybe you flew to Virginia and don't remember," I tried.

"No, Paul. Plane was in trouble. Everybody was screaming. I [unintelligible] then passed out. First thing I know, here I am in church."

This just kept getting crazier! Except for Gilbert, I'd never run into anything like this. I'd never even read about this sort of thing in any paranormal literature I'd encountered. I searched for what to ask next. Did the plane crash? There were no major crashes on the news. I later found that a small Skyline Aviation air taxi had crashed near Hampton, Virginia, on October 20, with the loss of four people.

"What kind of plane were you in, Bob?"

"Mohawk. Don't know what kind of plane. A few hundred passengers [unintelligible].

There were certainly no recent crashes like this, fortunately. And I knew Mohawk Airlines. I'd flown it myself. But something was wrong. Mohawk had merged with another airline a few years before and didn't exist anymore.

Then: "Paul, can you get me out of here. I'm hungry, and my right arm hurts!"

Hungry? Sore arm? Some ghost.

Bob's voice was moving to the right, and I could hear what sounded like footsteps.

"I'm scared! Can you help me, Paul? I know I'm here because God is mad at me. God hates me! What else can explain this? I think I must be going crazy! God, this has to be a dream!"

"Bob, calm down! I'll help in whatever way I can. God does not hate you! But I can hear you moving around. Are you moving?"

"Yes, I can walk around. I've been eating what I can find in the kitchen in the church basement. But there's no other sign of life here."

Kitchen?

"Bob, why can't you just walk out the door?"

"They don't open. They're all locked! The windows won't open either. Everything else is made of stone. I'm a prisoner. I tell you, God hates me!"

At this point, I was struck not only by the nature of this conversation, but by its length. Every *tête-à-tête* I'd ever heard about through a medium or electronic voice phenomena (EVP) came in one or two words at a time. At most, there were very short sentences, three-to-five words at most. Not so with Bob.

"Bob, why do you think God hates you?"

"My mom made me go to church when I was a kid, and I hated it! She said God would punish me if I didn't go, and look at me now. I think I died in a plane crash and this is hell! It's just too weird!"

This was hardly a time for a lesson in eschatology (the theology of "final things"), so I kept it simple.

"Bob, think about this. If you were dead, you'd be dead. You wouldn't be doing *anything*. You certainly wouldn't be talking to me, and you definitely wouldn't be hungry."

"Paul, I still can't see you."

I had an idea.

"Bob, I'll try to move around. See if you can see me then."

I heaved myself up from between the boxes, switched on the light, and moved to my right around ten feet.

"Bob, am I moving now? Did you see the light go on?"

"I see the cloud moving and something in it that looks like a figure! Is that you? You must be a ghost!"

"Bob, get off it! I'm no ghost! I believe we're experiencing a space-time displacement, kind of like Einstein talked about. Like parallel worlds. I research this stuff and I've had this happen one other time. So relax! I don't understand this, but I think you are making a transition from one physical life to another!"

I was surprised that this thought seemed to calm him down. And, luckily, Bob seemed to know who Einstein was. Evidently, Bob had reached a critical juncture. The more he accepted that he was in what I today refer to as a state of translation, the more he decided to "go with the flow," and the easier it became for him. Suddenly, something was different.

"Bob, in the world I'm in, there have been no major plane crashes, certainly not by Mohawk . . ."

"Paul, I'm glad to hear there were no crashes. Why do you bring that up?"

"Bob, you said you remember being in a plane that was in trouble."

Silence, then, "Paul, I haven't flown in five years."

"Uh, Bob, you said . . ."

The man's memory was changing as we spoke. This sent more of a shiver up my spine than anything else so far.

"Paul, now you're standing in the aisle . . ." Then, nothing. The connection was broken.

Now I knew how Alice must have felt in Wonderland. By that time, my own doctrines included "nothing in the paranormal is what it appears to be" and "don't trust anything a paranormal entity tells you." But would those rules apply in this case? Bob seemed clearly to be just a man, lost and upset, but still just a guy. He had a perfectly human, physical presence when I communicated with him. He was just in a different world. And there wasn't a whiff of a parasite.

Downstairs, Jack and Luba heard me walking around. They wanted to know what I was doing, and I had to tell them something.

"I think we're dealing with something far more interesting than a ghost. I think it's a kind of imbalance in time and space."

Blank stares.

"I think I can clear this up tomorrow night." I had no idea if that was true.

Day four. It took half an hour, but there was Bob once again. I had to try to resolve this tonight. Besides, back at St. Vlad's, I had papers due in Byzantine History and Liturgical Theology.

"Bob, we need to get you out of that church! Then maybe you can reach some kind of resolution," I declared, as if I knew what I was talking about.

Bob seemed perfectly used to me by now. But he didn't get what I was saying.

"Hi, Paul. Why would I want to leave? I have things to do. The choir director is sick!"

Either the man's memory had totally altered, he had lost his mind, or I had slipped through another brane and was talking with someone completely different.

"Who are you again?" I asked, more shivers than usual running up my spine.

"You don't have much of a memory for a seminarian! Bob [sounded like "Winther"] rector of Grace Episcopal Church."

What? Bob had changed to the point where he actually belonged in this church! Not only that, but he seemed to remember that I remembered he belonged there. And how could he possibly know I was a seminarian? I never mentioned that.

Bob started to say something else, when I suddenly heard a noise at his end. It was the sound of a heavy creaking, as of a huge wooden door opening. Then there were more sounds—people. It sounded like several male and female voices echoing in a large space.

The last I ever heard from Bob was a cheery, "Hello," apparently directed toward the new arrivals. That was it. The intersect was broken, and I never talked with Bob again. And Grace Episcopal Church? I later found at least six of them in Virginia. The ones in Alexandria, Keswick, and The Plains were made of stone, as opposed to brick. And any one of them could have had a Rev. Bob at some point. Or would. And what were those final sounds? People arriving for choir rehearsal?

I was numb. Jack and Luba thought I was sick when I came down from the attic that final time. Confused as I was, I had a certainty that their problem was over because the intersect was gone. The parallel worlds had detached, at least at that point in space occupied by their attic. I told them that things should be fine, and they wouldn't be hearing from their ghost again. They didn't understand what I'd done or how I'd done it, but they accepted my statement.

Luba checked in with me several times over the next six months, and all was quiet in Yonkers. They kept inviting me for dinner, but I politely declined. I didn't want to go back to that house. The experience was too weird, and in a way that exceeded what I'd gone through at St. Lawrence State Hospital. It wasn't that the Yonkers happenings were negative, and certainly not evil, as they were in Ogdensburg. It was the jarring nature of reality they seemed to reveal.

The run-ins with parasites I was more or less prepared for. The encounter with Gilbert as I sat in the hospital chapel shook me up, but it was straightforward, and it seemed to be another clue that parallel worlds are real. In Yonkers, however, my meetings with Bob, if they were what I perceived them to be, unveiled a new dimension to the entire multiverse experience.

Could it be that Bob really did die in a plane crash and had a consciousness shift to that church, where another facet of his superlife was already living a parallel existence as the pastor? Why had it taken his memory—perhaps his own collective subconscious—time to catch up? Had he become snagged on the overwhelming conviction that God hated him, and on our cartoonish ideas about death and an afterlife? And why did Bob think I was a ghost when we first met? Apparently, I was partly in his world and he was partly in mine.

Did I imagine this whole experience? If I had, then how and why did Jack and Luba's haunting end?

There were a hundred other questions. Not the least of these were: Are these parallel lives, these alternate realities, next to us all the time? Are there heaven and hell worlds right across the branes that we interact with every nanosecond of our lives? What keeps us from slipping into these heavens or hells? Are we already living parallel lives there? Who or what holds it all together?

I started out in life wondering where my father was after his suicide. Now I was wondering: Where is God in this gut-wrenching reality I was seeing hints of?

I returned to the seminary and holed up in my dorm room for three days, pretending to be sick. I considered dropping out of school. My roommates were worried, and Fr. Cyril Stavresvky, the dean of students, stopped by to see what was going on with me. How could I begin to tell him? He suggested that I see a doctor.

"Does this have anything to do with your paranormal involvement?" Fr. Cyril asked.

I wasn't about to be pumped for information, no matter how well-meaning the pumper. I can't quite recall what I said, but it was noncommittal. Two months later, I received a letter of expulsion, in which I was accused of having performed an exorcism on a fellow student, which was unmitigated nonsense. I wonder how much my post-Bob funk had to do with that. I would never entirely get to the bottom of that.

As for my fascinating friend, I strongly suspect that once Bob's memory solidified, and his consciousness settled, he dropped flawlessly into who he already is. In the world of Grace Episcopal Church, Rev. Bob doesn't remember the plane crash, one of millions of worlds that are his subconscious life in that facet of Virginia. His translation was complete.

Yet another question arises: If Bob went down in a plane crash in one parallel life, translated to another parallel life centered around that Virginia church, what the hey was he doing in an attic in Yonkers, New York? The best explanation I was ever able to come up with was that the multiverse is indiscriminate in its tendency toward Unity. Any world can intersect anywhere because its inhabitants, human or otherwise, are intimately connected anyway. I happened to be in the right place at the right time, with the right conditions, to connect with Bob.

THE SUPREME BEING AND THE NOBLE BEAR

Over the ensuing decades, I've seldom used the meditation/communication method through which I met Gilbert and Bob. I'm not entirely comfortable with it because you never know who or what you'll meet. And if I have the slightest hint that there's a parasite around, I don't open myself up at all.

That said, I've had some riveting encounters with beings I can't begin to identify, but who seem to be well aware of a Supreme Being. Trouble is, English, or even vocalization at all, isn't the primary form of communication in many, if not most, worlds. I communicate telepathically but verbally but can get by only in English, French, Spanish, German, and Latin, with some Greek and Hebrew, most tarnished with varying degrees of rust. So, the language barrier has been a roadblock for me in many, if not most, encounters that involve active, cross-brane communication.

When I *can* converse, the language may be recognizable to me, but factors such as word order (as with Gilbert), grammar, syntax, case endings, and some vocabulary might be quite different, presumably because of the way that language developed in that particular world family.

This was the case with the being I will always remember as the Noble Bear.

In the winter of 1980–1981, I received a phone call from an erstwhile seminary classmate from western New York.

"These people in Tonawanda are hearing heavy footsteps in their attic," he declared.

Not another attic!

So off I drove—for over seven hours—to Tonawanda, a northern suburb of Buffalo, not far from Niagara Falls. The first thing that struck me was that the family was more intrigued than frightened about what was happening. The couple was in their mid-twenties and had twin toddlers, a formidable task in itself without having to deal with "bumps in the night." There was a powerful presence in this attic, one that I'd never felt before. I settled in, and it took less than half an hour to hear from the presence.

"*Hic esten*," were the first discernible sounds I heard. The voice was low and commanding, but gentle.

Hic is Latin for "here," but *esten*? I won't threaten the reader with a Latin lesson, but this probably meant "you," meaning me. The case ending was wrong. It should have been *tu es* or just *es*.

I understood this as a direct statement to me: "You are here." And it clearly wasn't a question. The primary impression, now deeply implanted in my memory, was of an energy I can only describe as nobility, honor, courage, and goodness, and it was beaming from this being in waves. It was definitely a male presence. Around him was a huge sense of space. That's the best way I can describe it.

My very first thoughts: Could this be an angel, or a being responsible for our belief in angels? What did he mean by, "You are here"?

There followed two challenging but deeply fascinating afternoons communicating with a being I could only describe as bear-like. It had an ursine energy that shamans have easily recognized when I described it in later years. I'm certainly not claiming this was a real bear, but it was very definitely a non-human person.

For the first time in these multiversal exchanges, there was a visual. I could just make out the outline of a huge, upright figure. Also, for the first time in these encounters, I managed to snap a picture.

The one photo the author managed to get during the "Noble Bear" encounter appears man-like, with a shield-like object or a light carried in the left hand.

Unlike my encounters with Gilbert and Bob, my ursine friend seemed to have the proper spatial relationship to me. He was right where his voice came from. But there was something wrong with the geometry. The more I saw him over time, the more he looked as though his head should be several feet above the slanting attic roof, but it wasn't. It brought me an odd, out-of-place feeling.

I never got his name because I couldn't even begin to make it out. I don't think he got my name either. He probably heard Paul as *paulo,* a word meaning "little," even in his mutant Latin, I would think.

If I ferreted out his story and translated it correctly, I for the first time encountered a multiversal believer in a Supreme Being with strictly female energies. He referred to the Goddess (the word "Dea" was very clear) for the first time. And I got the impression that there was only one, because he said *Dea Summa Esa*, which I took as "Goddess the One Who Is" in his off-beat Latin. Even more riveting was his claim that She had sent him on a quest for a place called Renthusia, which I have never been able to find in any reference source, paranormal or otherwise.

Interestingly, he had been sent on this quest as a reward, not as a punishment. The reward was for acts of *carita et humilita*. Again, the wrong case endings, but the root words clearly translate as kindness (or love) and humility. Imagine a world where one is rewarded for humility, a virtue sorely lacking in our own.

He had passed across or through many worlds on his quest—his words were *per terrae*. And he had no idea that he was in an attic in Tonawanda, New York. He thought he was on a road in a forest, talking with one of many *alii viatori*, which I understood as "other travelers" on the road.

What was he going to do when he got to Renthusia?

Implera facta nova, or so it sounded. I took that as "achieve new deeds." Of kindness? Yes, but I somehow detected a sense that war or danger might be involved along the way, but we never got to that before he moved on. I literally felt him moving away.

All disturbances in the family attic ceased.

Between that time and 1987, there were five beings, both human and non-human, with whom I simply couldn't communicate. Two were non-verbal and three others spoke languages of which I have never heard the like. All five seemed just as flummoxed as I was with the encounter, and one seemed terrified of me.

I could fill another book with the questions that arose. Were these ghosts? Aliens? Both? What meaning do those words have in the living, eternal, and dazzling diversity of the multiverse? Were they from "other planets"? What does that even mean? Would they have had anything to say about God or Goddess? Probably. Everywhere I seemed to touch in the multiverse was shot through with a sense of divine presence, but it was far beyond anything I'd learned about in the seminary.

Also in those years, I had my first encounters with members of clearly identifiable species who are very giving and benign. These included what Ben and I would come to call the "Clerics" and the "Lion People." But those are stories for the next book.

WESUONK WALKS WITH GOD

In 1987, at an archaeological site not far from my home in Rhode Island, I met the First Nations (I think) woman who said that she "walked with God." At least that's what I think she said. I had to write down what I heard and look it up among the Algonquian language group's root words. I also memorized some basic vocabulary so I could at least initiate a conversation. In this way, I eventually got her name as Wesuonk.

That, however, is the word for "name"! This made me a little suspicious, but I was in no position to ask complex questions, and I wouldn't have known how to. Wesuonk's presence was entirely human and completely benign, so I let the name thing go. The deepest concepts I could get from her were that she doesn't believe in the existence of death (*kitonkquean*) and, like dear old Gilbert, routinely talks with people from parallel worlds.

I spoke with Wesuonk eight times between 1987 and 1989, at various times of day, when I was alone at the site. It didn't usually take long to intersect because she was always there. Ordinarily, this wouldn't have been easy because access to these sites is severely restricted, to the point of arrest. Under another hat as a journalist, however, I'm a historian. Conveniently, I was vice chairman of the town's Historic District Zoning Commission at the time and had influence with big cheeses at the Rhode Island Historical Society. So, I had blanket permission to enter the site, though the archaeological authorities had no idea what I was really doing.

Much like my conversation with an Aboriginal elder, Mindiluwi, in Australia ten years before, Wesuonk seemed to know all about the multiverse and had no sense whatsoever of time as we know it, from what I could tell. As in my conversation in Australia about the Aboriginal Dream Time, a sense of God or Goddess in one form or another was overwhelmingly present whenever I spoke with Wesuonk.

Then, in August 1989, Wesuonk was gone, and I never encountered her again, probably because intersect points move. It was a precious experience nonetheless. I learned some more about the multiverse and picked up a little Wampanoag vocabulary in the process.

PEOPLE IN DISTRESS

After encountering all these fascinating characters, there were still the distressed people who can come across very much like standard, garden-variety ghosts. These are humans who would be fodder for any old-time séance because some of them realize they've died in the last worlds they remembered. Unlike Bob, they don't know about translation. It's not that they don't realize they're ghosts, because they're not. The problem is they don't realize they're still people, albeit different people, or at least in different worlds.

What confuses them isn't the change from one body and one state to another; it's the narrow, cartoon-like ideas they carry over from childhood. God is an old man in the sky. He rewards the good and punishes the wicked. Be good, or just believe in Jesus or whomever, and you are saved. If this didn't happen after they translated, I have sometimes found them frightened and furious, like Bob in the beginning.

There was Vera, a young girl in Texas who remembered being abused by her uncle, then was killed in a traffic accident. I encountered her in the woods of Vermont. She was horrified because she had actual memories of being killed, so she said, but had encountered no heaven and no hell. She was searching frantically for God in a world that was suspiciously like the one she just came from.

"That's because you're not dead, just in a different world," I reassured Vera. That's why nothing has changed. God is everywhere. God is One. Drop your old ideas and open up. It's a new world! You'll find God."

It took time, but this actually worked. Vera calmed and, apparently, went on her way.

When I pulled off the road for a rest while traversing California's Imperial Valley in 2006, I met the eight wise children who claimed they lived with a Goddess in a beautiful world that sounded nothing like California to me. We had to do that one in a form of French. They were very aware of neighbors from parallel worlds, and they said they worried about us. I never found out if the Goddess had a name.

During that same book tour in 2006, I was at a hotel in Sedona, Arizona (where else?), and had an encounter that began in a dream. When I woke up, the encounter continued—with a Christian minister named Richard who apparently lost his faith *after* he died. His church was in Newry, in Northern Ireland. Things there were far from good in Richard's world.

At the beginning of the dream, I heard weeping, and there was a reverberation, as would take place in a large hall or church. This turned out to be Richard. One of the oddest things about this encounter, which took place in English, was that Richard reported frequent poltergeist-like phenomena inside and outside. As with Vera, Richard was bitter because he remembered dying and didn't get the heaven he expected.

Another bizarre aspect of this case was Richard's complete aloneness. He remembered dying, though not what he died of. He said, though, that he had no sense of actually being dead. Fascinatingly, Richard remembered going through other deaths, as well. If that's accurate, it backs up my contention that many facets of us in our superlives are undergoing the bodily death experience, in many forms, in many worlds, all the time. It's one of the root experiences of our existence.

I thought of the contention by mediums that they have to help dead people cross over because they don't know they're dead. Several "dead" people I've encountered, like Richard, are just the opposite: Because of the old beliefs about death and God that their societies drilled into them, they think they're dead but actually aren't.

What's more, Richard was alone in his old church. But when he left the building, there was no one outside either. This frightened him more than any other aspect of his situation, he said. I reassured Richard that he wasn't dead, which had begun to dawn on him anyway, and suggested that he remain quiet and pray, stop feeling sorry for himself, and that maybe he could bring about change.

Shortly, the intersect point broke, but not before the whole atmosphere in the hotel room lifted. To me, that was a sign that Richard had made a step toward taking charge of his future, and, maybe, to realizing that God is a lot bigger than he'd been taught.

THE REPENTANT DEMONS

I avoid parasites like the plague, and when Ben and I work on cases that involve them, we take great pains not to communicate with them. I've allowed myself only two exceptions to that rule since 1970. On both occasions, I encountered parasites who actually said they were sorry for the way they had to subsist. They both spoke perfect modern English.

"I am very sorry for how I live," said a female member of the Rogue parasite species during an Indiana case in 2010. "But, like you, I must eat. And the olders [that's what it sounded like] dominate with cruelty, feeding on what I do not."

In fact, this parasite wanted God to forgive her, so she claimed.

Three years later, another Rogue, a male this time, told me the same thing during a Massachusetts case.

Why did I believe them? I didn't, at first, and I'm sure there was more to the story. But there was a certain sincerity, and these two did not feel as alien as the parasites I encountered at St. Lawrence State Hospital, or the four I tangled with in the Bridgeport poltergeist case of 1974. Nor did they seem to have any fear about leaving their hosts if they had to.

Nevertheless, I have always believed both Gautama the Buddha's instruction to have compassion for all things, and the ancient Orthodox Christian contention that even demons can be saved. So, in both cases, I advised the human hosts not only to employ positive thinking and family love, but to direct compassion and love toward the parasites themselves. Both parasites left within a day.

A VERY SURPRISING GOD?

In any book that asks what ghosts have to say about God, most readers expect reassuring answers that comfortingly confirm their own belief systems. We want Aunt Jane, who died when we were a kid, to tell us that she's okay in the spirit world, that she's in heaven with God, that she can play spirit golf without having to pay spirit greens fees, and that she can eat all the spirit cookies she wants without getting spirit fat.

Most modern people have this concept, or something very like it, when it comes to heaven, or at least some kind of afterlife. But consider how physical these concepts are. Isn't the spirit world non-physical by definition? What we have in our modern concept could be a stubborn holdover of ancient ideas that we today would call the multiverse.

Just as when I encountered Gilbert, Bob, and the others in completely physical, albeit different, worlds, so our ancestors must have encountered multiversal intersects and had the same kinds of meet-ups. I believe that our ancestors' encounters with beautiful worlds and positive beings gave them their basic ideas about God, angels, and heaven, and that terrible worlds and parasites gave them their ideas about hell and demons.

These encounters were one thing, but communication would have been another, as I saw for myself. If ghosts, gods, aliens, or any beings from elsewhere or elsewhen actually do know about God or anything else, they had to somehow tell our ancestors, right? This was usually done through shamans or other people with deep spirituality, often while they were in altered states of consciousness. One result of this early communication was religion, which arose as a response to two things: ultimate questions and encounters with neighbors our ancestors thought were supernatural beings who had the answers.

Had I not known enough about quantum physics and the multiverse, and if I didn't have a suspicious nature, I would have thought that I was dealing with supernatural beings during at least some of the bizarre face-to-faces in this chapter.

Did I receive answers to any ultimate questions? I think Wesuonk gave it a shot, more so if we'd been able to understand each other better. And many of the benign non-human neighbors seem to have their own handles on what we're doing here and who or what God is.

While I follow my own rule of prayer and meditation, I wouldn't in a million years consider myself a shaman because I haven't walked that walk. My seminary education certainly didn't answer any ultimate questions. I was studying to be clergy, and clergy are teachers, preservers of doctrine, presiders over divine services, counselors, and administrators, but not shamans. Some clergy might have shamanic gifts. I know some who do, but these gifts are separate from their office as priests, ministers, rabbis, imams, or what have you.

If clergy have encounters with multiversal neighbors and tell people about it, it's likely their superiors will, at best, question their credibility and, at worst, do to them what was done to me. So, despite the fact that some represent ancient and venerable traditions of belief and worship, clergy might not be the best teachers when it comes to meeting God. But, despite their gifts, neither might shamans, mediums, monks, holy hermits, or whoever.

That's because it all comes down to interpretation, which is usually based on our own existing belief systems, and how honest we are with ourselves. Assuming that Gilbert was what he appeared to be when I encountered him at St. Lawrence State Hospital in 1975, Pat the medium and I came to totally different interpretations about what was going on.

So where *do* we turn for answers? I can speak only for myself. The multiversal neighbors I encountered, their nature, their purpose, and their status, if these were what they appeared to be, told me more about God than anything they themselves could have said or done. They came from many different worlds and were living under many different conditions, and even under different laws of physics. Whether they intended to or not, and no matter how confused they were themselves, all those I met taught me a great deal about God.

The first thing that hit me was the incomprehensible depth and breadth of Creation. My first such experiences, in the 1970s, took place in the context of the theological education I was receiving. Rather than contradict the basics of what I was learning, my encounters literally added new dimensions to it. One of the most basic official doctrines about God is that he is the Creator, and that he created the universe out of an explosion of infinite love that he couldn't contain. My encounters taught me that there is so much more to it: If God's creative love is infinite, wouldn't Creation be infinite, too? Rather than create one universe, enormous as it might be, wouldn't infinite love create an infinite multiverse, containing every possible reality? And wouldn't that multiverse, considered in total, be in perfect balance, a perfect Creation, in fact?

The second thing I learned was to find God, and any progress in knowledge at all, not by taking things apart but by putting them together. Despite their vast differences, all the neighbors I've met had significant commonalities; most obvious was the desire to survive and to move on to something fuller. When they didn't achieve this, there was sadness and disappointment, apparently even for the parasites. This taught me that we are all in the same boat, as the saying goes, not only here and now on planet Earth but in every world, everywhere and everywhen. No matter what our species, world, or state of being, we all desire love, life, and growth, and we desire each other, whether our purpose be positive or negative.

Those two basic realizations led me right to the idea of God and the Unity, and the idea that all things are tending toward that Unity, that eventually all the worlds will join in a perfect harmony, a great unification. This idea is right under our noses in both science and religion.

Science, specifically quantum science, has the Holographic Theory. As we noted earlier, this says that the matrix will eventually collapse into the great Unity. In more conventional science, especially in cosmology, there is a strong belief in the theory of the oscillating universe, that the cosmos will expand to a certain point (some scientists say the expansion is already slowing down), then reverse so that the universe eventually returns to the singularity whence it came. The "Big Bang" and the "Big Crunch," as it were.

Religion, while fragmented into thousands of sects and belief systems, is still saturated with realizations of the Unity. Buddhists and Baha'is pull no punches about a desire for universal oneness. Even in Christianity, the theology of Teilhard de Chardin sees all Creation eventually drawing into unity with the Cosmic Christ.

From the paranormal standpoint, Ben and I believe that bizarre experiences are taking place in greater numbers because, among other things, parallel worlds with different laws of physics and different inhabitants are collapsing into each other in greater numbers, creating more and larger flap areas.

When it comes to God, this might all sound very impersonal, but it's not. Whether we approach it through science, theology, the paranormal, or however we like, the Unity, as we said in the last chapter, puts God closer to us than we are to ourselves. Our own superlives are a Unity across the worlds. By extension, in the cosmic logic of the multiverse, we literally are each other. Even as illustrated by the horrific possession phenomenon, here is the Unity as well, for better or worse.

What I've learned from "ghosts" is that we must answer our own ultimate questions. This is far more difficult and dangerous than you might imagine. As we should see by now, we are not islands. We can neither live nor learn on our own. But where do we go for our teachers? There are self-appointed mystics and coaches on every street corner, and many are charlatans, delusional, or both. There are almost as many sages and teachers with advanced degrees from accredited colleges and universities. But this group, which includes scientists, can be rife with agendas and narrow thinking, along with academic, industrial, and scientific politics.

My own answer has always been an old spiritual rule, which I believe is based on the paradoxes that make up life in the multiverse. The greatest spiritual masters, from the Buddha to Jesus and beyond, all knew about it and lived it. It's based on the realization that the Unity is already there, and you just have to accept it.

The rule is simply this: Embrace the paradoxes! Let your questions go, and the answers will come to you on their own. Forget yourself and you will fulfill yourself. Be empty of ego, and you will be full of life and compassion. Forget what you think you know, and you will be full of knowledge. Be humble, and this will help you see things as they really are. It will make you honest, and that's the only way to find truth. This is everything our fiercely self-centered society tells us not to do.

Let your subconscious do the work. And what is your subconscious? As I've said, it's the totality of all the lives you are living—your superlife—across all the worlds. Will the answers you receive be the correct ones? If you cling to humility and Unity, I believe they will be.

Don't just whistle past the graveyard. Dance, and do so with joy and wisdom.